YOUTH GANGS IN LITERATURE

Recent Contributions in
Exploring Social Issues through Literature

Literature and the Environment
George Hart and Scott Slovic, editors

YOUTH GANGS IN LITERATURE

Claudia Durst Johnson

Exploring Social Issues through Literature
Claudia Durst Johnson, Series Editor

GREENWOOD PRESS
Westport, Connecticut • London

Library of Congress Cataloging-in-Publication Data

Johnson, Claudia D.
  Youth gangs in literature / Claudia Durst Johnson.
    p. cm.—(Exploring social issues through literature, ISSN 1551–0263)
  Includes bibliographical references and index.
  ISBN 0-313-32749-1 (alk. paper)
  1. American fiction—History and criticism. 2. Gangs in literature. 3. Juvenile
delinquents—United States—Biography—History and criticism. 4. Borges, Jorge
Luis, 1899—Characters—Juvenile delinquents. 5. Young adult fiction, American—
History and criticism. 6. Literature and society—United States. 7. Juvenile delinquency in literature. 8. Juvenile delinquents in literature. 9. Social problems in
literature. 10. Youth in literature. I. Title. II. Series.
PS374.G35J64 2004
810.9'3556—dc22   2004009406

British Library Cataloguing in Publication Data is available.

Library of Congress Catalog Card Number: 2004009406
ISBN: 0–313–32749–1
ISSN: 1551–0263

First published in 2004

Greenwood Press, 88 Post Road West, Westport, CT 06881
An imprint of Greenwood Publishing Group, Inc.
www.greenwood.com

Printed in the United States of America

The paper used in this book complies with the
Permanent Paper Standard issued by the National
Information Standards Organization (Z39.48–1984).

10 9 8 7 6 5 4 3 2 1

The editors and publisher gratefully acknowledge permission to reprint excerpts
from "Seven Hurt in Chinatown Shooting: Police Blame Gang Dispute over Fireworks," by Kevin Fagan, Stephen Schwartz, and J. L. Pimsleur in the *San Francisco
Chronicle,* July 1, 1995.

Contents

Series Foreword

Exploring Social Issues through Literature was developed as a resource to help teachers and librarians keep pace with secondary school curriculum developments in the language arts such as integrated studies and teaching literature across the curriculum. Each volume in the open-ended series confronts an important social issue that has both historical ramifications and contemporary relevance to high school students. The initial topics developed for the series reflect the 'hot button' issues most requested by educators. Themes—such as environmental issues, bioethics, and racism—encompass a considerable body of literature. The books in this series provide readers with an introduction to the topic and examine the differing perspectives offered by authors and writers from a variety of time periods and literary backgrounds.

This resource was developed to address students' needs and appeal to their interests. The literary works selected range from standard canonical works to contemporary and multicultural adult fiction that would be familiar to teens and to young adult fiction. Many titles are found on curriculum reading lists; other considerations in selection include pertinence, interest level, subject and language appropriateness, and availability and accessibility of the text to the non-specialist. The authors of these volumes, all experts in their fields, also sought to include a wide spectrum of works offering as many differing perspectives on the issue as possible.

Each volume begins with an introductory essay tracing the historical and literary developments related to the identified social issue. The chapters provide brief biographical information on the writer and present critical analysis of one or more work of literature. While the focus of the chapters is generally full-length fiction, it is not limited to that and may also include poetry, short stories, or non-fiction—such as essays or memoirs. In most chapters works are arranged chronologically to reflect the historical trends and developments. In other cases works are grouped according to thematic sub-topics. The analysis includes discussions of the work's structural, thematic and stylistic components and insights on the historical context that relates the work to the broader issue. Chapters conclude with bibliographic information on works cited and a list of suggested readings that may be helpful for further research or additional assignments.

Educators looking for new ways to present social issues will find this resource quite valuable for presenting thematic reading units or historical perspectives on modern problems of conflict. Students of literature as well as general readers will find many ideas and much inspiration in this series.

Preface

Exploring Social Issues through Literature is a unique series developed by Greenwood Press that allows readers to encounter single important social issues throughout history in a wide range of literary representations. *Youth Gangs in Literature,* a volume in the series, has been written with secondary-school students, educators, and librarians in mind. Although the book will be used primarily by teachers, it has been designed and written to be accessible to young students as well. The problems that issue from the literature examined in this volume invite an interdisciplinary study of that literature—whether sociological, psychological, or historical. Thus, *Youth Gangs in Literature* is entirely appropriate for use in English, American Studies, History, or Social Sciences classrooms.

The aim of the book is to generate informed discussion by providing information about the many issues involved in the formation, operation, and effect of youth gangs.

The volume analyzes street gangs as they are portrayed in novels, memoirs, and short fiction. The works selected for study—both canonical and contemporary fiction, both adult and young-adult titles—were chosen to represent major periods of gang activity and major cultures involved in gangs in the United States. They are arranged chronologically. Included here are studies of western gangs along the Mississippi River and on the southwestern frontier, Irish gangs in New York City and Chicago in the nineteenth and twentieth centuries, Jewish gangs in New York City in the 1940s, African American gangs in Harlem and New York in the 1940s through the 1960s, girl gangs in the industrial Northeast in the 1950s, prep-school and military-school gangs in the 1960s, African American and immigrant gangs in South Central Los Angeles in the 1970s and 1980s, Hispanic gangs in East Los Angeles from the 1960s to the 1990s, and Asian gangs in New York City's Chinatown and Houston, Texas, in the 1990s.

Consideration has been limited as nearly as possible to works appropriate to the classroom. But given the subject matter of gangs, it is virtually impossible to exclude all offensive language. The assumption here is that instructors will use their discretion in deciding which books to require for classroom discussion, which to place on an optional reading list, and which to exclude altogether.

Preceding each analysis is a primary document—from newspaper articles, histories, and interviews—that has a specific bearing on the discussion that follows. For example, a newspaper account of a shootout between Vietnamese and Chinese gangs on the streets of San Francisco's Chinatown introduces the discussion of *Shadow of the Dragon,* about Vietnamese gangs.

Each analysis begins with the historical background pertinent to gang activity in the work under discussion and then traces the story of gangs within the narrative. Each essay ends with an analysis of prominent, gang-related issues. Essays are followed by a list of suggested readings.

ORGANIZATION OF THE BOOK

This study of the gang experience as it developed in different times and places (chiefly in the United States) and among different populations is organized chronologically. It begins with the ascendancy of gangs in the lawless frontier along the Mississippi River, which provided a convenient escape for the gangs of Lazarus Morell, whose story is told by Jorge Luis Borges, and the gangs parodied by Mark Twain in *Adventures of Huckleberry Finn.* From the Mississippi River, this study proceeds to the streets of nineteenth-century New York, where Irish gangs held hostage areas of the city like Five Points and Paradise Alley, and where youthful gangsters graduated to positions of authority in local government. Their stories are told in Herbert Asbury's *The Gangs of New York* and in Kevin Baker's *Paradise Alley.*

William Bonney, known as Billy the Kid, moved as a child from the gang-infested streets of New York to the equally lawless new settlements of the Southwest. Larry McMurtry's *Anything for Billy* is the story of one of many western outlaw gangs that came to define American values, both good and bad.

In the early nineteenth century, gangs thrived, not only in New York City, but in Detroit, Chicago, and other urban areas, chiefly among the children of Irish and Jewish immigrants. With the prohibition of alcohol sales in the 1930s, Chicago, with its large immigrant population and its proximity to the Great Lakes and Canada, became notorious as a center of gang activity. James T. Farrell's *Studs Lonigan* is the classic story of that period.

Within a similar climate in Brooklyn's Jewish Brownsville neighborhood in the 1940s, an equally notorious group of gangsters, called Murder, Inc., arose. Irving Schulman's *The Amboy Dukes* is the story of the younger generation of street gangs that were produced by and that fed into the adult crime scene.

By the 1930s and 1940s, more than a century of degradation and disruption had produced segregated areas of poverty in the northern cities to which southern African Americans had relocated. The poverty and desperation that became the breeding ground of gangs is the subject of Richard Wright's *Rite of Passage*.

In the late 1930s and early 1940s, Adolph Hitler's Nazism reminded the world that the gang mentality often permeated the highest levels of government. Hitler's atrocities led William Golding to a fictional premise about the evil inherent in human nature in the savage gangs of *Lord of the Flies*.

Foxfire, by Joyce Carol Oates, is a portrait of a female gang that formed in the urban poverty of the 1950s. This is the first portrait of a gang in this collection of essays that is made up of neither ethnic minorities nor immigrant children. The period after World War II is marked by widespread suburban prosperity and the government's deep fear of social unrest. Both these situations overshadowed the existence of pockets of continuing urban poverty among workers in the lowest-paid jobs.

The 1960s were identified with youthful rebellions against all authority, many of which resulted in the formation of gangs. Three works set in the 1960s are like *Foxfire* in that they go against the stereotype of gangs, their characters being Caucasians in the traditional mainstream of American society. S. E. Hinton's *The Outsiders*, while set in the 1960s, looks back to the personal rebellions of the late 1950s (the film *Rebel Without a Cause* comes to mind). But rival gangs in the novel form along social and economic lines, the rich against the poor.

The Civil Rights movement and the secrecy, manipulation, and self-interest that kept alive America's unpopular military involvement in Vietnam forms the undercurrent of Pat Conroy's portrayal in *The Lords of Discipline*. In a military academy, a highly secret pernicious gang holds sway with the help of the gang's alumni in high places.

The corruption in government that came to be known as the Watergate scandal of the early 1970s figures in Robert Cormier's novel, *The Chocolate War*. In this novel set in a prep school in New England, the deputy headmaster is equivalent to President Richard Nixon and the president's "men" are a cruel school gang who do his bidding.

Unlike the Jewish and Irish immigrants, most of whom moved away from the poverty of their old neighborhoods, African American communities, like the one portrayed in Walter Dean Myers's novel *Scorpions*, continue to be cursed by conditions that create gangs and, thus, continue to be destroyed by violent criminals.

New York City had once been considered the capital of youth gangs, an assumption ironically perpetuated by the romanticized stage play and film *West Side Story*. But by the 1970s, Los Angeles had begun to replace New York as the gang capital of the United States. Frank Bonham's *Durango Street* takes place in the early 1960s. By this time, its setting of South Central Los Angeles was already a battlefield, the city's African American population held in terror by its own sons. In *Monster*, a memoir by Kody Scott, the horrors of African American gangs in South Central Los Angeles make the New York Scorpions look like a Sunday-school class. Drug taking and drug dealing had been part of the gang scene for decades, but in the 1980s, with the introduction of crack cocaine, the toll that gangs took on their communities grew to astonishing levels.

By the 1960s, Chicano youth gangs had risen to notoriety in East Los Angeles. The comparatively harmless barrio clubs of the first half of the century had evolved into killing machines that, like their African American counterparts, were decimating their own people. Luis Rodriguez's *Always Running* is a memoir of his years in the barrio gangs of East Los Angeles in the 1960s and 1970s. It also details the grim subsequent history of gangs in Los Angeles and in Chicago.

Other minorities of color whose families immigrated to California were also sucked into the gang scene in Los Angeles. *American Son*, by Brian Ascalon Roley, is about two teenage boys whose mother has immigrated to the United States from the Philippines in the wake of the terror, poverty, and chaos in her homeland.

At the same time, from the 1970s to the present, Asian youth gangs, fewer in number but even more violent than Chicano and

African American gangs, were making greater inroads into any United States city with an Asian population big enough to support a Chinatown, or more accurately, an Asia Town. The Vietnam War looms in the background of Sherry Garland's *Shadow of the Dragon*, about Vietnamese gangs and skinheads in Houston, Texas.

The Two Chinatowns, by former policeman Dan Mahoney, situates Chinese and Vietnamese youth gangs of the 1990s within a complex system of international crime run by Asian mobs known as triads.

ISSUES

In approaching the literature of gangs of different cultures throughout history, several patterns or similarities emerge. Foremost among these is the extent to which young men and women are instructed in negative values by the unscrupulous behavior of powerful adults. These adults may be part of the government, like the discriminatory Anglo Americans in nineteenth-century New York City; those who made up the ruthless merchant ring in Billy the Kid's New Mexico; or those known as the "President's Men" in the 1970s Watergate scandal. Or they may be lesser figures of authority, like the social services arm of New York City in *Rite of Passage*, the school deputy headmaster in *The Chocolate Wars*, or the military academy president and trustees in *The Lords of Discipline*.

Economics is also usually at the center of an understanding of the gangs discussed here. Poverty is a result of and a breeding ground for discrimination and degradation. The desperation for sheer survival sometimes makes the gang an irresistible choice. In the slums, in times when unemployment is high, poor young men and women are lucky to get jobs—sometimes backbreaking, sometimes dangerous, usually demeaning—paying starvation wages. This is the situation that prevailed in *Paradise Alley, Foxfire, Rite of Passage, The Outsiders, The Scorpions, Durango Street, Always Running, American Son,* and *Shadow of the Dragon*. Yet these same young men and women can, through gang connections, make lots of easy money stealing and working for drug dealers. In this way, they can pay not only for family essentials but also for adolescent pleasures.

Gangs flourish wherever displacement and immigration has created a class of outsiders who see little hope of joining mainstream society. Their solution is to band together for social purposes as well as survival. This was the impetus for gang formation among the children of Irish and Jewish immigrants in New York City in the nineteenth and early twentieth centuries, for the children of African Americans who moved from their homes in the South to the urban North, and for Chicano, Chinese, Vietnamese, Filipino, and other immigrants to all parts of the United States.

The works analyzed here show that, for youths, gangs hold out additional promises beyond survival and money. In *Studs Lonigan*, gangs offer adventure and excitement. In *Rite of Passage, Lord of the Flies, The Outsiders, Foxfire, Durango Street*, and *Always Running*, the gang provides protection from physical attacks. In *The Amboy Dukes, The Chocolate Wars*, and *The Lords of Discipline*, the gang promises respect and power.

The boy or girl who joins a gang often reasons that the gang serves as a family, his or her own family having either fallen apart or failed to provide material or emotional sustenance. This theme is repeated in *Studs Lonigan, The Amboy Dukes, Rite of Passage, Foxfire, The Outsiders*, and *Scorpions*. Often it is the family, usually an older brother, who pulls a boy down into the gang life, as in *Scorpions* and *American Son*. Conversely, it is the cohesive strength of his family that allows the protagonist of *Shadow of the Dragon* to resist gangs.

These works never let us forget that, despite the lure and support of the gang, the damage they wreak on the innocent, their own communities, their own families, and each other is horrendous.

Introduction

> The media likens Los Angeles to a "Beirut by the Beach." For 1991, police cited these statistics: 100,000 gang members, 800 gangs, nearly 600 young people killed.... By 1990 the various law enforcement "operations" to destroy gangs (using helicopters, infra-red lights and made-over armored vehicles—not far behind what was used in "Desert Storm") detained or arrested 50,000 youth, in South Central alone. (6)

Thus writes former gang member Luis J. Rodriguez in the preface to *Always Running,* a memoir of his gang days in California. At the time of this writing, there were other timely stories:

- In 2001, gang-related deaths in Los Angeles totaled more than 300, and many of the victims were innocent bystanders, including little children.
- In August 2002, high-school students in New Jersey were arrested for beating initiates into a fraternity so badly that they required hospitalization. One observer quipped, "Gangs or fraternities, what's the difference?"
- On September 10, 2002, the *San Francisco Chronicle* reported that a witness to a gang slaying in San Francisco had been killed. He was the last of the three witnesses willing to testify to the murder. Both the others had also been murdered.
- In January 2003, a college student at San Jose State was killed in what was described as "a rumble" between rival fraternities, a fight that started with fists and ended with knives.

- In April 2003, in what appeared to be a gang killing for revenge, a gunman armed with an assault weapon shot into a high school in New Orleans, killing one person and wounding three.
- In spring 2003, it was reported that from 1993 to 2003, an estimated 10,000 youths had died in gang-related deaths in Los Angeles alone.
- In April 2003, South Central Los Angeles, to counter its notorious reputation as a gang-ravaged area, proposed changing its name.
- In April 2003, a story out of Chicago told of a former gang chief and ex-convict who took DePaul University students on tours of gang-ruled territory on Chicago's West Side.
- Police reported that 10 people were murdered and 15 wounded in South Central Los Angeles by gang gunfire in a single week in mid-May 2003.
- On June 4, 2003, on a typical day in South Central Los Angeles, in what is presumed to be a gang killing, three innocent bystanders were shot and two wounded in a drive-by shooting.

Turning from reality to art, one finds that one of the most widely advertised movies, released in late 2002 and nominated for numerous Academy Awards, was a film set in the nineteenth century entitled *Gangs of New York*. The film prompted spectacular sales of the reissued 1928 book on which it was very roughly based. Moreover, two other books about nineteenth-century New York gangs were published to considerable acclaim in 2001 and 2002: *Paradise Alley* by Kevin Baker (HarperCollins) and *Five Points* by Tyler Anbinder (Penguin Putnam).

There is little doubt that the topic of youth gangs is one of pertinence and abiding interest. And this volume, a collection of essays on fiction, memoirs, and histories of gangs, is intended to encourage discussion of what could be termed homegrown terrorism, this scourge that destroys its own.

DEFINING TERMS

Because the term *gang* is inexact, the term must be defined, the parameters clearly drawn, before any meaningful discussion can commence. On the benign extreme, gang is used to refer simply to a group of friends or workers. According to some definitions, the term may also embrace social fraternities or other secret societies.

Law-enforcement agencies define gangs in a fairly uncomplicated, straightforward way: they are simply organized groups that gather together for the purpose of criminal activity. This definition would encompass pirates on the high seas, members of organized crime like the Mafia, and groups of outlaws like the gangs of Jesse James in the Old West and Pretty Boy Floyd in the 1930s. Our focus here is on youth gangs. Mobsters, like motorcycle gangs and prison gangs, are usually made up of adults, who often have their beginnings in youth gangs. The connection between youth gangs and adults involved in organized crime is strong, for adult criminals actively foster youth gangs and recruit from their numbers.

Sociologists have attempted to define youth gangs in particular as groups of criminals that pose one of the greatest, fastest-growing threats to contemporary society. They are defined as highly organized, cohesive, secret, and violent. Operating on the outer boundaries of society, they have common interests, commit crimes for revenue, and defend a particular territory or business, or their group reputation.

Gangs are technically differentiated from mobs. Mobs often act spontaneously in a single incident as a group of disorganized individuals, many or most of whom don't know each other. But in the literature considered here, mobs, as in the case of the nineteenth-century Draft Riots in New York City and the Los Angeles riots, were largely composed of gangs. Gangs are also somewhat distinguished from what are known as "tagger crews" or graffiti bands that operate as loose groupings of individuals with little organization and less violence.

TYPES OF GANGS

Gangs are largely segregated by sexual orientation and ethnicity. Most gangs are made up exclusively of males. There are considerably fewer "girl" gangs. Females associated with male gangs are often there as hangers-on to serve at the pleasure of the males. Girls are brutally and humiliatingly initiated as official groupies, rarely as members.

Most gangs take their identity from their ethnicity; they are separated, for example, into Chicano, African American, Chinese, Vietnamese, Korean, and Caucasian gangs. In a few instances, what brings a gang together is a narrow, all-consuming interest that may, in a few cases, cross ethnic lines. Such is the case of surfer gangs, biker gangs, and skinheads. By contrast, what are called street gangs are, as groups, only secondarily devoted single-mindedly to politics or a particular activity such as surfing.

Street gangs are divided into several different types. "Scavengers," sometimes referred to as wanna-be gangs, are typically made up of white suburbanites whose chief activity is bullying and intimidating other juveniles. Latino or Spanish gangs, whose primary incentive is to gain respect, are called territorial gangs. African American and a few Spanish gangs are called hardcore gangs because of their focus on making money at all costs and wiping out their rivals through violent, criminal activity.

Members of a single gang typically share common goals, backgrounds, and turf. Although there are many different kinds of youth gangs, most have certain elements in common: Their membership is made up of juveniles, and they are involved in criminal activity of many kinds. They defend particular territory or turf, from street corners to neighborhoods. They develop elaborate methods of communication. And they have typically been local and independent of any larger, national organization.

CRIMINAL ACTIVITY

Juveniles have been attracted to gangs in part because gangs hold out the promise of money, thus prestige. Gangs provide a setting where youths can learn skills useful in conducting thievery and extortion, where schemes can be contrived, and where members can find a measure of protection, whether or not they are engaged in criminal activity. Moreover, rather than ostracizing and censuring its members for felonious activity, gangs value and reward criminality. Theft, drug dealing, violent assault, and the murder of rivals are the offenses that eventually land most gang members in jail.

GANG STRUCTURE

Gangs have a hierarchical structure with a strong leader and council at the top, although both the leader and council members are constantly changing as they move to other locations, get arrested, or grow too old for the gang. Typically, there are several categories of gang members or potential gang members. The "O.G.s" (or Original Gangsters) are the party-faithful members of long standing. They are also called the hardcores, and they usually constitute the top 10 percent of the membership. The hardcore leaders are the most violent gang members. One step below them are the regular or associate members, 14-to-17-year-olds who have been formally initiated into the gang and support themselves and the rest of the gang with armed robbery, extortion, and drug deals. The wanna-be's are the 11-to-13-year-old hangers-on who, not yet initiated into the gang, continually try to prove themselves with the commission of petty crimes, chiefly thefts. The members of the bottom category are the prospects, boys under 10 who are viewed as future recruits because they live in gang-dominated turf or have gang members in their families.

INITIATION

Initiation into a gang is called being "V'd in" or jumped in. The process usually includes successfully perpetrating a crime at the direction of the gang leadership and surviving a 10-minute beating in which all members of the gang participate.

GANG IDENTITY AND METHODS OF COMMUNICATION

Like sports teams, gang members develop identity and loyalty by using specified names, hand signs, graffiti, tattoos, codes, and meaningful colors. For example, the colors of the sect called the People are red, black, and white; one of their important symbols is a pitchfork turned down. Their rivals, in the sect called Folks, use the colors blue, green, and black, and a symbol of a pitchfork turned up. Gang symbols, then, become identifiable tattoos. These become statements of gang members' identity and loyalty, as well as their mode of communication with one another.

GANG DRESS

Gangs place inordinate importance on dress and appearance. Members of all three major gang sects identify themselves by "dressing to the left" or "to the right." The brims of their hats, for instance, will be turned to the left or right, their shirt collars turned up or down to the left or right. They wear earrings in the left ear only or the right ear only. Other identifiers include scarves hung from belt loops or tied around the left or the right leg, eyebrows shaved off or lines shaved through them, tattoos on the palm of the hand or between the thumb and index finger, or marks burned onto some part of the body.

Particular gangs are known for wearing the team shirts and caps of athletic teams, usually using initials related to their gang names. The

People wear Chicago Bulls regalia, and the Crip Nation and Cobra Nation wear shirts and caps emblazoned with North Carolina insignia. The Disciples wear Detroit Tigers shirts and hats.

HISTORICAL DEVELOPMENT

Gangs, that is, groups who band together in antisocial behavior, are almost as old as human history itself. One of the earliest allusions to gangs comes from India in about 1200 A.D. Called *thugz* (from which we get the word thugs), these groups wandered across the country disrupting communities. Like gangs throughout history, *thugz* had their own emblems, codes, and jargon. Another early reference to gangs comes from Saint Augustine, who, in his *Confessions*, mentions the criminal activities of youth gangs in Italy between 354 and 430 A.D.

As early as medieval times, a combination of factors set the stage for the later bonding together of rebellious juveniles to produce havoc in established communities. In the first place, children were expected to behave as adults. There was little consideration that they were vulnerable and ignorant in the ways of the world. Children were often regarded as little more than work animals or lowly slaves. The seeds of unrest among them were sown with the brutality and violence to which they were routinely subjected. In the second place, a shift in population encouraged juveniles to group together in rebellious behavior. Total life expectancy was comparatively low (about 32 years in 1640), as the population of adults was depleted by disease and accidents. At the same time, the fertility rates were high. The result was a population in which youths were in the majority, with some 50 percent of the population below the age of 20. These young, working-class people were typically forced to go out on their own to work from ages as young as 7. They were late in marrying and having homes of their own, so for 10 or 20 years, they were without the cohesiveness of home and family, without established lives inside traditional structures. Desperately poor, completely on their own, often looked down upon by the community's adults, these youths banded together to seek familial support, loyalty, esteem, power, economic relief, and revenge against an oppressive adult society. An early example was James Coterel, a young man in fourteenth-century England who, with his brothers, terrorized the countryside with all manner of violence, including murder. Juvenile delinquency surfaces in the sixteenth century with the so-called *charivari*, or the lords of misrule, who as a group attacked weak, deviant adults, including wife beaters, debtors, and idlers, demanding money to cease their harassment. Communities actually condoned the *chari-vari*'s actions, seeing them as relatively harmless ways to channel the energy of the large, restive population of youths who, at the same time, were administering social correctives. These groups called themselves the Hectors, the Bugles, and the Dead Boys. Similar young lords of misrule also held sway in France and Germany. But young people eventually moved from attacks on deviant individuals to attacks on the establishment. Some became revolutionaries.

One famous gang, actually called a band, in the late fourteenth or early fifteenth century was the one led by Robin Hood, who operated in Sherwood Forest in Nottinghamshire and in Yorkshire. This legendary group had the reputation of robbing the rich and giving to the poor.

Another unlikely medieval group of gangs was composed of university students throughout England and Europe. Students carried all manner of weapons with them and attacked their teachers and fellow students. As a group, students waged war on the towns in which their universities were located. At the end of the thirteenth century, one group of 3,000 Oxford students and teachers attacked townspeople and their businesses, killing 3 people and wounding more than 50.

While gangs were developing in the Old World, they were taking root in the New World as well, even in areas overseen by the pious Puritans. In seventeenth-century colonial New England, young servants, often indentured to their masters for 10 years or more, banded together during rare leisure time to drink, fight, gamble, experiment with sex, and fatten their lean pockets with petty theft. The fastest acceleration of group delinquency came in the eighteenth century with the Industrial Revolution, bringing with it the rise of the factory system, migrations from rural to urban areas, the development of slums, and the appearance of the apprentice system. To feed the demand for laborers in increasing numbers of factories and trades, children were required as apprentices to learn needed skills and to perform the lowliest and most arduous chores. Children as young as 7 were taken from home and located with employers, usually in areas of concentrated population. Here, a boy or a girl learned a trade and received room and board in the employer's house, more often than not living in squalid conditions. They were overworked, deprived of food, and beaten mercilessly. If they attempted to escape, their legal status was the same as that of an escaped slave. Under such conditions, the apprentices often banded together for solace and company. One firsthand account of the lives of apprentices comes from the pen of

Benjamin Franklin in eighteenth-century Boston. Young Ben, apprenticed to an older brother who mistreats him, gets no understanding, even from his father who consistently takes Ben's brother's side. Many years later, Ben declares that his brother's tyranny prepared him to rebel against King George III, with whom he compares his brother. In such an oppressive atmosphere, Ben and his young friends kept each other company. Like the gangs that came much later, they had both good and bad influences on one another; most fell into bad behavior and habits, drinking heavily and keeping company with loose women.

The growing urban slums in England and the United States in the nineteenth century and the chasm between rich industrialists and poor laborers led to the first wholesale development of extensive, organized, criminal subcultures among the young. Loss of parental control (not to mention loss of parents and family); youthful independence; admiration of older, more rebellious thugs; and simple desperation gave rise to the recruitment of scores of homeless youths to make money for adult criminals by committing petty crimes. In England, the usual criminal activities were begging, picking pockets, and cutting purses. These youths named themselves the Redskins, the Black Hand, the Beehives, the Fagins, and the Swell Mob. Charles Dickens's *Oliver Twist* is a fictionalized account of how the country's economic system inevitably led to exploitation and disruption. By midcentury, many British youth gangs had taken on formal structures, identifying attire, and names—like the Scuttlers, the Ikeys, and the Pesky Blinders. Their chief pleasure, until the outbreak of World War I, seemed to be harassing authority. By the turn of the twentieth century, outright "hooliganism" was the bane of the British police. After World War I was over, hooligans again arose in England, under the names of the Razor Boys, the Wide Boys, the Spivs, the Cash Boys, and the Teddies, the last of which dominated the gang scene in Britain in the 1950s.

In the United States, youthful gangs held sway on the western frontier as well as in the eastern cities. Out west, where the law was non-existent or, more often than not, corrupt, gangs like that of Billy the Kid protected their own and terrorized their enemies. Mexican gangs also appeared on the southwestern scene in the early 1900s.

One of the most colorful periods of gang history occurred in the late nineteenth and early twentieth centuries in areas of New York City known as the Bowery, Five Points, Paradise Alley, and Hell's Kitchen. Gangs made up of Jewish, Italian, and Irish immigrants contributed to the character of the city. During the American Civil War, the gangs' violent turf battles added to the national chaos, and in the

1870s, the 19th-Street Gang and the Short Boys terrorized the entire city. The Irish gangs included the Dead Rabbits, the Forty Thieves, and the Pug Uglies. The Dead Rabbits used as their flag a dead rabbit impaled on a stick. The Pug Uglies were named for their hats, called pugs, which they stuffed with paper to create a bizarre, oversized appearance. The most famous Jewish criminal leader, who operated in the late nineteenth and early twentieth centuries, was Monk Eastman. Eastman, who had connections to saloons and political machines, ruled over New York gangs of juveniles who were groomed for his vast criminal network, to which they graduated when they reached adulthood. Italian gangs were produced in the Bowery. From their youthful ranks the Sicilian Mafia recruited its members, like Al Capone and Lucky Luciano.

New York was not the only city to be plagued by gangs in the early decades of the twentieth century. In the 1920s and 1930s, gangs arose wherever illegal liquor was in demand, notably in Chicago and Detroit, where the trade from Canada flourished during Prohibition. In Chicago, African American gangs, linked to the race riots of 1919, specialized in petty gambling and theft. Gangs of white immigrants in Chicago specialized in extortion, murder, and bootlegging. In Detroit in the 1920s, the notorious Sugar House Gang was operated by Jewish youths. Asian and Hispanic gangs appeared in the 1920s and 1930s as well, Asians dominating the Chinatowns of San Francisco, Los Angeles, and New York City, and Mexicans arising from the barrios of Los Angeles. In the late twentieth and early twenty-first centuries, the Latin Kings and Vice Lords ruled Chicago, and African American and Hispanic gangs, especially the Bloods and the Crips, presented problems for law enforcement in western cities, notably Los Angeles.

The 1980s and 1990s saw the rise of "super gangs," with memberships of more than 1,000. Unlike the older, local gangs, super gangs, notably the Latin Kings, the Bloods, the Crips, and the Gangster Disciples, spread into multiple states and developed immense drug networks.

ISSUES AND PERSPECTIVES

Social Problems and the Attraction of the Gang

Young people throughout history have been attracted to gangs for many of the same reasons. The young *thugz* of ancient India, the medieval lords of misrule in England and Europe, the young outlaws of the Old West, the immigrant youths of the nineteenth century, and the ethnic gangs of the twenty-first century share a craving for security, protection, respect, revenge, adventure, and money, none of which seems within reach through other avenues of their lives. They also share a desire for escape. In older societies, the means of escape was alcohol; today, it is more likely to be drugs, which are easier to attain through gang membership.

With few exceptions, the root of the gang problem has always been primarily socioeconomic. Most gangs have flourished in situations of crushing poverty, crowded slums, joblessness, inadequate wages, dehumanizing racial and ethnic discrimination, and rank injustice, the last so graphically manifest in the great chasm between rich and poor. The ranks of nineteenth- and early-twentieth-century gangs in both England and America came largely from orphans who lived on the streets of the cities, little boys and girls who were described by the humanitarians of polite society as members of the "dangerous classes." Gangs did, and do, attract their numbers from children of immigrants, whose families barely eke out a living in a new country where they feel isolated, with their self-esteem and ethnic identity constantly under assault in the predominant culture.

In such a demoralizing situation, the gang offers to members both a haven and an opportunity—money to assuage their economic distress; respect, at least within their own communities, to assuage their battered egos; drugs and alcohol to escape the grim realities; and adventure to substitute for the travel, sports, and other activities so readily available to children of middle- and upper-class parents.

However, poverty is not always the only force drawing young men and women to gangs. In a few cases, gangs have formed in middle- and upper-class communities. These youths, who do not lack material necessities, not to mention comforts, join gangs that offer them danger, the opportunity to bully others, and the availability of drugs and alcohol.

THE DAMAGE INFLICTED BY GANGS

Although the formation of gangs seems inevitable and understandable, given the inequities and hardships in societies, it is absurd to romanticize or condone gang activity. Gangs devastate society, schools, families, neighborhoods, young people not in gangs, and the individuals who are caught up in gang life. The ruin is as deadly and pervasive in our society as systemic cancer.

In the broadest sense, the gang mentality has infected the values of the areas where they thrive. Gangs perpetrate, reward, and glorify violence, war, fighting, cruelty, physical force, rank materialism, and defiance of the law. They show little regard for those attributes that humanize society and lift it above the level of dumb animals: intellectual excellence, gentleness, kindness, compassion, and peace. The violent, antisocial values they uphold are the ones that, by example, the youth around them learn to honor and perpetuate because they see that actions based on these values lead to material goods, instant gratification, and, for the moment, esteem in their small worlds.

Although most gang members are taught not to victimize very young children, the elderly, and the clergy, the treatment of young women by male gangs reinforces the worst, most hideous side of society's violent misogyny, influencing not only a young girl's view of herself but also the society's view of females. Rape and gang rape, always without protection and frequently by HIV-infected men, are crimes that gang members engage in with impunity. Impressionable young girls, often from families in which fathers, brothers, and uncles are, or have been, gang members, are taught that their worth in the community depends upon ingratiating themselves with gangs.

Gangs are often formed as a response to racial and ethnic discrimination found in mainstream society. Ironically, however, racial and ethnic segregation and hatred are exacerbated by the gangs themselves. Most gangs are rigidly, narrowly ethnic, and their enemies are those unlike themselves: the Vietnamese gangs battling the Chinese gangs, and the African American gangs battling the Mexican gangs.

Gangs wreak heartbreaking and unrelieved damage on the neighborhoods of their own people, and on community projects and institutions intended to help the underprivileged. Gangs inculcate hostility to academic learning and disrupt schools and the whole system of education with bullying, intimidation, extortion, and violence, turning schools into battlegrounds. The one sure place where a poor child can find opportunity, not to mention fulfillment, is laid waste by the gang that terrorizes and assaults student and teacher alike.

The same can be said of areas with affordable housing units—the projects. Gangs have turned them into prisons, intimidating and frightening their own people, their own neighbors, and ensuring that the underprivileged children who live there begin their lives on a battlefield of violence and drug dealing.

Moreover, gangs pose a constant threat to innocent citizens in poor neighborhoods where children and uninvolved bystanders are killed on a weekly basis by drive-by shootings and firebombings.

Finally, if drug dealing and drug addition kill, destroy lives, and perpetrate violence, then contemporary gangs, which thrive on both, magnify the problem more than does any other single element in society.

CURRENT PERSPECTIVES AND PLANS FOR INTERVENTION

The prospects for diminishing the damage done by gangs are grim. The first few years of the twenty-first century has seen an increase in the number of gangs and gang members, an increase in the number of cities and communities in which gangs are located, and a steady rise in violence, drugs, and the number of handguns held by gangs. Furthermore, gangs have developed in rural areas rarely troubled by organized juvenile crime until recently. The expectation is that in the future gangs and violence will continue to escalate. Nor do those who have studied gangs have hope that the old solutions to control gang activity will work any better in the future than they have in the past.

Although intervention tactics are necessary to combat gangs, most of the tactics yield only limited results. They identify students at risk for recruitment by gangs and counsel them, provide drug- and alcohol-abuse prevention programs and job training, pass legislation to give law-enforcement officers greater latitude in prosecuting gang members, enforce zero-tolerance policies regarding gangs in schools, prohibit gang insignia in schools, support and enforce greater gun-control laws, and introduce more sports and other after-school programs into targeted communities. One of the problems is that these programs lack adequate funding, and, according to many sociologists, none of these programs, as essential as they are, targets the root of the problem; none proposes the fundamental social changes that make gangs irresistible lures for young people suffering from physical and spiritual deprivation.

BIBLIOGRAPHY

Bernstein, Saul. *Youth on the Streets.* New York: Associated Press, 1964.

Bloch, Herbert. *The Gang.* New York: Philosophic Library, 1958.

Cartwright, Desmond S., ed. *Gangs and Delinquency.* Monterey, CA: Brooks/Cole Publishing, 1975.

Cloward, Richard A. *Delinquency and Opportunity.* Glencoe, IL: Free Press, 1960.

Cohn, Albert. *Delinquent Boys: The Culture of the Gang.* Glencoe, IL: Free Press, 1963.

Covey, Herbert C. *Juvenile Gangs*. Springfield, IL: C. C. Thomas, 1992.

Cummings, Scott, and Daniel Monti. *Gangs: The Origins and Impact*. Albany: State University of New York Press, 1993.

Donahue, Sean. *Gangs*. New York: Thunder Mouth Press, 2002.

Goldstein, Arnold P. *Delinquent Gangs*. Champaign, IL: Research Press, 1991.

Huff, Ronald, ed. *Gangs in America*. Thousand Oaks, CA: Sage Publications, 1996.

Klein, Malcolm W. *The American Street Gang*. New York: Oxford University Press, 1995.

Knox, George. *An Introduction to Gangs*. Bristol, IN: Wyndham Hall Press, 1994.

Rodriguez, Luis. *Always Running, La Vida Loca: Gang Days in L.A.* New York: Simon & Schuster, 1993.

Sheldon, Randall G. *Youth Gangs in American Society*. Belmont, CA: Wadsworth Publishing, 1997.

Spergel, Irving. *The Youth Gang Problem*. New York: Oxford University Press, 1995.

Outlaw Gangs in an Outlaw Society: Jorge Luis Borges's "The Dread Redeemer Lazarus Morell" (1972) and Mark Twain's *Adventures of Huckleberry Finn* (1884)

FROM MARK TWAIN,
LIFE ON THE MISSISSIPPI.

1883. New York: Oxford University Press, 1990.

There is a tradition that Island 37 was one of the principal abiding places of the once celebrated "Murel's Gang." This was a colossal combination of robbers, horse-thieves, negro-stealers, and counterfeiters, engaged in business along the river some fifty or sixty years ago. (199)

. . .

[Twain quotes from "a now forgotten book which was published half a century ago." This book was Captain Frederick Marryatt's *A Diary in America* published in 1839. Marryatt made use of *History of the Detection, Conviction, Life, and Designs of John A. Murel,* published in Athens, Tennessee, in 1835. It contains what is reputed to be an interview with Murel.]

Myself and a fellow by the name of Crenshaw gathered four good horses and started for Georgia. We got in company with a young South Carolinian just before we got to Cumberland Mountain, and Crenshaw soon knew all about his business.... Crenshaw had traveled the road before, but I never had; we had traveled several miles on the mountain, when he passed near a great precipice; just before we passed it Crenshaw asked me for my whip, which had a pound of lead in the butt; I handed it to him, and he rode up by the side of the South Carolinian, and gave him a blow on the side of the head and tumbled him from his horse; we lit from our horses and fingered his pockets; we got twelve hundred and sixty-two dollars. Crenshaw said he knew a place to hide him, and he gathered him under his arms, and I by his feet, and conveyed him to a deep crevice in the brow of the precipice, and tumbled him into it, and he went out of sight; we then tumbled in his saddle, and took his horse with us, which was worth two hundred dollars.

We were detained a few days, and during that time our friend went to a little village in the neighborhood and saw the negro advertised (a negro in our possession), and a description of the two men of whom he had been purchased, and giving his suspicions of the men. It was rather equally times, but any port in a storm: we took the negro that night on the bank of a creek which runs by the farm of our friend, and Crenshaw shot him through the head. We took out his entrails and sunk him in the creek. [New York: James R. Osgood, 1883]

He had sold the other negro the third time on the Arkansas River for upwards of five hundred dollars; and then stole him and delivered him into the hand of his friend, who conducted him to a swamp, and veiled the tragic scene, and got the last gleanings and sacred pledge of secrecy; as a game of that kind will not do unless it ends in a mystery to all but the fraternity. He sold the negro, first and last, for nearly two thousand dollars, and then put him forever out of the reach of all pursuers; and they can never graze him unless they can find the negro; and that they cannot do, for his carcass has fed many a tortoise and cat-fish before this time, and the frogs have sung this many a long day to the silent repose of his skeleton. (202–203)

Jorge Luis Borges's short fiction "The Dread Redeemer Lazarus Morell," in *A Universal History of Infamy*, and Mark Twain's *Adventures of Huckleberry Finn* are both useful in setting up the complexities and essential paradoxes of gang behavior. Both works, set in the slaveholding South of the nineteenth century, ask what legality and criminality are, what the difference is between institutional and illegal violence, and in what ways the outlaw gang merely parallels an inhumane state or nation. These questions, although asked in the nineteenth century, are pertinent to modern discussions of youth gangs.

"The Dread Redeemer Lazarus Morell," a fictionalized tale of a historic person named John A. Morell, is divided into eight brief sections, beginning with "The Cause," a fictional explanation of the importation of black slaves into the New World and a list of some of their contributions to American culture and folklore. One of the legends that arose in this period involved Lazarus Morell, a poor white boy who grew up to ply his trade as a horse and slave stealer along the Mississippi River in the 1830s and 1840s. In the section entitled "The Man," the narrator provides the reader with a thumbnail sketch of Morell, known as "an adulterer, a Negro stealer and a murderer" (22) who, nevertheless, could preach so eloquently that he brought his audience to tears. In his old age, he became the very image of the southern gentleman.

Morell's reputation rested on a swindle of mind-boggling complexity, which the narrator describes as the sordid, "deadly manipulation of hope" (23). It was carried out by Morell's gang of 1,000 men, 200 of whom were the leaders and 800 of whom—many of them of mixed race—took the real risks, did the dirty work, and were killed as scapegoats when any trouble arose. The plan was this: The Morell gang roamed the South, promising to help selected slaves to escape, on one condition—that the slave would allow himself to be sold by Morell to another owner and would remain there for a short time. The slave was told that after a short time, he would have to escape and be rescued by Morell again. The slave was promised that he would receive a percentage of his sale price and be relocated to a free state. But Morell never intended to keep his part of the bargain. After the slave had been sold, Morell insisted that the slave needed to escape and be sold a second time and that the expenses incurred in carrying out the escape had left little or no money from the sale for the slave himself. Many of the slaves were forced into three sales and were invariably killed by Morell's gang to avoid detection.

After Morell is betrayed by a gang member, who has done the unthinkable in breaking his oath to Morell, he is cornered in New Orleans by the authorities. But he escapes and plans to lead an army of blacks (who have been deceived into thinking he is the slaves' friend) to take over the Louisiana Territory. But five months later, in a Natchez, Mississippi, hospital bed, he dies of lung disease, neither the death of an outlaw nor the death of a liberator. Coincidentally, an uprising of slaves, seemingly unconnected to Morell, is put down at the same time.

Borges's story of Morell raises the following questions, which beg to be asked of his gang in particular and of gangs in general: How does one define lawful and unlawful behavior? Is our treatment of other people determined by personal conscience or by the government and those in authority? What does one do when the two are in conflict? Is it possible for the government itself, which makes the laws and dictates behavior, to be outside the law of personal conscience and what we would call human decency? Are we really surprised when a society that violates human decency breeds gangs that break all laws? Is "goodness" distinguishable from "greatness"?

Borges shaped his fiction from historical accounts in Mark Twain's *Life on the Mississippi* and historian Bernard de Voto's *Mark Twain's America*. His tale, especially its historical context, so powerfully suggested by Borges, effectively evokes the irony and paradoxes that pervade stories of gangs universally. By the 1830s, slavery had become a thriving institution in the United States. The entire economy of the American South depended upon labor-intensive crops such as cotton, rice, tobacco, and sugar cane, and black slaves provided the great plantations with the cheapest possible labor. Nor was the South alone enriched by slavery. Northern textile mills like the one in Lowell, Massachusetts, had no compunction about buying slave-produced cotton from the South.

The primary abomination for the slave was the situation of being owned. When slaves who had been freed were reminded that their lives "were better" under slavery, most declared that they would rather die free than live as slaves. Even with the plantation owner's incentive to protect his investment, the lives of slaves were appalling. Excavations in the second half of the twentieth century showed that they typically lived in huts with dirt floors and had to supplement the rations provided to them with hunting and fishing. Overwork, disease, and misuse depleted their ranks. On plantations run by cruel owners and overseers, they were beaten, chained, raped, and sold away from their families.

Violence was an everyday occurrence in the slaveholding South. Not only was violence directed against slaves, it pervaded all other aspects of the slave-owner's life as well. The genteel southern plantation owner turned to violence on many occasions to settle disagreements or to defend his honor when someone had "insulted" him or a member of his family. The southern gentleman felt himself honor bound either to thrash the perpetrator or to challenge him to a duel. Making dueling a crime did little to halt the practice, which was universally condoned in the South. In inland frontier areas, outlaws like Morell, no more or less violent than the society out of which they sprang, plundered settlements up and down the Mississippi River.

Morell operates within a setting of state-approved slavery, murder, kidnapping, and rape. It is a context that underscores the complexities of gang formation and behavior. Morell is a vicious criminal who preys on black slaves by offering them their only hope and then luring them to certain death, a man who thinks nothing of shooting and then disemboweling an innocent man whose only crime is owning a horse that Morell wants. He and his gang, in short, are the epitome of infamy. But the truth is that this vicious outlaw is a product of, a reflection of, and parallel to the conventional plantation owners who rule and control his society. Morell trades in human beings and so do the plantation owners. Morell resorts to cruelty and so do the plantation owners. Is the slave owner who works, starves, or beats his slaves to death any less heinous than the outlaw who ties a rock to the slave's ankles and throws him in the Mississippi River?

In such a society, the perception of law and outlaw is confusing, a fact underscored by the narrator's reference to the abolitionists, who really struggled to free the slaves, unlike Morell, who only pretended to. In order to follow God's law and the law of individual conscience, abolitionists believed that they had to break man's law. So slaveholders, seeing no difference between factions that threatened their way of life, classed these true "redeemers" with Morell, the false redeemer.

Morell's gang in particular and gangs in general throughout history arise from and reflect the mores of the society they oppose. One example is found in society's materialism. We live in a society that declares money making to be of supreme importance, a culture that admires a company CEO above others and that produces legislation to facilitate a single individual's accumulation of millions of dollars. Gangs that emerge from such a society generally adopt the same materialistic values, which are reflected in the gang names Cash Boys and Cash Flo. Is the gang member who seeks easy money and the esteem that money brings with it so different from a ruthless, greedy CEO?

Borges suggests the similarities between the outlaw gang and the genteel society the gang opposes by making clear parallels between the gentleman slaveholder and Lazarus Morell. The slaveholders are described in the tale as "idle, greedy gentlemen with flowing locks" (21), who are able to live in mansions by overworking their slaves "under the over-seer's lash" (21) and by "tracking them down with snarling packs of hounds" (21) when they escape. Toward the end of his career, Morell himself becomes a southern gentleman like those who had sustained the plantation system and created the misery of his own childhood as a poor white. "Thereafter, the years conferred upon him that majesty peculiar to white-haired scoundrels and daring unpunished criminals. He was an old Southern gentleman, despite a miserable childhood and an inglorious life" (22). Clearly, prestige had been bestowed on both outlaw and owner because of the financial success that they enjoyed as a result of their crimes.

The irony of an outlaw gang in an "outlaw" society is underscored in Borges's language, beginning with the oxymoronic title (in which one word seems to cancel out the other), referring to Morell as "The Dread Redeemer." Ironically, Morell has a reputation among slaves as a savior because no one outside the gang ever lives to tell the story of how he actually kills those to whom he promises redemption.

Reflected in the narrator's phrase, "the great and blameworthy life of the nefarious redeemer Lazarus Morell" (20), is the dreadful reality of gangs in general—the fact that greatness has little to do with goodness. The local esteem that many a gang leader enjoys is built on crime, not integrity.

There is also irony in Morell's leadership, which is anything but benevolent. His lowliest followers are virtual slaves, members who are turned in when law-enforcement officials or plantation owners get too close. Even worse, Morell and his leaders throw their followers into the Mississippi River to drown when they become liabilities. The contradiction in terms—dread redeemer—is pertinent, not solely to Morell, but also to gangs in general. The gang leader makes false promises to young men contemplating membership in the gang: join us and you will be rescued from a life of insignificance and poverty. This is the message. The reality is that the lowliest gang members are often sacrificed to protect gang leaders and that most gang members end up dead or in prison.

Another dimension of the redeemer irony is apparent in Morell's success as a preacher of the gospel. At the same time that he is captivating audiences with his explications of the Bible, his gang, at his instruction, is stealing their horses.

Borges reverses the usual meaning of various symbols to further demystify and deromanticize Morell and his gang, reminding the reader that most gang members, people who are attracted to the romantic illusion of gang life, eventually encounter a grim reality. The black slaves equate the Mississippi River with the Jordan River of biblical times, seeing it as their avenue of liberation. The river is also, like the Jordan, traditionally a watery means of baptism and symbolic renewal. In this case, however, the Mississippi River is death, not new life, a place where the gang can conduct the worst of its activities, escaping up the river after plundering houses along the way, crossing the river with the horses it has stolen, and drowning in the Mississippi anyone, black or white, who gets in its way. Drowning in the Mississippi River would have been appropriate for Morell, who plied his nefarious trade there and whose name, Lazarus, suggests triumph over death; however, the teller of the tale denies him this "poetic symmetry."

ADVENTURES OF HUCKLEBERRY FINN

Set in precisely the same time as "Dread Redeemer" and precisely the same locations of Missouri, Arkansas, and Louisiana, Mark Twain's *Adventures of Huckleberry Finn* is a treatise on gangs in the same kind of "outlaw," slaveholding society along the Mississippi River.

Adventures of Huckleberry Finn, a story told by its major character, is the journey of a 13-year-old boy and an escaped slave who inadvertently joins him on a raft on the Mississippi River. At the beginning of the novel, Huck Finn, son of a drunken vagrant called Pap, and Tom Sawyer, Huck's friend, escape from the tediousness and hypocrisy of civilization by forming a gang that satisfies Tom's insatiable hunger for adventure. Soon after, to escape his abusive father and his pious-mouthed overseer, Miss Watson, Huck fakes his own death and heads for an island in the Mississippi. There he is joined by Miss Watson's slave, Jim, who intends to reach a free state and work to buy his enslaved wife and children. Huck and Jim take off on a raft down the river, planning to go up the Ohio where it meets the Mississippi near Cairo, Illinois.

On the way, Huck and Jim have encounters with two real gangs, in sharp contrast to Tom Sawyer's romanticized childhood gang. When an empty frame house floats down the river toward them, they manage to board it, looking for food. Clearly this had been a house of prostitution, once inhabited by a vicious gang that has left a murder victim behind. Jim, who discovers the body and identifies it as Huck's "Pap," warns Huck not to look at it.

Then on a sinking ship named the *Sir Walter Scott*, they meet another dangerous gang (likely patterned on Morell's), a group that makes its living by thievery. The gang members are in the process of planning the murder of one of their own, who they have accused of betrayal. Huck and Jim spy on this frightening gathering and manage to steal the gang's little boat to get off the sinking ship alive. But Huck's conscience will not rest until he has approached a ferryman to rescue the scoundrels.

On a foggy night, Huck and Jim miss the chance to move up the Ohio to a free state. Instead they find themselves being carried farther down the Mississippi, even deeper into slave territory. When their raft is capsized by a steamboat that rolls right over them, Huck makes his way to a community where two seemingly respectable families have for decades been engaged in a bloody feud, not unlike the feuds between rival gangs. The murder, in one of these wars, of Buck, the young boy Huck has come to regard as a brother, traumatizes and grieves him. The event impels him to leave the Grangerford family to which he had become devoted and to reconnect with Jim on the river. Huck is again met with a scene of violence and death when he witnesses a murder on the main street of an Arkansas town in broad daylight. The town patriarch, Colonel Sherburn, guns down the unarmed town drunk for insulting him.

Shortly after, Jim and Huck and their raft are taken over by a gang of two—river rats who call themselves the King and the Duke. They participate in several con games to extort money from the communities they pass. On the outskirts of one town, the King, pretending to be a reformed ship's captain, cons a devout audience with a sermon about his own conversion and missionary work, ending by sending around the hat for money. The scene is another echo of the Morell gang.

After Huck foils a scheme of the King and the Duke's to extort money from an innocent family by posing as long-lost English relatives, the two wastrels are arrested and eventually tarred and feathered. Jim is captured and chained in a shack behind a house that coincidentally belongs to Tom Sawyer's aunt and uncle. Here, Huck finds Jim and plans to rescue him. His plans are threatened with indefinite delay when Tom Sawyer shows up and insists that the rescue be staged according to the rules of his own romanticized gang and formulated on the pattern of French and English romances.

To see his plan succeed, Tom keeps from Huck and Jim the news that Jim has already been freed by Miss Watson on her deathbed and can no longer be legally imprisoned as a slave. The story ends when Jim is finally able to go to a free state in the North; when we see Tom, who, for all his rapscallion escapades, proves himself to be a lover of western romance and hence a figure of civilization; and when Huck, who has seen enough of civilization in Tom and in the community, leaves civilization behind in heading west.

Mark Twain's novel is largely a bitter satire of gangs and the society that produced them. The remarkable thing about his 1884 satiric commentary is that he attributes characteristics to gangs in the 1830s and 1840s that are applicable to gangs in the twentieth and twenty-first centuries. These include copying the fantasies found in literature and, in recent times, in movies and music; the importance of codes and secrecy; the love of militaristic hierarchy and trappings; the importance of securing money by lawless means; the importance of a reputation for courage and loyalty; violence; and the element of the games boys play in gang activity. In examining these similarities between nineteenth-century gangs in *Adventures of Huckleberry Finn* and contemporary gangs, it is useful to consult Professor Larry Watts's 1995 interview with a gang member called Ted (in Johnson 195–219).

Literary Fantasy

Tom Sawyer's gang, with which Twain's novel begins and ends, thrives on the devices Tom finds in romantic literature. In chapter 2, "Our Gang's Dark Oath," Tom explains that he got a "beautiful oath" from "pirate-books and robber-books." He gets the idea of kidnapping people and holding them for ransom from books. Note the reference to "the authorities," meaning books, in Tom's conversation with his gang members:

> "Must we always kill the people?"
> "Oh, certainly. It's best. Some authorities think different but mostly it's considered best to kill them—except some that you bring to the cave here, and keep them till they're ransomed."
> "Ransomed? What's that?"
> "I don't know. But that's what they do. I've seen it in books, and so of course that's what we've got to do."
> "But how can we do it if we don't know what it is?"
> "Why, blame it all, we've got to do it. Don't I tell you it's in the books? Do you want to go to doing different from what's in the books, and get things all muddled up?" (11)

· · ·

"Why can't a body take a club and ransom them as soon as
they get here?"

"Because it ain't in the books so—that's why....Don't
you reckon that the people that made the books knows
what's the correct thing to do?" (12)

Inspired by Cervantes's *Don Quixote,* Tom directs a raid on a
Sunday-school picnic, which, he tells the gang, is actually a group of
Spanish merchants and Arabs.

At the end of the novel, the only remnants of Tom's gang are himself and Huck. Tom, as the leader, is inspired by numerous romantic
novels to create difficulties in the freeing of Jim. He tells Huck:

Why, hain't you ever read any books at all?—Baron Trenck,
nor Casanova, nor Benvenuto Chelleeny, nor Henri IV, nor
none of them heroes? Who ever heard of getting a prisoner
loose in such an old-maidy way as that?...The Iron Mask
always done that and it's a blame' good way, too. (304)

Ted, in Dr. Watts's interview, provides a telling perspective on the
connection between gangs and literature and "the movies," a state-
ment that could be just as well applied to Tom Sawyer: "You see it in
the movies and what not.... It's like your chance to really experience
it" (in Johnson 217). So the gang creates for itself and actually lives
the fantasies found in literature and film.

Codes and Secrecy

Codes and secrecy are essential to gangs in both the nineteenth and
twentieth centuries. They are in evidence in many secret gang-like societies such as the Ku Klux Klan. In imitation of adult gangs, Tom insists that Jim must send coded messages scratched on the bottom of a
plate. Ted speaks of graffiti that marks territory and serves as a means
of secret communication. He says his gang has "quite a literature" (in
Johnson 215), meaning the various secrets and rituals that any member must master to communicate with his brothers in the gang. These
codes are to be guarded with one's life. Ted will not divulge any aspect
of his gang codes to his interviewer, even under the promise of
anonymity. Similarly, Tom ridiculously spells out the dire punishment
for any member who reveals gang secrets:

And if anybody that belonged to the gang told the secrets, he must have his throat cut, and then his carcass burnt up and the ashes scattered all around and his name blotted off the list with blood and never mentioned again by the gang. (10)

Hierarchy

Adventures of Huckleberry Finn takes place in a South inspired by the knights and princes in the literature of Sir Walter Scott, which Twain ridicules in the characters of the King and the Duke. Southerners, even before the Civil War, loved military titles and bestowed the title of "colonel" on well-to-do gentlemen who had never ever seen a day of battle. One such character in Twain's novel is "Colonel Grangerford," who intimidates everyone in his clan, and "Colonel Sherburn," who kills an unarmed drunk. Gangs found this system of rank extremely attractive and incorporated it into their organizations, as is apparent in Morell's gang.

The same could be said of Ted's street gang, which has "generals" and "enlisted men." The "high supremes" are the generals or kings of Ted's gang—those who have risen to the top, are supposed to be most wise in the ways of the streets, and are to be obeyed without question.

Getting Money Illegally

The "business" of gangs in *Adventures of Huckleberry Finn* is thievery by violent means. When Ben Rogers asked Tom Sawyer, "What's the line of business of this Gang?" Tom makes it clear that they will be robbing stagecoaches. Moreover, they plan to hold hostages to collect money and rob the children on the picnic, pretending that they are Spanish merchants. Tom's illegal activities are romantic fantasies that are in contrast to the two real gangs that Jim and Huck chance upon. The gang that was once inside the house floating down the Mississippi has left behind masks and stolen loot, as well as one of its victims. And a gang has boarded the *Sir Walter Scott* looking for loot to steal. The two-person gang of the King and the Duke is less vicious, but still intent on conning people out of their money.

Ted, who tells Dr. Watts that "it's all about making money," explains that his gang's chief business is "selling dope" and pimping for prostitutes (in Johnson 207).

Reputation for Courage and Loyalty

The driving force behind a gang's code of honor is reputation—what others think of you. And reputation rests on the appearance of courage and loyalty in the communities through which Huck moves. We see it reflected in Colonel Sherburn's taunt to the mob ("you're afraid to back down—afraid you'll be found out to be what you are—cowards" [188]) and in Buck Grangerford's pride in the courage of both his own clan and that of his enemies. Tom also concocts activities for his gang that are designed to test the courage of the members, and he is most proud of himself when his own courage is in evidence when he is shot in helping Jim escape. Likewise, Ted insists that courage is the essential value of any gang member.

Loyalty is described by Ted as one of the most important qualities of a gang member. Betrayal is dealt with swiftly and mercilessly. Tom Sawyer's view of the way his gang should work is a parody of the importance of loyalty that one sees reflected in the feud of the Grangerfords and Shepherdsons. The gang Huck and Jim see on the *Sir Walter Scott* have tied up one of their members, whom they first contemplate shooting and then plan to let drown, because they believe he has betrayed them and intends to betray them again:

> "Oh, please don't, boys; I swear I won't ever tell!"
>
> And another voice said, pretty loud:
>
> "It's a lie, Jim Turner. You've acted this way before. You always want more'n your share of the truck and you've always got it, too, because you've swore't if you didn't you'd tell. But this time you've said it jest one time too many. You're the meanest, treacherousest hound in the country." (89–90)

Violence

Huck encounters violence repeatedly: in Hannibal, in his father's shack, in the house floating down the river, on the sinking ship, among the Grangerfords, on the street where Colonel Sherburn shoots the drunk Boggs, and in the streets where the King and the Duke are tarred and feathered. Such violence is incorporated into and romanticized in Tom's gang, which has plans for knifings, shootings, and kidnappings. So it is with Ted's gang, where any insult or threat might "get handled," as Ted says—someone might well find himself "in cement shoes" (in Johnson 216).

Gangs and Boys' Games

Twain's description of Tom Sawyer's antics parodies the deadly gangs of the adults by portraying them as the games of little boys who raid a Sunday-school picnic and capture a turnip cart, using the laths and broomsticks that they pretend are swords and guns. Similarly, Ted confesses that the truly deadly activities and ceremonies of the 1990s gang were much like the games of little boys. Little boys, he says, like to play and fight and break things up and love their toys of war.

GANGS AND SOCIETY

Like Borges, Twain compares the slaveholding society of Huck's age with both the childish and the deadly gangs that grow out of that society. They are all prone to violence, all obsessed with reputation, all greedy for material possessions. With Tom Sawyer's gang, Twain points up the silliness of the southern code of honor, with its oaths, vows, chivalry, feuds, and duels.

The outlaws and outlaw gangs in *Adventures of Huckleberry Finn*, while they reflect the same violence found in mainstream society, are actually less heinous than society in general—its outlaws less vicious than the community patriarchs. The establishment employs wholesale violence to maintain its slaves, beating and raping them and using dogs to track down runaway slaves like wild beasts. All the evidence points to members of the genteel, slaveholding society as bigger thieves and murderers than the outlaw gangs. Huck says at one point, for example, that the rascally King and Duke probably aren't as bad as real kings and dukes.

Evidence of the materialism of mainstream society members is their history of owning, not just things, but people. Their society was founded on the buying and selling of human beings, a materialism and greed much more far-reaching than the petty thievery of the river gangs and the cons of the King and the Duke.

Because of the certified thievery and murder on the part of society, Twain's novel turns matters of honor, conscience, and legality on their heads. Honor on the part of Colonel Sherburn and the Grangerfords is an atrocity that results in wholesale murder. And Huck considers himself a dishonorable outlaw and sinner for shielding Jim. He thinks of himself as a thief who has stolen Miss Watson's property. If he had listened to his "conscience" and done the "right" thing, he would have turned Jim in to the authorities. He truly believes he will go to hell for helping Jim escape. Obviously, what the author and reader regard as "right" is, in the view of this society, illegal and morally wrong.

Finally, the society common to "Dread Redeemer" and *Adventures of Huckleberry Finn* that facilitates and condones large-scale murder, violence, thievery, and materialism is more vicious in nature than that of the outlaw gangs it spawns, making the crimes of these gangs appear to be child's play in comparison.

BIBLIOGRAPHY

Bancroft, Frederic. *Slave-Trading in the Old South*. Baltimore, MD: J. H. Furst Co., 1931.

Berlin, Ira. *Many Thousands Gone: The First Two Centuries of Slavery in North America*. Cambridge, MA: Belknap Press, 1998.

Borges, Jorge. "The Dread Redeemer Lazarus Morell." *A Universal History of Infamy*. New York: Dutton, 1972.

Boyett, Gene W. *Hardscrabble Frontier*. Landham, MD: University Press of America, 1990.

Cash, Wilber J. *The Mind of the South*. New York: Alfred A. Knopf, 1946.

De Voto, Bernard. *Mark Twain's America*. Boston: Little Brown, 1932.

Dixon, Bruce D. *Violence and Culture in the Antebellum South*. Austin: University of Texas Press, 1979.

Foster, Francis. *Witnessing Slavery*. Madison: University of Wisconsin Press, 1994.

Johnson, Claudia Durst. *Understanding* Adventures of Huckleberry Finn. Westport, CT: Greenwood Publishing, 1996.

Oakes, James. *The Ruling Race: A History of American Slaveholders*. New York: Alfred A. Knopf, 1982.

Pessen, Edward. *Jacksonian America: Society, Personality and Politics*. Urbana: University of Illinois Press, 1985.

Tadman, Michael. *Speculators and Slaves: Masters, Traders, and Slaves in the Old South*. Madison: University of Wisconsin Press, 1989.

Twain, Mark. *Adventures of Huckleberry Finn*. 1884. New York: Grosset and Dunlap, 1948.

Wyatt-Brown, Bertram. *Southern Honor: Ethics and Behavior in the Old South*. New York: Oxford University Press, 1992.

2

The Irish Immigrant: Herbert Asbury's *The Gangs of New York* (1927)

FROM CHARLES DICKENS, *AMERICAN NOTES.*

London: Chaucer Press, 1842.

Let us go on again; and plunge into Five Points....

This is the place: these narrow ways, diverging to the right and left, and reeking everywhere with dirt and filth. Such lives as are led here, bear the same fruits here as elsewhere. The coarse and bloated faces at the doors have counterparts at home, and all the wide world over. Debauchery has made the very houses prematurely old. See how the rotten beams are tumbling down, and how the patched and broken windows seem to scowl dimly, like eyes that have been hurt in drunken frays. Many of those pigs live here. Do they ever wonder why their masters walk upright in lieu of going on all-fours? and why they talk instead of grunting?

So far, nearly every house is a low tavern....

What place is this, to which the squalid street conducts us? A kind of square of leprous houses, some of which are attainable only by crazy wooden stairs without....

Ascend these pitch-dark stairs, heedful of a false footing on the trembling boards, and grope your way with me into this wolfish den, where neither ray of light nor breath of air appears to come.... The match flickers for a moment, and shows great mounds of dusty rags upon the ground; then dies away and leaves a denser darkness than before, if there can be degrees in such extremes.... Then the mounds of rags are seen to be astir, and rise slowly up, and the floor is covered with heaps of negro women, waking from their sleep....

Here too are lanes and alleys, paved with mud knee-deep...ruined houses, open to the street, whence, through wide gaps in the wall other ruins loom upon the eye, as though the world of vice and misery had nothing else to show: hideous tenements which take their name from robbery and murder: all that is loathsome, drooping, and decayed is here. (136–38)

While the uncharted West provided the world with gang heroes like Billy the Kid and Jesse James, the province of the gang in the twentieth and twenty-first centuries would not be the wild frontier but the urban jungle, where gangs were inevitably linked to poverty, immigration, ethnic hostility, and lawless brutality. At the same time that outlaw gangs were riding the range in the far West, forerunners of contemporary gangs were forming in the streets of New York City. *The Gangs of New York,* first published in 1927 and written by journalist Herbert Asbury, is the classic story of the history and legend of early gangs. Asbury's book was reissued 70 years after its first appearance and is the inspiration for a highly publicized motion picture released in 2002, directed by Martin Scorsese and starring Leo DeCaprio.

THE GANGS OF NEW YORK

The following discussion of Asbury's book proceeds chronologically, roughly from 1840 to 1920, to look at accounts of some of the neighborhoods and conditions from which the major gangs sprang and at the character, activities, and leaders of this seminal and colorful chapter in street-gang history. The gangs of the period are distinctive in their patronage of every aspect of show business and in their notorious criminal collaboration with the city's political bosses. They were, however, similar in fundamental ways to the gangs that followed them, up to and including the twenty-first century: they were generated by a killing cycle of poverty and discrimination, especially in immigrant neighborhoods, beginning at midcentury with Irish and Eastern Europeans and later including Chinese and Italians.

Although Asbury refuses to excuse or rationalize the behavior of the Irish who dominated gangs in this period, the rise of the Irish gang must be viewed in the light of the outrageous discrimination leveled against Irish immigrants at this time. The Irish poor escaped to the United States from abject poverty in their homeland. They arrived in the new land ignorant, filthy, brutalized, and often alcoholic. To make matters worse, Ireland had taught them disdain for law. Once here, they found that they had taken up in a country overwhelmingly Protestant—like their bitter enemies in Northern Ireland and England—where their Catholicism was powerless, misunderstood, and despised. Even in circles where there was compassion for black slaves, the Irish were belittled and segregated as subhuman.

In the following chronological discussion, it is to be noted that several neighborhoods produced the most notorious gangs in New York City:

- Five Points, centered in what is now the southwest corner of Columbus Park, near the intersection of Baxter, Worth, and Park streets, where, ironically, the New York County Courthouse now sits;
- The Bowery, the neighborhood still known as the Bowery, located just northeast of Five Points;
- The East River waterfront, located on Water and Cherry streets, near the East River on the Lower East Side;
- The West Side, the center of which was the end of Charlton Street on the Hudson River, due west of what is now Washington Square and New York University;
- Hell's Kitchen, located in an area near where Madison Square Garden now stands;
- Corlear's Hook, an area near the Williamsburg Bridge on Delancey Street, several blocks east of the older East River waterfront; and
- Chinatown, an area adjoining the old Five Points near what is now Confucius Plaza.

FIVE POINTS

The area known as Five Points, of which a park named Paradise Square was the center, was originally settled by respectable members of the working class, but in 1820 native working men and their families moved out as the buildings there fell into disrepair and poor drainage turned the streets and yards into swamps. Howard Zinn, in *A People's History of the United States,* describes the conditions that prevailed there in the 1820s and 1830s:

In New York you could see the poor lying in the streets
with the garbage. There were no sewers in the slums, and
filthy water drained into yards and alleys, into the cellars
where the poorest of the poor lived, bringing with it a ty-
phoid epidemic in 1837, typhus in 1842. In the cholera
epidemic of 1832, the rich fled the city; the poor stayed
and died. (213)

The sordid conditions of the nineteenth-century Five Points neighborhood produced the earliest gangs in New York City history. Within
20 years, the area had become the most crowded, filthy, and crime-
infested slum in the country, the only affordable neighborhood in the
city for freed slaves and poor immigrants from Ireland. A census taken
in the 1860s found that 3,000 people lived inside a half-mile area of
Five Points, and that around Paradise Square were no less than 270 saloons, in addition to houses of prostitution and liquor stores. English
novelist Charles Dickens's description of the area in 1842 in *American Notes*, which Asbury quotes, is an excellent explanation of the
breeding ground of gangs:

Let us go on again, and plunge into the Five Points.... This
is the place: these narrow ways diverging to the right and
left, and reeking everywhere with dirt and filth. Such lives as
are led here, bear the same fruit here as elsewhere. The
coarse and bloated faces at the doors have counterparts at
home [in England] and all the world over. Debauchery has
made the very houses prematurely old. See how the rotten
beams are tumbling down, and how the patched and broken windows seem to scowl dimly, like eyes that have been
hurt in drunken frays....
    From every corner, as you glance about you in these dark
streets, some figure crawls half-awakened, as if the judgment hour were near at hand, and every obscure grave were
giving up its dead.... [M]en and women and boys slink off
to sleep, forcing dislodged rats to move away in quest of
better lodgings. Here, too, are lanes and alleys paved with
mud knee-deep; underground chambers where they dance
and game;...ruined houses, open to the street, whence
through wide gaps in the walls other ruins loom upon the
eye, as though the world of vice and misery had nothing
else to show; hideous tenements which take their names

from robbery and murder; all that is loathsome, drooping
and decayed is here. (136–40)

From several accounts of the time, Asbury puts together a picture
of one of the most notorious Five Points tenements called the Old
Brewery, a five-story building that he said resembled "a giant toad,
with dirty, leprous warts, squatting happily in the filth and squalor of
the Points" (12). On one side of the tenement was an alley that led to
a room without plumbing, appliances, or furniture where 75 children
and adults lived, many of them prostitutes who plied their trade in the
room. At one time, 1,000 people lived in the Old Brewery, many of
whom were known murderers, thieves, and prostitutes. Asbury writes:

> Fights were of almost constant occurrence and there was
> scarcely an hour of the day or night when drunken orgies
> were not in progress; through the flimsy, clapboard walls
> could be heard the crashing thud of brickbat or iron bar,
> the shrieks of the unhappy victims, the wailing of starving
> children and the frenzied cries of men and women and
> sometimes boys and girls, writhing in the anguish of delir-
> ium tremens. Murders were frequent; it has been estimated
> that for almost fifteen years the Old Brewery averaged a
> murder a night. (14)

From the beginning of gang activity in New York City, the gangs
were marked by ethnic exclusivity and ethnic hatred based not only on
race and national animosities but arising also from economic competition for jobs. Until about 1820, the lowest-level jobs, which often involved clearing the city of garbage and sewage, were filled by freed
black slaves for whom few other jobs were available. But with the influx of masses of equally poor, equally illiterate Irish, the conflict between former slaves and immigrants for the little work available
became ugly.

The gangs, all of them Irish, that sprang from the squalor of Five
Points were among the most colorful to grace the streets of New York
City. Most of them were organized out of and had their meetings in
various grocery stores in Five Points where alcoholic beverages were
the chief commodities. The first group to have structure and leadership were the Forty Thieves. One assumes that the gang's name describes its activities. The Forty Thieves were followed by the
Kerryonians, so named because they were from County Kerr in Ire-

land. The Kerryonians were mainly interested in undermining any British or Irish Protestant presence in city life. The three most outrageous Five Points gangs were the Roach Guards, named for a liquor store, the Pug Uglies, and the Dead Rabbits. Only very big, tall Irishmen entered the ranks of the Pug Uglies, who were known for their huge hats stuffed with wool and pulled down close around their ears to offer some modicum of protection in fights. They were armed at all times with a brickbat, a bludgeon, and a pistol. The Dead Rabbits, the early enemies of the Roach Guards, were named for going into battle with a dead rabbit impaled on a stick. A few notorious girls were associated with these gangs, the most famous of whom was Hell-Cat Maggie, supporter of the Dead Rabbits. In the 1820s and 1830s, these gangs were primarily known as brawlers and street fighters rather than killers for hire, like those who followed in midcentury.

However, the ever present Irish hostility toward blacks broke out in early July of 1834, in an especially ugly series of gang-war aggressions. At this time, the Five Points gangs directed their viciousness not only at blacks but at abolitionists who were working to end the system of slavery and free individual blacks held as slaves in the South. Throughout 1833, the Five Points gangs had launched sneak attacks on the homes and businesses of known abolitionists, breaking windows with rocks and bricks. The gangs were temporarily diverted by turbulent city elections, but again directed their violence against Englishmen, freed slaves, and abolitionists in mid-1834. On July 7 of that year, a gang mob attacked two theaters managed by an Englishman. After the police had routed them from the theaters, they roared as a mob to an upper-class neighborhood where they stormed the house of well-known abolitionist Lewis Tappan, sacking it and burning the furnishings in the street. The Five Points gangs continued their rampages throughout the week, eventually turning their attention to the freed slaves living in the Five Points area. Dozens of buildings frequented by blacks were burned, including two houses of worship. The horrible extent of the gangs' activity is graphically described by Asbury: "Throughout the night [of July 10, 1834] the screams of tortured Negroes could be heard, and an Englishman who was captured by the thugs had both eyes gouged out and his ears torn off by the frenzied rioters" (37).

THE BOWERY

In the early 1840s, gangs sprang up in another neighborhood of the city—the Bowery, which adjoined the Five Points area. The Five Points gangs, who had spent decades bitterly fighting one another, now began to join forces to fight the Bowery gangs. The Bowery gangs, also made up of Irish immigrants, included the True Blue Americans, who were known for delivering anti-British speeches on street corners; the American Guards; the O'Connell Guards; and the Atlantic Guards. But the most famous of the Bowery gangs was the Bowery Boys, led by the legendary Mighty Mose. All the gang members, but especially the Bowery Boys, were enthusiastic volunteer firemen, sponsors of the Bowery and other working-class, Americanized theaters, and devoted workers for Tammany Hall, the New York City political machine. They were also working men, often apprenticed to mechanics and butchers, often bouncers. Like their counterparts and enemies in Five Points, they were also street fighters. According to Asbury, their leader, Mose, was as much a legend as a reality, in the tradition of Paul Bunyan. A play about him, now lost, was produced in the Bowery, and songs about him were sung by soldiers from the Bowery in the Civil War. He was reportedly eight feet tall and had gone into battle against the Dead Rabbits wielding a lamppost.

By the 1850s, there were well-established gangs of boys and girls from 10 to 12 years old in the Bowery and Five Points areas, each of whom was associated with a gang of older members in their teens. They were known simply as the Little Pug Uglies, the Little Dead Rabbits, and so on, a few of which were led by girls. The leader of the Little Forty Thieves of Five Points was Wild Maggie Carson, a child of 7, who reportedly had never had a bath until she was 9 and was finally rescued from the slums at the age of 12. While Maggie rose from the most degrading background, Jack Mahaney, another child-gang leader, was reared in wealth. Mahaney consistently got into trouble with the law and eventually deserted his home for life on the streets in a Five Points gang made up of 9- to 15-year-olds under the brutal rule of Italian Dave. These boys, like Fagin's gang in Charles Dickens's *Oliver Twist*, were trained as pickpockets and purse snatchers.

In 1849, the Five Points and Bowery gangs united to lead a violent demonstration against a common enemy at the Astor Place, a theater that booked English actors and catered to Anglophilic, upper-class audiences. For the lower-class Irish immigrants, led by the well-armed fighters in their neighborhoods, the elegant, ostentatious Astor Place was the prime symbol of the economic, political, and cultural oppression of the poor. Beginning on May 7, 1849, in a siege that continued for several days, members of the working-class poor attacked the theater and the police with paving stones and bullets. Henry Irving, the eminent English tragedian who had been booked for a performance in the Astor Place, escaped to England, never to return. The state militia and the National Guard were called in to quell the uprising, but not before 21 people were dead and 31 seriously injured.

EAST RIVER WATERFRONT GANGS

In the mid-1840s, more deadly youth gangs emerged in an area southeast of Five Points on the East River. The spawning ground for these waterfront gangs was often described as the unhealthiest place in the city because the main sewers, often open, ran beneath its tenements, located in a place called Gotham Court. By the mid-1840s, Gotham Court had replaced the Five Points Old Brewery as the most dangerous area of the city. The buildings of Gotham Court were in such bad shape that they were condemned by the city in 1871, but were not forcibly vacated until the 1890s. Most of the building's 1,000 residents were, as in Five Points, Irish or black. Asbury tells us that literally hundreds of saloons, houses of prostitution, and gambling dens were situated on its main thoroughfare, Water Street. In one of the most notorious establishments, called Kit Burns's Place, the sport of choice was setting rats and dogs on one another.

The East River waterfront gangs that were headquartered in these dives included the Daybreak Boys, the Buckoos, the Hookers, the Swamp Angels, the Slaughter Housers, the Short Tails, the Patsy Conroys, and the Border Gang. Their members were not just petty thieves and brawlers. They were also brutal killers, kidnappers, and river pirates. Murders, usually of outsiders who wandered into the neighborhood, occurred on a regular basis. The chief occupations of the gangs were specific to their location on the waterfront. They easily lured sailors into their saloons, houses of prostitution, or boardinghouses and then robbed and murdered them, dumping their bodies in the East River. They also shanghaied sailors by drugging, kidnapping, and selling them to unscrupulous ship captains who were low on manpower. Waterfront gangs were also notorious for piracy, at first traveling in rowboats to rob houses along the river and later boarding ships to kill the crew and steal valuable cargo.

The Daybreak Boys, which included members as young as 10 years old, ruled the waterfront from 1850 to 1852. They were reportedly responsible for thefts of more than $100,000 and close to 50 murders. Most of their victims were found robbed, stabbed, and floating near the wharves in the East River. With the arrest of some gang leaders and the formation of a squad of harbor police in 1858, many of the waterfront gangs around Gotham Court moved out to other areas.

BIBLIOGRAPHY

Anbinder, Tyler. *Five Points*. New York: Penguin Putnam, 2001.

Asbury, Herbert. *The Gangs of New York*. 1927. New York: Thunder Mouth Press, 1990.

Brace, Charles Loring. *The Dangerous Classes of New York*. New York: Wynkoop and Hallenbeck, 1872.

Gordon, Michael. *The Orange Riots*. Ithaca: Cornell University Press, 1993.

Headley, Joel Tyler. *The Great Riots of New York, 1712–1873*. Indianapolis: Bobbs-Merrill, 1970.

No Irish Need Apply. Dir. and Prod. Marcia Rock. (video recording). Cinema Guild, 1993.

O'Sullivan, John, and Alan Meckler. *The Draft and Its Enemies*. Urbana: University of Illinois Press, 1974.

Zinn, Howard. *A People's History of the United States, 1492–Present*. New York: Harper Perennial, 1995.

3

The Draft Riots: Kevin Baker's
Paradise Alley (2002)

FROM CHARLES LORING BRACE, *THE DANGEROUS CLASSES OF NEW YORK*.

New York: Wynkoop and Hallenbeck, 1872.

The intensity of the American temperament is felt in every fibre of these children of poverty and vice. Their crimes have the unrestrained and sanguinary character of a race accustomed to overcome all obstacles. They rifle a bank, where English thieves pick a pocket; they murder, where European *proletaires* cudgel or fight with fists; in a riot, they begin what seems about to be the sacking of a city, where English rioters would merely batter policemen, or smash lamps. The "dangerous classes" of New York are mainly American born, but the children of Irish and German immigrants. They are as ignorant as London flash-men or costermongers. They are far more brutal than the peasantry from whom they descend, and they are much banded together, in associations, such as "Dead Rabbit," "Pug-ugly," and various target companies. They are our *enfants perdus*, grown up to young manhood. The murder of an unoffending old man...is nothing to them. They are ready for any offense or crime, however degraded or bloody. (27)

. . .

[T]he young ruffians of New York are the products of accident, ignorance, and vice. Among a million people, such as compose the population of this city and its suburbs, there will always be a great number of misfortunes; fathers die, and leave their children unprovided for; parents drink, and abuse their little ones, and they float away on the currents of the street; step-mothers or step-fathers drive out, by neglect and ill-treatment, their sons from home. Thousands are the children of poor foreigners, who have permitted them to grow up without school, education, or religion. All the neglect and bad education and evil example of a poor class tend to form others, who, as they mature, swell the ranks of ruffians and criminals. So, at length, a great multitude of ignorant, untrained, passionate, irreligious boys and young men are formed, who become the "dangerous class" of our city. They form the "Nineteenth-street Gangs," the young burglars and murderers, the garroters and rioters, the thieves and flash-men, the "repeaters" and ruffians, so well known to all who know this metropolis. (28)

. . .

Seventeen years ago, my attention had been called to the extraordinarily degraded condition of the children in a district lying on the west side of the city, between Seventeenth and Nineteenth Streets, and the Seventh and Tenth Avenues. A certain block, called "Misery Row," in Tenth Avenue, was the main seedbed of crime and poverty in the quarter....The parents were invariably given to hard drinking, and the children were sent out to beg or steal. Besides them, other children, who were orphans, or who had run away from drunkards' homes, or had been working on the canal-boats that discharged on the docks near by, drifted into the quarter, as if attracted by the atmosphere of crime and laziness that prevailed in the neighborhood. These slept around the breweries of the ward, or on the hay barges, or in the old sheds of Eighteenth and Nineteenth Streets....Herding together, they soon began to form an unconscious society for vagrancy and idleness. Finding that work brought but poor pay, they tried shorted roads to getting money by petty thefts, in which they were adroit. Even if they earned a considerable sum by a lucky day's job, they quickly spent it in gambling, or for some folly. (319)

. . .

If any of my readers should ever be inclined to investigate a very miserable quarter of the city, let them go down to our "Corlear's Hook."... Here they will find every available inch of ground made use of for residences, so that each lot has that poisonous arrangement, a "double house," whereby the air is more effectually vitiated, and a greater number of human beings are crowded together. From this massing-together of families, and the drunken habits prevailing, it results very naturally that the children prefer outdoor life to their wretched tenements, and, in the milder months, boys and girls live...on the docks and wood-piles, enjoying the sun and the swimming, and picking up a livelihood by petty thieving and peddling.

Sometimes they all huddle together in some cellar, boys and girls, and there sleep. In winter they creep back to the tenement-houses, or hire a bed in the vile lodgings which are found in the ward....Ragged, impudent, sharp, able "to paddle their canoe" through all the rapids of the great city—the most volatile and uncertain of children; today in school, to-morrow miles away; many of them the most skillful of petty thieves, and all growing up to prey on the city. (331)

On the first day of New York City's Draft Riots, the key event in Kevin Baker's historical novel, *Paradise Alley*, journalist Herbert Willis Robinson, one of the novel's narrators, notices a cheerful little boy with blood on his face trying to sail a homemade paper boat in the watery gutter made red by the slaughterhouse and butcher shops. When the boy's first boat soaks up blood and falls over, he makes another one. At the height of mob frenzy on that same day, the little boy turns up again as he rushes into the Black Joke Fire House to tell the fire company that the rioters against the draft are raging toward the Fourth Ward. He is recognized as one of the boys that the gang-associated fire company uses to race ahead of the engines to locate water hydrants. On this occasion, he grins "ecstatically," helping open the firehouse doors so the firemen can join the riot—not to put out fires but to burn the draft records. On the second day of rioting, the child—"the white boy with blood on his face" (477)—makes another appearance, this time helping the victims of the rioters. He is leading a group of black orphans, whose orphanage is being attacked, through a labyrinth of alleys and tunnels to the safety of a precinct house. One of the adults with them observes that the boy seems to be performing this heroic act as if it were a game. After the children are safely ensconced in the basement, the child disappears.

Journalist Robinson sees the smiling boy, once bloody-faced, again, after the riot is over. This time he is seated on top of his parents' wagon, moving out of New York City toward the uncharted West, supposedly out of the atrocities created by the Irish gangs in the streets and toward a place "where boys don't daub their faces with blood like so many savages" (658).

The boy is known as Henry McCarty, assumed to have been the given name of William Bonney, or Billy the Kid, whose parents, at the end of *Paradise Alley,* are rescuing the family from the violence of New York City after the Draft Riots. What the reader doesn't see in the novel is that, as a teenager, the boy will again encounter the same murderous official corruption as that out of which he came, in New York City's Tammany Hall. Only this time it will be in New Mexico, and this time he will understand it and lead the most notorious Robin Hood–like gang to fight the "machine" in the Old West.

The existence of the government's officially sanctioned, criminal "gang" that teaches, exploits, and fosters the terror of savage Irish youth gangs in nineteenth-century New York City is the foremost issue in *Paradise Alley.*

THE HISTORICAL CONTEXT

The story of New York City's Irish gangs begins with the plight of the Irish in their own country, before immigrating to the United States. Politically and legally, the native Irish Catholics were regarded as little more than animals by their Protestant English occupiers, who owned most of the land and administered government in Ireland. As Catholics, the Irish were forbidden from participating in the governance of their own country, forced to pay rent to their English landlords, and forced to pay taxes for the support of the English Church. Without land, powerless, and reduced to penury, the Irish lived on a single crop—potatoes—while their English landlords, many of them absentee, consumed and exported everything else produced on Irish land, including a variety of crops and meats. More and more native Irish were required to live on less and less land. By the 1840s, the same amount of land that had supported 42 people a decade earlier now had to support 294. But in the 1840s, their poverty turned to atrocity when blight attacked the potato, spreading rapidly from one section of Ireland to another. The Irish objected to these years being called "a famine." They chose the more honestly descriptive term— "the starvation"—because foodstuffs other than the potato were plentiful enough but unavailable to the native population, which saw them being exported to Britain by the cartloads. The extent of the suffering in the 1840s was almost unimaginable. An estimated one million Irish died of starvation between 1845 and 1850, and an estimated three million died of diseases. During the worst years of the starvation, England refused to extend food to the Irish. Instead, armed soldiers kept the hungry from stores of food, and the landlords drove their starving tenant farmers off the land, tearing down or torching their shanties so they could not return. Seven hundred people were driven from just one estate in the Irish county of Tipperary. To stay alive, they ate worms, dogs, rats, and grass. Bodies were said to have littered the roads where the carriages of the landlords rolled over them in the dark. Starving dogs and other animals consumed the unburied dead.

To escape, two million Irish fled their homeland, most going to America, where many already had friends and relatives. Their passage was an eight-week trip on what were called "coffin ships" that had once been used to transport slaves. Like slaves, they traveled in the most squalid of conditions below decks. One in six, a total of sixteen thousand, died in a six-year period, their bodies dumped overboard without ceremony by the ship's crews in the night. Even though their destinations were cities like New York and Boston, most of the coffin ships had to land in Canada, which had more lenient inspections than did the United States. Upon their arrival, the Irish were quarantined in miserable hovels called "fever sheds" before being released. Twenty thousand Irish died in Canadian fever sheds, primarily on Grande Isle.

With these harrowing experiences behind them, the Irish poor flooded into northeastern urban areas. By 1850, 40 percent of the Irish immigrants lived in New York City. But America did not prove to be the Eden they might have anticipated. Without education or skills, the men were restricted to the dirtiest, most demeaning, dangerous, and physically arduous work, when work was available. In villages and small towns, they were isolated in areas of dilapidated lean-tos. On the outskirts of towns, they lived in caves. In New York City, they were restricted to and crammed into ghettoes of poverty and crime, like Paradise Alley.

The lives of the many Irish Catholic immigrants were made miserable, not only by poverty, but prejudice. The United States, from its New England inception and throughout the nineteenth century, was a Protestant country characterized by fear and suspicion of foreigners, especially those who were Catholic. Ruth's attack by members of the political party called the "Know-Nothings" is historically based: riotous rampages attacking Catholic churches, convents, and Irish communities occurred throughout the 1830s and 1840s in cities throughout the northeast. Because of their religion and culture, their lack of education and marketable skills, the Irish were regarded as uncivilized, little more than animals. Indeed, because they were neither German nor Anglo-Saxon, many Americans regarded them as nonwhite members of an inferior race—"stupid, negligent, and abominably filthy" (in Moran 77). Signs warning that "No Irish Need Apply" were common wherever they settled. In *Paradise Alley,* a joke among the Anglo natives goes like this: "Question: Why is the wheelbarrow the greatest invention of all time? Answer: Because it taught the Irish how to walk on two feet" (45). The Irish had their own joke about their lowly position in Protestant America: they said mainstream America would rewrite the United States Constitution to read, "The right to life, liberty, and the Pursuit of Irishmen" (Moran 95).

Although the New York Irish poor lived in ghettoes with blacks, and some even intermarried with them, their gangs were notorious for their hatred of blacks (as the novel illustrates), much of which arose from their competition with them over low-level jobs. But at least some of the racism on the part of Irish gangs has been attributed to their desire to validate their "whiteness" in the minds of mainstream America by vociferously severing themselves from blacks. In *Paradise Alley,* when Ruth first arrives in the city, the Know-Nothing gangs called her "nigger" (108).

So the forces of a common, destitute past and the ostracism and humiliations of the present drove the young Irish together into rowdy gangs devoted to the securing of capital by criminal means and the intimidation of anyone they perceived as a threat. Part of gang building was to secure status and identity, and part of it was the desire for revenge.

Paradise Alley is the story of the most notorious gang-led riots in American history, the Draft Riots. The leaders and most-prominent participants in this rampage, which lasted for three days, were the members of Irish gangs from Five Points, the Bowery, Paradise Alley, and the docks of the East River. It was not the first gang-led riot. Gangs had caused massive destruction to the property of abolitionists and blacks, and had driven black residents from their neighborhoods in rampages, the worst of which occurred during 1834 and 1835. Also aimed at government officials, abolitionists, and free blacks, the Draft Riots were started in response to the Civil War Conscription Act, passed by the United States Congress in March of 1863. With high casualties and declining volunteers, Congress instituted a draft for soldiers to fight in the Union army. But, as was true in the Confederate army as well, the act decreed that those with money could hire themselves a substitute or buy their way out for $300. It was a flagrant act of governmental class and economic discrimination. Objections to the act erupted immediately in Ohio, Indiana, Iowa, Vermont, New Hampshire, and Massachusetts. The poor immigrants of New York also regarded the Conscription Act as discrimination against the Irish, for rumor had it that those who had applied for citizenship would be subject to the draft. To make matters worse, the Irish, who as a group despised their neighbors of color and had a history of antiabolitionist rage, had never had any sympathy with the Union cause and were incensed that they would be subject to draft for a war in which they did not believe. In July, draftees began to be chosen in New York City. On July 13, 1863, under the leadership of Irish gangs, an antidraft demonstration erupted and was soon out of control. For three days, no member of local government, no abolitionist, no black person was safe from the frenzied mob. For three days, the gangs raged through the streets, setting fire to buildings, torturing and killing their victims, even attacking an orphanage. The devastation did not end until Union troops, fresh from the Battle of Gettysburg, entered the city to put down the riot. Black residents were entirely driven out of some parts of the city. In the next year, the onerous Conscription Act was repealed.

THE NARRATIVE OF *PARADISE ALLEY*

Paradise Alley is the story of three women, their husbands and lovers, and people connected with them as they struggle for existence during the crucial three days of the gang-led Draft Riots of New York City on July 13, 14, and 15, 1863. It concludes with the account of one day—April 24, 1865—indicating how the riots affected the characters two years later and pulling together the threads of the plot.

The story is told from multiple points of view as the riot itself grows in intensity, shifting from wild celebration to savagery as the rioters begin mindlessly to loot, burn, torture, and kill anything that offends them. In the end, the mob even beats and tortures Irish women in a mindless orgy of destruction and cruelty.

While the action of the novel is limited to only those three days of the riot and its aftermath on April 24, 1865, flashbacks, memories, and subjective introspection afford additional information on American Civil War battles, Irish nationalism, and the massive starvation in Ireland stemming from the potato blight of the late 1840s.

Paradise Alley, where most of the characters live, was located in the Fourth Ward of New York City adjoining what was called Gotham Court, in the southeast area of Manhattan, on the East River. However, the rebelling mob covers most of the city on those three days, gradually moving down toward the homes of the three women in Paradise Alley.

Ruth, one of the three main characters, is married to Billy Dove, a former slave. She is paid $4.00 a week as a ragpicker, employed by Germans who turn the scraps into dolls. In flashbacks, she reveals what has brought her to the United States. In Ireland, in the late 1840s, she left her dead and dying family to wander the roads, almost dead of starvation herself and passing many bodies of the dead as she aimlessly searched for food. At a crucial moment, a stranger named Johnny Dolan saved her from being killed and consumed by hungry dogs. Dolan, a brutal man and a killer, considered her his property and beat her frequently at the same time that he provided her with protection. He secured passage for the two of them on a ship headed for America, where Johnny already had an older sister, Deirdre, in residence. The ship was little better than a floating coffin; and, once more, people died in great numbers from starvation and disease. But Ruth and Johnny finally arrived safely in New York. Here they were confronted with another exploitive, cold-blooded society. To survive, Dolan, like other young Irishmen like himself, joined a savage gang. He killed one man for his food and ultimately killed another, in the process gouging out the man's eye with a corkscrew. Friends of Dolan's sister Deirdre then forcibly put Dolan onto a ship headed for the Pacific, to protect him from the police. Now, as the present action begins, 14 years after he has left New York, "Dangerous Johnny Dolan" is headed back to New York from California, intending to reclaim all that was his, including Ruth. Even before Dolan's departure, Ruth had become the lover of and then had married the former slave Billy Dove, who, while under his master in South Carolina, had been a shipbuilder and sailor. Billy, a tall, handsome man, had taken her into the house that he had built in a black neighborhood called Seneca Village. When it was subsequently torn down for a park, the two had moved to Paradise Alley. The novel opens with the sentence, *"He is coming,"* ominously referring to the imminent arrival of Johnny Dolan, a fearful event that parallels the rising intensity of the Draft Riot mob, slowly making its way across New York City.

A second woman, Dolan's sister Deirdre Dolan O'Kane, is a former domestic and a devoutly religious woman who wants above all to live a decent, respectable life. To further this ideal, she has accumulated a tidy, well-furnished house. She is married to Tom O'Kane, who, at her encouragement, is now a soldier in the Fighting 69th. Tom was one of those who had helped pack Dolan away onboard a ship. As the story opens, the Battle of Gettysburg has just occurred. It is soon revealed that certain soldiers are being shipped directly from Gettysburg to New York City to help restore order; among them is Tom O'Kane.

The third of the key women in the story is Maddy Boyle, a prostitute. While selling hot corn on the streets, Maddy, a very pretty girl, had caught the eye of Herbert Willis Robinson, a reporter for the New York *Tribune*, Horace Greeley's paper. Robinson, paying her an excessive amount for the hot corn, had first taken her to a house of prostitution, then to a house of her own in Paradise Alley.

When Robinson proved unresponsive to Maddy's suggestion that they marry, she returned to prostitution while, at the same time, continued her relationship with Robinson. In pursuit of his own ambition, Robinson writes a novel dealing with the scenes of the gang-infested life he has witnessed.

As the story opens and the mob moves further down toward Paradise Alley, Johnny Dolan, seeking revenge, fortuitously becomes the leader of the mob. Robinson, who is covering the action as a reporter, is increasingly anxious about Maddy's safety. Billy Dove, unable to reach Ruth, makes his way to the colored orphanage where he works. Finding it under attack, he attempts to help the orphans escape the fury of the mob.

As the rioters rage on, Maddy, Ruth, and Ruth's children seek safety in the home of Deirdre, who valiantly tries to save them all as the mob, by this time little more than an insane killing machine, descends on Paradise Alley. In one harrowing scene, the mob begins beating to death Ruth's oldest child, Milton. In an attempt to save him, Ruth throws her own body on top of his, taking upon herself all the blows, the killing one administered by Johnny Dolan. Milton lives, but Johnny's mob beats Ruth so savagely that she dies a few days later.

Two years later, an equally ugly fate awaited her ex-lover Johnny Dolan, the leader of the Draft Riot mob, now down on his luck. Entering a dive to escape a policeman and have a drink, he is directed to a "Velvet Room," described as a place for sailors to rest, only to find himself falling through a trap door to be shanghaied—sold to work as a common sailor aboard a ship.

Immediately after the riot and Ruth's death, Billy Dove enlists in a colored regiment, leaving his children behind with Deirdre. Nine months later, he was listed as missing after the Battle of Cold Harbor. Deirdre also takes care of Maddy, whom she had found dirty, sick, and disoriented after the riot.

A GANG-DOMINATED GHETTO

Paradise Alley was dominated by gangs of Irish immigrants when the novel's characters first come to the United States. Upon their arrival, they notice the prominence of a gang called "the Roach Guards," whose members distinguish themselves by wearing pants with a blue stripe down the leg. With his friend Snatchem, Tom, Deirdre's husband, had "run with the Break O' Day Boys" (330), at one point stealing a schooner from the East Side docks and sailing it up the East River. Deirdre forced Tom to break his ties with the gang when they married, but had no success in stopping her brother, Johnny Dolan, from running with gang members after he arrived. He takes up with Tom's disreputable friends in the Break O' Day Boys and with a gang-run group of firemen called the Black Jokes. Each gang had its own fire brigade and was more interested in competing with one another than putting out fires. When a fire alarm went up, gangs would race each other to the scene to get control of the water from the hydrant. The Black Joke brigade, Johnny among them, races against the Big Six brigade to a fire and gets control of the water. The Black Jokes, by forcing the Big Six to get water through them, deliver the ultimate humiliation, called "washing" them. The connection between the Irish gangs and the politicians is suggested by the information that the Big Six were made up of youths from the old gang of New York's most powerful and corrupt politician, Boss Tweed.

Johnny gains the respect of powerful gangs like the Dead Rabbits and the Gamblers when he finishes 50 rounds of a rigged prizefight. They put him on their shoulders even while he is still unconscious and carry him around like a hero. But Johnny's involvement with gangs becomes more than recreational when he begins to engage in piracy with the river gangs; as Baker narrates, he was "away only on night jobs with the river gangs, that he did not talk much about" (287). Still, after Johnny commits a murder, his greatest fear is of the gangs, the Break O' Day Boys or the Swamp Angels, who might sell him out. But Tom, his brother-in-law, and Billy Dove are able to get him out of town secretly by appealing for help from the Break O' Day Boys.

When Johnny runs into one of his old gang members upon returning to New York, he kills him in cold blood, on the chance that the man might inform on him.

A GANG-LED RIOT

The Draft Rioters were composed primarily of draft-age Irish gang members from Five Points, the Bowery, and Gotham Center—men who despised the free blacks who lived in their midst and competed with them for jobs, men who were being forced to fight for the Union because they didn't have the $300 to buy their way out of service as the wealthy could do. The gang's rage over the draft is foreseen when Deirdre's husband, Tom, decides to enlist. He encounters crowds of "gang b'hoys" who deride the recruiters and those like Tom who are signing up to fight for the Union.

Dolan quickly assumes leadership of the growing mob because in their eyes he is the "Mose," the larger-than-life hero of the Irish gangs. Looking "grizzled and hideous," he is welcomed as the embodiment of Mose, "the old stage perennial, Mose, the Bowery Boy, hero of the gangs and the firemen" (153). And the mob's rage is fed with rumor bred of distrust of the corrupt machinery of government: They are putting Irish soldiers in the front lines to save the native Anglo-Saxon Americans. They are sending in 100,000 freed slaves to take the jobs of the workers (34).

When Tom is in Hoboken, New Jersey, on his way up from Gettysburg with other soldiers to help quell the riot, his friend Snatchem warns him that the violence is frightening, "more than some Dead Rabbits riot" (506). Snatchem is correct. It isn't just one gang, but all the city's competing Irish gangs that in this instance have joined together to turn their objection to the draft into a violent melee. Later, when Tom makes his way through the city, he realizes that a man in uniform will face his greatest danger from "any stray b'hoy from the river gangs" and "the Old Maid's Boys," made up of hundreds of men and boys who were so ruthless that they amused themselves by setting fires and then beating up the firemen who came to put them out and smashing their fire engines. On one day of the riot, Billy Dove is blocked from reaching Ruth by hordes of "men and gang b'hoys just looking for trouble" (178). Upon reaching the orphanage, he temporarily distracts the "gang b'hoys" from attacking the building by performing the dances and tricks that whites expected of black men. As he attempts to find Ruth in all the chaos by traveling through tunnels and streams, he hopes that he won't emerge in "one of the hideouts of the river gang" (603).

Robinson, the reporter, also notes the prevalence of gang members among the rioters. He writes, "Up from the wharves and the Five Points come others, with no intention of fleeing. These are the professional gangsters and the river thieves, the housebreakers and crimps and killers" (302). Near Canal Street, he notes "roving gangs of gang b'hoys" looking for trouble (306). In the Bowery, he sees eight drunk gang b'hoys with a coffin marked, "Old Abe's Draft Died Monday, July 13, 1863" (433). Later, he witnesses the torturing and killing of O'Brien by a mob of "gang b'hoys" (453).

ISSUES

The gang issues that arise in the nineteenth-century story told in *Paradise Alley* are universal ones. They include: the brutalization of once-decent individuals by poverty and desperation; the formation of gangs as a response to being ostracized and discriminated against by mainstream society; the connections between outlaw and law itself, in which gangs feed on and are fed by corruption at the highest levels of government; the pervasiveness of antisocial behavior in gang life, wherein members, in their cold-blooded sadism, lose all sense of humane sympathy and social responsibility, and tend to display a malignant hatred of other races and nationalities.

An atmosphere of general corruption, callousness, and even cruelty pervades the entire society that Baker portrays. "Elections" are fraudulent; voters are bought; politicians are strangers to any sense of morality or virtue. The genteel society that exists far above that of the wretched immigrants, who come in like pigs in rotten boats, employs members of the same wretched class as menials or servants. At the same time, they make sure that immigrants and their kind never quite make it as true human beings, even in their "kindness" displaying an invidious variety of callous cruelty. With only a few exceptions, the entire complex of people or castes that make up this seething culture value only the drive for profit, creating a universal atmosphere of a city about to explode. Robinson, commenting on the "gangs at the top," refers to "our unspeakable aldermen and councilmen, better known as The Forty Thieves," and then amends that to "eighty two" thieves (15). He characterizes the government as a "legislature of bicameral crooks" and the society as a "vast, imponderable hive of crooked street commissioners and demagogues, dead horse contractors and confidence men, hoisters and divers, shoulder-hitters and fancy men, ward-heelers and kirkbuzzers and harlots" (15, 16). At one level down, there are the crooked fire departments. "The Black Joke and other fire companies are the breeding swamps of our wonderful new democracy. There are dozens of such companies, supposedly protecting our highly combustible city. In fact, they are little more than headquarters for our street gangs and political machines—you go tell the differ-ence" (20). There is, he notes, "so much corruption that even if you wanted to clean it all out you could not do it" (15–16).

Paradise Alley records the corruption at the highest levels in New York City, as capitalists make fortunes on the Civil War, many by sell-ing shoddy goods to the Union army. The gangs were merely poorer versions of the same kind of criminality they observed in high places. It is not surprising that Irish gangs were recruited by politicians to carry out unsavory acts of intimidation and that youth gangs became the training grounds for many a politician.

The newly rich, who suddenly leap into luxury by cheating the gov-ernment, illustrate nicely the gangster element in local government and business that fosters criminality and shoddy values among youth gangs. The newly rich sell incredibly shabby material, perpetrate outright fraud, and charge exorbitant prices. Something of the tone they set is represented early in the story. At 11th Street, Robinson passes a spot where a contractor is putting up a double tenement in the place where an old mansion had been torn down, for the sake of progress and profit. As he watches, the tenement collapses, killing the Irish poor inside, be-cause in the summer heat the "worthless mortar" had liquefied: an ex-ample of sheer corruption and greed on the part of callous contractors. Instantly, the "whole neighborhood" is there. And immediately people leap into the dangerous mass, vainly hoping to dig the victims out. Robinson himself leaps in, without thinking (45–48). By contrast, Robinson notes that "swaths of gold and magenta shimmer along the dollar side of Broadway." He calls it "All this golden lust" (55).

Once the Civil War comes, with its inevitable taint of chaos, mass butchery, and driving necessity, this unsolvable pattern of cruelty is propelled forward. War, with its automatic corruption and cruelty, de-vours everything and everyone; and in this atmosphere, noble words or slogans emerge as hollow and even violently hypocritical—to those at the bottom of this putrid mass. The society has the smell of an open sewer. Those with money, like the newly rich, rise to wealth during the war by cheating the government, the soldiers, and their fellow human beings; the rich have all the natural concern of highwaymen or predatory gangs. In the same way, the shabby politicians who climb to power in wartime provide a living example for those at the bottom. These are the eternal victims exploited by everyone, including their own kind. In this case, it is the Irish immigrants, people who have escaped from one life of starvation, death, and total exploitation in their own country by a foreign people only to face total exploitation and cruelty in a new world. Now they were being asked to fight, and probably to die, for the country that despised them and turned them into urban slaves.

Through the eyes of Baker's intellectual observer Robinson, as well as through intrinsic action in the story, he makes the point that government and gangs are all alike. And while he concentrates primarily on the lives of the three women and those connected with them, it is Finn McCool, the brutal assistant foreman of the Black Joke Volunteer Fire Company and Tammany ward heeler, who serves as an example to the young gang members of how one rises to positions of influence and power in this world.

Gangs and gangster values exist pervasively in this society at the bottom, and gangs foment the trouble that results in the massive riot. The young Irish men and women of Paradise Alley are brutalized by their experiences in Ireland at the hands of the British and by their degradation in America. With few exceptions of those who strive to live decent, moral lives of kindness and concern for others, the brutalization they endure is continued in their unspeakable cruelty to others: gouging out eyes, biting off ears, slow castration, and burnings alive.

BIBLIOGRAPHY

Baker, Kevin. *Paradise Alley.* New York: HarperCollins, 2002.

Bernstein, Iver. *The New York City Draft Riots: Their Significance for American Society and Politics in the Age of the Civil War.* New York: Oxford University Press, 1990.

Connery, Donald S. *The Irish.* New York: Simon and Schuster, 1968.

Cook, Adrian. *The Armies of the Streets: The New York City Draft Riots of 1863.* Lexington: University of Kentucky Press, 1974.

Ignatiev, Noel. *How the Irish became White.* New York: Routledge, 1995.

Moran, William. "From across the Irish Sea" and "Wretched Refuse." *The Belles of New England.* New York: St. Martin's Press, 2002.

O'Connor, Richard. *The Irish.* New York: G. P. Putnam's Sons, 1971.

Wittke, Carl. *The Irish Experience in America.* New York: Russell and Russell, 1970.

4

New York Gangs around the Turn of the Twentieth Century: Jorge Luis Borges's "Monk Eastman, Purveyor of Iniquities" (1972)

FROM J. C. FURNAS, *THE AMERICANS: A SOCIAL HISTORY OF THE UNITED STATES, 1587–1914.*

New York: G. P. Putnam's Sons, 1969.

Probably the real trouble was numerical. Volume of influx very likely was outrunning capacity to assimilate. Though it was not much higher proportionate to existing population than it had been before the Civil War, the situation had changed internally. Free land had ceased to be available with the famous closing of the frontier in the early 1890s. Industrial employment was increasingly the economic prospect for all inhabitants of America, native or immigrant. Labor was correct in feeling that the annual flooding-in of the ignorant and unskilled hampered its struggles toward power and leverage equal to the boss'.

. . .

To see boys in their earliest teens acting as uniformed messengers late at night in New York City also struck H. G. Wells hard. He laid it down that "Nocturnal child employment is a social abomination." . . . Of the three occupations the messenger boy's may have been most destructive to judge by the high rates of venereal disease and commitments to reformatories among them in Philadelphia as well as New York City. New York State had laws against sending minor messengers on errands for patrons of inmates of brothels, but nobody bothered to enforce them, and the boys preferred such assignments because of the fat tips often entailed. Doubtless it could be almost as destructive, however, to be an Italian or Greek urchin dodging about the streets cajoling passersby into letting him shine their boots in order to take home enough day's gains to avoid being skinned alive by the *padrone*—the enterprising Neapolitan who bought such boys from their parents in Italy.... [I]t did society little good and him [the newsboy] less to have him...doing odd errands for shady characters as occasion served, and, when he lacked a family to absorb his earning, living in loose colonies of other such derelicts in flophouses or patched-together shanties. (842–43)

After the Civil War, soldiers returned to New York to find a city and an economy in collapse. There was no way to make a livelihood, and starvation and disease were rampant. Moreover, the city had been ravaged by the fires of various riots during the war. One hundred thousand people were living in tenement cellars, and garbage, alive with rats, was piled two feet deep in the streets. Thousands of women had been forced into prostitution by poverty. With these conditions, it is scarcely surprising that gang activity, especially robbery, rose dramatically. New gangs arose throughout the city, prominent ones located in such neighborhoods as Hell's Kitchen, the West Side on the Hudson Bay waterfront, Corlear's Hook, north of the old gang area on the East River, and Chinatown. Italians, chiefly from immigrant families, now swelled the ranks of gangs. The specialty of the Hudson River gang, called the Charlton Street Gang, was piracy. The gang's leader for a time was a young woman named Sadie Goat (so named for butting her victims with her head). In 1869, under her direction, the Charlton Street Gang acquired a boat, which they sailed under the pirates' Jolly Roger banner. Immediately after the Civil War, two other kinds of robbery increased dramatically among gangs: bank robbery and grave robbery. Stolen corpses were not only sold to medical schools but were held for ransom.

WHYOS

Near Five Points, one of the city's most vicious gangs arose shortly after the Civil War, reaching the height of its power in the 1880s and

1890s. The members, Irishmen all, called themselves the Whyos, and one of the requirements for membership was the committing of a murder. The Whyos ran a protection racket and gambling establishments, but they also had a business of beating and killing for hire. Among the papers found on one of their members arrested by the police was a list of crimes the Whyos were willing to commit and the amount of money they required for doing each job:

```
Punching . . . . . . . . . . . . . . .$2
Both eyes blacked  . . . . . . . . 4
Nose and jaw broke  . . . . . . .10
Jacked out [knocked out]  . . .15
Ear chawed off . . . . . . . . . . .15
Leg or arm broke . . . . . . . . .19
Shot in leg . . . . . . . . . . . . . .25
Stab . . . . . . . . . . . . . . . . . . .25
Doing the big job  . . . . . . . .100 and up (Asbury 211)
```

CHINATOWN

From about 1860, Chinatown was also ruled by gangs, called tongs (as Asian gangs are called to this day). The birthplaces of the tongs were the gambling and opium dens of Chinese immigrant Wah Kae, who had a monopoly over illegal activities in the area in the 1860s. The number of Chinese in the area grew from 12 in 1872 to 10,000 in 1910. The notorious tong wars that ravaged Chinatown from 1899 to 1918 were fought chiefly over competing gambling establishments. The main tongs were the On Leongs, led by Tom Lee, the Hip Sings, whose leadership was always a matter of contention, and the followers of Mock Duck. They warred with each other, wearing chain mail into battle. Often the shoot-outs in Chinatown streets resembled Wild West confrontations.

GANGS OF CHILDREN

After the Civil War, burgeoning numbers of juveniles from slum neighborhoods committed crimes not only at the direction of adult gang leaders, but in independent gangs of their own. They inflicted enormous disruption and terror on the populace. Some of these gangs found adventure in throwing rocks through the windows of missions and schools. Other young thieves were the bane of shop owners throughout Greenwich Village. Many solicited customers for prostitutes. The Italian children who formed gangs, often pathetic musicians begging in the streets, were under the control of adult thieves to whom they had often been sold by their parents. An enterprising juvenile street gang called the Dudes created their own theater in a tenement basement and wrote and performed plays for money, until rival gangs and their refusal to pay patronage to the local politicians resulted in the theater's closure. At the turn of the century, the most notorious juvenile gang of pickpockets and purse snatchers was led by a young man named Crazy Butch who at eight years old had been in jail. Despite the growth of social services and educational opportunities in the early days of the twentieth century, juvenile gangs entered their battles with wooden swords and something like garbage-pail lids used as shields.

CAUSES OF GANGS THROUGH WWI

All the gang activity from the end of the nineteenth century to World War I was kindled by a volatile social situation of cultural clashes and unemployment. In the 1880s, there were 5.5 million immigrants in the United States; in the 1890s, 4 million, a mix of Irish, Germans, Italians, Chinese, Russians, Greeks, and Eastern Europeans, many of whom settled in New York City, where they landed. An economic collapse in 1893 left one-fifth of the work force unemployed. In addition, there were throughout the country more than 1 million children less than 16 years old in the work force.

These conditions, which prevailed throughout the nineteenth century and well into the twentieth, accelerated further gang activity. Hopeless poverty taught children that they had nothing to lose and that they should grab pleasure where they could find it. Unemployment led them to crime and attacks on their rivals for work. Discrimination led them to band together. Illiteracy, ignorance, and the need for scapegoats led them to ethnic violence.

"MONK EASTMAN, PURVEYOR OF INIQUITIES"

Of the multiple gangs that arose in New York's immigrant neighborhoods in the two decades that ended the nineteenth century, none was more crude and brutal than the Eastmans, a gang of 1,200 males led by Monk Eastman, a man of many aliases. Eastman is the subject of a fictionalized sketch by Argentine writer Jorge Luis Borges. To accentuate Eastman's crudeness and perhaps Eastman's refusal to romanticize killing, Borges opens his sketch with a contrast to Eastman: the description of a graceful dance performed by elegantly dressed Argentine gang members just before they butcher each other. The story of Eastman that unfolds has none of this romance and refinement, for he is personally as coarse and repugnant as the killings he carries out. Instead of the slim, darkly handsome and elegantly dressed Spanish killers, for example, Monk is repugnant and slovenly:

> He was a battered, colossal man. He had a short, bull neck; a barrel chest; long scrappy arms; a broken nose; a face, although plentifully scarred, less striking than his frame; and legs bowed like a cowboy's or a sailor's. He could usually be found without a shirt or coat, but not without a derby hat several sizes too small perched on his bullet-shaped head. (54)

Eastman's background was not typical of that generally associated with a gang member. He was not a neglected and abused child of the slums, but the son of a reasonably successful, religious Jewish businessman. When Eastman was a young man, his father set him up in a business to his liking: a great animal lover, Eastman was able to run his own pet store. He accumulated a shop full of birds and cats, which he refused to sell, and, for the rest of his life, he strutted around the streets of New York with cats at his feet and under his arms and birds perched on his head and shoulders. In contrast to St. Frances of Assisi, another monk evoked by this picture, Monk was crude, sadistic, and arrogant. While he was curiously attracted to the innocence of the birds and cats with whom he was always surrounded, he was equally attracted to the darkest arenas of human activity: houses of prostitution, gambling dens, and the backrooms of sinister saloons where thefts, maimings, and murders were planned. The birds and cats who accompanied him on his strolls through the slums he controlled might have been innocent creatures, but Eastman himself was a snarling, dangerous brute of a human being. One example is his behavior in securing a job and operating as a bouncer in a saloon. To convince the reluctant saloon owner to hire him, he beat up the men who seemed to be the favored candidates for the job. Once hired, he put a notch on his bludgeon for each man he had beaten up and thrown out. When he wanted an extra notch for his stick—to make it an even 50—he cracked open the head of an innocent customer who was quietly drinking his beer.

The collaboration of gangs with government is shown in Eastman's dual roles. He served as a ward captain in the same area of the city where he led a gang of 1,200 to fill contracts to steal, break arms and legs, and kill. He was rarely arrested for his atrocities and only once served time.

His gang's chief rivals were members of the Five Points gang, an Irish gang led by Paul Kelly. As a result of Eastman's infringement on Kelly's territory, a deadly war was launched between the two gangs, leaving seven wounded and four dead. The political machine put pressure on Kelly and Eastman to make peace, and they met and decided to settle their differences with a boxing match. As to be expected, it was an especially dirty fight with no holds barred, and it ended in a draw. The acrimony, with many arrests and shootings, escalated until politicians at Tammany Hall, who were little more than criminals themselves, turned Eastman over to the courts, and he was sentenced to 10 years in Sing Sing Prison.

This was the end of the gang called the Eastmans. What was left of his organization was taken over by a Jewish immigrant, equally bloody, named Big Jack Zelig. When Eastman was released from prison, he started over, operating on his own, often terrorizing, "chawing off an ear," and murdering for hire all by himself. In 1917, to avoid another arrest, Eastman joined New York's 106th division of the National Guard and was promptly sent to Europe to fight in World War I.

Though he hated military policies, especially the practice of making captives prisoners instead of just shooting them, he hungered as much for action on the battlefields of Europe as he had for action in the New York City streets. At one point, he insisted that he had run across more danger in some Bowery dance halls than he had found under fire in Europe. Even when he was wounded in battle, a parallel to his being hospitalized with a wound in New York, he escaped from the hospital in the war zone to return to fight in the worst battles in France. After the war, his superiors attested to his ferocity and bravery in battle, but he was never officially decorated.

In "The Mysterious, Logical End," Borges describes Eastman as dying of five gunshot wounds on the streets of New York shortly after the end of World War I.

Aside from the irony of Eastman's apparently gentle association with animals, other themes that run through Borges's sketch are especially telling. Borges portrays Eastman without any redeeming features. His barbarism and crudeness is untempered by rules of decency or human compassion. As a consequence, the reader sees his cruelty for what it is, unromanticized by elegance, unmitigated by a history of social injustice. The graceful, stylized dance of death performed by the Argentine dancers at the beginning of the sketch is controlled and refined by tradition, by rules of how things should be done beautifully— even the slaughter of another human being. By contrast, Monk Eastman is an ugly, uncontrollable, raging bull with no iota of shame, no constraints, no sense of decency. Perhaps Eastman's hideous legend of killing is to be preferred over the romanticized version of it.

Borges's choice of the language of battle on every page and his reference to Eastman's experience in World War I remind us that all of this gangster's life was involved in killing enemies over territory on some sort of battlefield. Both nations and gangs protect their turf and kill to maintain boundaries. In the section entitled "The Battle of Rivington Street," Borges compares the street fighters with the Greek and Trojan soldiers fighting at Troy and with the Confederate and Union soldiers fighting in the Civil War at Bull Run.

These comparisons lead to an ironic inevitability: the behavior that makes Eastman a distinguished soldier in World War I is the same behavior that makes him a heartless animal on the streets of New York.

BIBLIOGRAPHY

Asbury, Herbert. *The Gangs of New York*. 1927. New York: Thunder's Mouth Press, 2001.

Berrol, Selma Cantor. *The Empire City: New York and Its People 1624–1996*. Westport, CT: Praeger, 1997.

Borges, Jorges Luis. "Monk Eastman, Purveyor of Iniquities." *A Universal History of Infamy*. New York: Dutton, 1972.

Feldstein, Stanley, and Lawrence Costello, eds. *The Ordeal of Assimilation*. Garden City, NY: Anchor, 1974.

Friedman-Kasaba, Kathie. *Memories of Migration 1870–1902*. Albany: State University of New York, 1996.

Haswell, Charles Haynes. *Reminiscences of an Octogenarian of the City of New York*. New York: Harper and Brothers, 1896.

Mohl, Raymond. *Poverty in New York*. New York: Oxford University Press, 1971.

Morris, Lloyd. *Incredible New York: High Life and Low Life from 1850–1950*. Syracuse, NY: Syracuse University Press, 1996.

5

A Heritage of Guns: Larry McMurtry's *Anything for Billy* (1998)

FROM "THE KID CALLED THE BEST KNOWN MAN IN NEW MEXICO."

Las Vegas Gazette, *December 28, 1880.*

With its accustomed enterprise the GAZETTE was the first paper to give the story of the capture of Billy Bonney, who has risen to notoriety under the sobriquet of "the Kid," Billy Wilson, Dave Rudabaugh, and Tom Pickett. Just at this time everything of interest about the men is especially interesting and after damning the party in general and "the Kid" in particular, through the columns of this paper, we considered it the correct thing to give them a show.

Through the kindness of Sheriff Romero, a representative of the GAZETTE was admitted to the jail yesterday morning....

"Billy, the Kid" and Billy Wilson who were shackled together stood patiently up while a blacksmith took off their shackles and bracelets to allow them an opportunity to make a change of clothing. Both prisoners watched the operation which was to set them free for a short while, but Wilson scarcely raised his eyes and spoke but once or twice to his compadre. Bonney, on the other hand, was light and chipper and was very communicative, laughing, joking and chatting with the bystanders.

"You appear to take it easy," the reporter said.

"Yes! What's the use of looking on the gloomy side of everything? The laugh's on me this time," he said. Then looking out the placita, he asked, "Is the jail at Santa Fe any better than this? This is a terrible place to put a fellow in." He put the same question to every one who came near him and when he learned that there was nothing better in store for him, he shrugged his shoulders and said something about putting up with what he had to.

He was the attraction of the show, and as he stood there, lightly kicking the toes of his boots on the stone pavement to keep his feet warm, one would scarcely mistrust that he was the hero of the "Forty Thieves" romance which this paper has been running in serial form for six weeks or more.

He did look human, indeed, but there was nothing very mannish about him in appearance, for he looked and acted a mere boy. He is about five feet eight or nine inches tall, slightly built and lithe, weighing about 140; a frank open countenance, looking like a school boy, with the traditional silky fuzz on his upper lip; clear blue eyes, with a roguish snap about them; light hair and complexion. He is, in all, quite a handsome looking fellow, the only imperfection being two prominent front teeth, slightly protruding like squirrel's teeth, and he has agreeable and winning ways.

A cloud came over his face when he made some allusions to his being made the hero of fabulous yarns, and something like indignation was expressed when he said that our Extra misrepresented him in saying that he called his associates cowards. "I never said any such a thing," he pouted. "I know they ain't cowards."...

A final stroke of the hammer sent the last rivet on the bracelets, and they clanked on the pavement as they fell.

Bonney straightening up and then rubbing his wrists, where the sharp edged irons had chafed him, said:

"I don't suppose you fellows would believe it but this is the first time I ever had bracelets on. But many another better fellow has had them on too." (1)

The youth gangs of the twenty-first century are directly traceable to the mythic elements of guns, violence, youth, and lawlessness that, of necessity, were engendered in and associated with the nineteenth-century settlement of the Old West. For more than 100 years, people from all over the world have found the gangs of the American West to be fascinating and compelling. In the nineteenth century, gang leaders became cult figures, legends in their own time, when they were immortalized and idealized in copious so-called dime novels depicting their exploits. They were the first subjects of the newly developed movie technology and continued to be the most frequently portrayed types in film and television throughout the twentieth century. After the emergence of Popular Culture and American Studies as academic disciplines in the last decades of the twentieth century, many historians joined the general populace in turning their attention to western outlaws.

No figure from the Old West has been more often the subject of historical scrutiny than the controversial young gang leader, probably christened Henry McCarty, but known as William Bonney, or Billy the Kid—the inspiration of many novels, a ballet, an opera, and more than 40 motion pictures. One hundred years after his death in 1881, he is the roughly fictionalized model for the protagonist of a novel entitled *Anything for Billy,* by one of America's most prolific novelists of the West, Larry McMurtry.

Billy the Kid was produced by and epitomized a culture of guns and violence that has marked youth gangs ever since. And it was the peculiar conditions faced by those who went West in the nineteenth century as well as the character of the population attracted to the West that gave rise to Billy and other outlaws.

American culture was shaped by the Old West and by the circumstances that led to the development of a peculiar western culture. They included

- the absence of the trappings of European civilization, that is, written law, a measured system of justice, cultural limitations, religious and educational institutions, and traditional society;
- the endless turf wars, in an invaded territory that was up for grabs, between Indians and Europeans, Anglos and Hispanics, cattlemen and homesteaders, rustlers and cattlemen, cattlemen and sheepherders, big and small farmers, and farmers and the railroad;
- the prevalence of firearms, the advantage enjoyed by those with access to the greatest number of firearms, and the settling of disputes with guns rather than the law;
- corruption in government and law enforcement; and
- a large population of single men in an area that offered man's work predominantly, including mining, cow herding, cattle driving, and scouting—and, for the less particular, gambling, rustling, gunslinging, and running saloons and brothels.

To this wild area, so vastly different from the cultivated east coast of the United States, many men, especially young men, were attracted. There were, of course, many families who moved west in search of land to farm and veterans who tried to leave behind the devastation of the Civil War. But it was a different kind of person who was attracted to the West that left the most distinctive mark on America: these were the young men, who like the young gang members today, were in search of adventure, reputation, and quick riches, inside or outside the law. Some sought new identities and escape from debts, responsibilities, and, often, criminal pasts.

WESTERN ROOTS OF AMERICAN GANGS

Perpetual War over Territory

Areas of the Old West like New Mexico are roughly comparable to poor urban areas of the twenty-first century where multiple gangs are constantly at war with each other and the police. The first wars in the West were between Native American tribes. For instance, the Apaches fought the Navajos and the Sioux invaded Crow territory. As those of European and English extraction moved into the West, there were conflicts between Native Americans and invaders of their territory. By the 1870s, southwestern Indians, who for centuries had seen Spanish, French, British, and Americans invade and occupy their lands, were partially confined to reservations, where they lived wretched and slowly disintegrating lives. In addition, ethnic tensions were high and often led to violence. The older Spanish settlers especially resented the dominance of newly arrived Anglos.

Some of the worst conflicts were between small ranchers and the big ranchers whom they resented. John Chism, for instance, claimed as his ranch a vast area of what had been open rangeland along the Pecos and then solidified his claim with a force of some 100 cowboys armed with six-guns. Billy the Kid's perception that Chism had failed to keep his word provoked him to rustle some of Chism's cattle, leading Chism to place a bounty on Billy's head. Also in New Mexico was Pete Maxwell, who commanded an equally large spread inherited from his father, Lucien. Billy knew the Maxwells well, even supposedly romanced Lucien's daughter, Paulita. Billy was also ambushed at the Maxwell's compound, leading some historians to speculate that Pete Maxwell, resenting Billy's attention to his sister, had betrayed him. In *Anything for Billy,* Isinglass, the land owner and enemy of Billy Bone, appears to be based on a combination of Maxwell and Chism.

Where Guns Were the Law

The American long rifle was the first gun carried by pioneers and lawmen in the West. But the necessity of loading the gun for each shot, which took a full minute, made it a poor weapon to use from horseback. So Westerners began to carry three firearms on horseback: a loaded rifle and two loaded pistols. In 1838, however, a six-chambered repeating gun was manufactured in the United States. This was the Colt revolver, the weapon first used by the Texas Rangers. By 1840, it had been introduced to the western territories. Within 10 years, it had become the weapon of choice for the cowboys out on the trail. And for the rest of the nineteenth century, some kind of repeating firearm was carried at all times by almost every adult male in the West. Throughout the nineteenth century, in a country where government was nonexistent or corrupt, it was said that the only law was the six-gun. Having and knowing how to use a gun to kill game was essential to survival in the wild. And in a land without law, where rugged individualism prevailed, knowing how to use a gun was essential for self-protection.

THE LINCOLN COUNTY WAR

The Lincoln County War in New Mexico, in which Billy Bonney (on whom Billy Bone is roughly based) played a major role, illustrates the pervasiveness of outlaw behavior, the greed for control of territory and power, the widespread use of guns, and the perpetual gang wars—all of which were not unlike a contemporary urban neighborhood torn by gang wars. The formula for disaster in Lincoln County began when an ex-soldier named Lawrence Murphy set up a general store in the northern part of Lincoln County and established a monopoly on all phases of trade. In what came to be known as the Murphy-Dolan Gang, Murphy, in consort with two younger men, James Dolan and Pat Riley, operated closely with a ruling clique in the territory known as the Santa Fe Ring. With the cooperation of judges, businessmen, and state government, the Murphy-Dolan Gang was able to profit from lucrative contracts with the army, from its monopoly as sole supplier of goods to reservation Indians, and from its monopoly on banking for all small ranchers and farmers within the area. Not surprisingly, they cheated the Indians, the army, and the public. They falsified records in dealing with the army, charged maximum rates for all loans while seldom granting extensions or mercy, and suppressed all competition. As de facto Indian agents, they watered the grain, short-weighted supplies, doctored the scales, and issued them rotten food. They were legalized thieves, operating in a symbiotic relationship with all facets of power, including judges, bankers, politicians, local sheriffs, miscellaneous functionaries, and the Santa Fe Ring.

The monopoly of the Murphy-Dolan Gang was seriously challenged in the 1870s—when John Tunstall, a young Englishman determined to get rich in the American Southwest, invaded their turf. Among the cowboys hired by Tunstall was a young man of about 17 known as William Bonney, sometimes called Kid Antrim or Billy. After months of seething friction between Tunstall and the Murphy-Dolan Gang, Sheriff William Brady and his posse, which included notorious killers, were ordered by the Murphy-Dolan Gang to arrest John Tunstall on a trumped-up charge of horse stealing. In the ensuing encounter with the Englishmen, Tunstall was shot dead. Billy Bonney vowed revenge for the death of Tunstall, whom he later declared was the "only man who ever treated me decent," and the Lincoln County War began.

For two years, bloody and indiscriminate slaughter prevailed in the hills and among the scattered ranches and farms of Lincoln. In addition, it was an opportunity for private revenge and predatory raids motivated by nothing but greed in a country long-accustomed to the law of the gun. On one side was the unscrupulous Murphy-Dolan Gang, which controlled the law in Lincoln. On the other side was Billy Bonney; his gang; Alexander McSween, an ex-minister and lawyer; and, in the background, John Chism, the powerful rancher who dominated the plains just as the Murphy-Dolan Gang dominated the hills in the northern part of Lincoln County.

The conflict came to a head when McSween and his supporters, including Billy, were trapped in the McSween house by William Brady, the Murphy-Dolan-owned sheriff; his men; and the army based at nearby Fort Stanton, whose help Murphy had enlisted. After five days, someone set fire to McSween's house, leaving those inside with the quandary of facing death by fire if they remained or death by gunfire if they sought to escape. In this situation, Billy is said at last to have assumed leadership. Under what McSween thought was a flag of truce, he walked out the front door unarmed to surrender and was immediately cut down by bullets. With flames raging inside the house and a circle of guns waiting outside, Billy at last took action. He ran out the back door, past a fence, down to the small river than ran behind the house, mounted a horse, and galloped away to safety. This feat made him an instant outlaw hero throughout the nation.

When Sheriff William Brady was shot on the streets of Lincoln, Billy was charged with the murder. Pat Garrett, who was elected sheriff after Brady's death, trailed Billy and his gang to a shack at Stinking Springs and ultimately forced his surrender. His trial for murder was conducted outside the Lincoln jurisdiction because it was well known that many people in and near Lincoln, especially Hispanics, supported Billy. After being found guilty and sentenced to hang, he was brought back to Lincoln. But before the sentence could be carried out, someone hid a gun for Billy in the jail's outhouse. He managed to shoot two deputies, take a gun from the jailhouse case, saw off his shackles, and ride out of town. A few months later, Pat Garrett went to Fort Sumner on the trail of Billy the Kid. Placing deputies on the porch for protection, Garrett went into a bedroom of landowner Pete Maxwell's ranch to seek information about Billy. While he was in the dark room, the figure of Billy appeared in the doorway. Sensing someone there, Billy asked, *"Quien es?"* or "Who's there?" Garrett immediately shot and killed the man who had once been his friend.

McMurtry makes use of the historical details of Billy's escape from jail. Tully Roebuck, in the novel, bears some resemblance to Pat Garrett.

MCMURTRY'S STORY OF A WILD WEST GANG

The narrator of *Anything for Billy* is Ben Sippy, a well-born Philadelphian with a wife and nine daughters. He enjoys all the luxuries and comforts of a wealthy man living in a well-established eastern city, including a chambermaid to whom he is attracted and a butler who fetches him dime novels about the West. These novels often immortalized the adventures of young outlaws only weeks after the incidents had occurred. So obsessed is Sippy with the stories of the West that he himself begins to write, soon becoming one of the best-known authors of the genre made famous by Ned Buntline. Two events change the direction of Sippy's life forever. The butler dies, and Sippy comes home to find that his domineering wife, Dora, has sent his entire cherished collection of dime novels to be destroyed. These events lead Sippy to strike out for the American Southwest, the area that has long been the center of his life and dreams. Recognizing that he is going to an area ruled by weaponry, he stops in Galveston, Texas, to buy himself a small arsenal of firearms and knives. In New Mexico, Sippy immediately makes a dubious reputation for himself as a failed train robber. His first and only attempt is a disaster when the engineer merely waves at the gun-pointing Sippy. Sippy is reduced to trotting down the railroad track on his mule in pursuit of the train disappearing ahead of him. By the time he reaches New Mexico, the fiasco has already provided comic relief for the outlaws he soon encounters.

Billy Bone, whom Sippy takes credit for naming Billy the Kid, is the title character of Sippy's story. Sippy becomes his loyal friend and companion, following Billy from one dangerous encounter to another through New Mexico, Mexico, and Texas. In a bizarre turn, the naïve boy takes the lead, and the older, educated man, a father of nine daughters, becomes the sometimes reluctant follower.

Shortly after meeting Billy and his solicitous sidekick, Joe Lovelady, Sippy finds himself in the middle of a range war. On one side is the Greasy Corners Gang, a colorful but seedy group of gunfighters and buffalo hunters who have as their headquarters a saloon called the China Pond in a remote spot called Greasy Corners. Among this group are Billy; Lovelady; Tully Roebuck, a sometimes friend who also works as a sheriff for their enemy; Des Montaignes, who owns the saloon; La Tulipe, Montaignes's wife, who is a fortune teller; and Vivian Maldonado, a former Italian acrobat.

On the other side is Will Isinglass, a vicious, invincible old owner of a 3-million-acre ranch called the Whiskey Glass. Isinglass has under his control an army of cowboys from his ranch, hired guns from Texas, a hired assassin, an African giant named Mesty Woolah, and Bloody Feathers, his son by an Indian woman.

Filling out the cast of characters that Sippy encounters is the free-spirited Katie Garza, Isinglass's daughter by a Mexican woman, and the aristocratic Cecily Snow, whom he holds captive on his ranch. Katie is a revolutionary leader of one of the deadliest gangs in the West called (in English) the Turkeys. Cecily is an unscrupulous egomaniac who by day gathers botanical information for a book and by night plots the murder of Isinglass.

The wide-range war that encompassed all of New Mexico and part of Texas is known as the Whiskey Glass War. Isinglass's immense spread had once been the home of numerous Native American tribes, all of whom he has largely obliterated, sending them to reservations in other areas. Now Isinglass's project is to rid his 3 million acres of the wild "sweethearts" in the Greasy Corners Gang who remain on his land.

When the Texas guns are seen approaching, Billy and the Greasy Corners Gang ride away in retreat, despite a great deal of blustering and posing. They leave behind the buffalo hunters, who have no way out because they have eaten their horses. The Texans kill all the buffalo hunters and the Greasy Corners gunmen scatter.

Billy, after an idyllic affair in Mexico with Katie Garza, tries to rejoin the gang to fight Isinglass, taking Lovelady and Sippy with him.

Only Lovelady and Billy escape after the rest of the Greasy Corners Gang is wiped out in the battle. Sippy is captured by Isinglass, who takes him to his castle. There, Cecily Snow seduces Sippy and later, when Billy shows up, seduces him as well. Claiming that her moronic half-brothers are trying to kill her, she persuades Billy to murder them so that she won't have to share her inheritance. During Sippy's enforced stay with Isinglass, Lovelady is captured and beheaded by Mesty Woolah.

Although Katie is the woman who comes to his rescue and nurses him back to health when his horse falls on his leg in the escape from the law, it is the devious Cecily Snow with whom Billy plans to elope. He brings her to Greasy Corners where a few cowboys, Sippy, and La Tulipe have holed up awaiting another attack by Isinglass, Bloody Feathers, Tully (now a sheriff), and Long Dog (an assassin hired by Isinglass). Just as the attackers ride into camp, however, Katie Garza appears out of nowhere and shoots Billy dead, because, she says, she thought someone who loved him should be the one to shoot him.

After returning to Lincoln and writing a best-selling version of Billy's death, Tully is ambushed and killed. As a very old man, Isinglass is killed when he starts his car but can't figure out how to stop it.

Only Sippy remains to tell the stories of Billy, the Greasy Corners Gang, and the Whiskey Glass War. He shortly finds that no one wants his Wild West novels anymore, but he finds a new medium in film, and he writes scenarios for Hollywood. His favorite is *Sweethearts of Greasy Corners,* which he sees (and cries through) 25 times.

The Greasy Corners Gang and the Contemporary Urban Gang

Like Mark Twain in *Adventures of Huckleberry Finn,* McMurtry comically satirizes the gangs of the nineteenth century, at the same time showing the dark underside of an American Southwest that provided the myth and values perpetuated in the urban gangs of the twentieth and twenty-first centuries. From the Old West as it is depicted in *Anything for Billy* came the culture of death, violence, guns, and youth; the sanctioning of lawlessness; and the fascination with bands of outlaws, the leaders of which achieved heroic status. Billy's world also shares with the modern gang the members' obsession with their reputations as killers and the defense of their turf against outsiders.

At the start, Sippy learns from Joe Lovelady that Greasy Corners and its gang are identified with killing and dying. Sippy, after witnessing three violent deaths in three days, concludes that the Old West is a hard place to survive. Consistent with gangs throughout history, the members of the Greasy Corners Gang are, ironically, as likely to kill their own members as they are their enemies. As Billy, Lovelady, and Sippy first enter the China Pond, the saloon that serves as their headquarters, Vivian Maldonado and Happy Jack are killing a man who hasn't fit into the gang adequately. Billy himself later shoots at Nute Rachael in a disagreement and later kills the saloon owner, Des Montaignes. And it is Billy's lover Katie Garza who kills him. From the moment Sippy meets the Greasy Corners Gang until he returns to Philadelphia, he sees one violent death after another, including one man who is disemboweled and one who is beheaded. And it is not only the members of the warring gangs who are killed; like innocent victims of drive-by shootings, bystanders in the Old West are also killed, including a little boy of 10. In McMurtry's novel, as in actual communities of New Mexico, most of the characters die violent deaths. Only Sippy and one or two cowboys live to tell the stories.

Gang wars of various kinds constitute the whole way of life in New Mexico, and most of these, as depicted in the novel, are fought over turf. In *Anything for Billy,* Isinglass represents the white capitalistic invaders who accumulated great amounts of land and threw off Native Americans and others not in their employ. And the Greasy Corners Gang is intent on defending what they have come to regard as their turf in Skunkwater Flats and Greasy Corners.

McMurtry's depiction of the gun culture of the Old West begins with Sippy's understanding that he will have to amass an arsenal before he enters New Mexico. La Tulipe seems to be the only major character in the novel who isn't heavily armed. Cecily Snow and Katie Garza, however, are among the deadliest shots in New Mexico. All the men carry weapons with them at all times, and they steal and kill for weapons. Further, they are as closely identified with the weapons they own as they are with the horses and mules they ride. Moreover, their reputations are built on perceptions, often erroneous, of their skills with guns.

As in the antebellum South, men in the Old West did anything to secure their reputations. One of the members of the gang, Hill Cole, "is finished" when he fouls up in a shooting contest and feels driven to go to great lengths to prove himself thereafter. After Billy decides to leave Katie in Mexico, she explains that, "He thinks he's got to make a reputation.... That's all it's about—as if he ain't famous enough already" (166).

The gangs that predominate in *Anything for Billy* operate outside traditional law because no such law exists in the territory. Isinglass, who owns most of the land and has a gang even more ruthless than the Greasy Corners Gang, owns law enforcement—figureheads like Tully Roebuck—and uses them not to exact justice but to murder, bully, and steal to further Isinglass's own interests. The confusion of outlaw and lawman is seen in the figure of Tully, who at times is a member of the Greasy Corners Gang and at times is in the employ of Isinglass as a sheriff of Lincoln, New Mexico. It is understandable in a place where the law is inevitably corrupt that boys like Billy have a "determination to defy any order, no matter who it came from, or what the consequences" (211).

Although in *Anything for Billy* all the outlaws except Billy are adults, the Greasy Corners Gang is as much a youth gang as any of those in the twentieth century. In the first place, all the gunmen follow Billy, "the prince" of Greasy Corners, a 17-year-old who is repeatedly described by Sippy as a boy or a kid who looks about 12 when he is asleep. And the other characters (although they are adults, and a few like Lovelady and Tully have wives) are, in essence, boys playing deadly boys' games. Most of them have deserted or rejected the domesticity and work of adulthood to roam the countryside with other "boys," unburdened by responsibility, living, as Sippy repeatedly observes, for the moment. Such an existence accentuates a cult of death, in a place where there is little hope of life associated with having children and growing crops.

McMurtry layers his satire over these darker, violent elements of his story, beginning with Sippy's sudden desertion of his family when his wife throws out his collection of dime novels and his subsequent attempt to rob trains for a living. Further parody can be seen in Billy's reputation as one of the most formidable gunmen in the West, a name that is firmly established even before he has ever shot anyone. Furthermore, Billy and the other gunmen are portrayed as mediocre shots. They fire at their targets repeatedly and generally miss. In a shooting contest, the sophisticated easterner, Sippy, and the girl-gang leader, Katie Garza, outshoot all the gunmen of Greasy Corners. When Mesty Woolah is found shot to death with a single bullet from a considerable distance, Sippy automatically knows that the killer could only have been Cecily Snow, because Billy did not have the skill to perform such a feat.

The gunmen are, moreover, reluctant to engage in gunfights. Billy, especially, says repeatedly that he is going to kill Isinglass or Mesty Woolah but instead wastes no time in clearing out with the rest of the gunmen when their attackers approach, at one time even abandoning their friends, the buffalo hunters.

Despite the parody, the narrative frame of *Anything for Billy* rests on the tendency of the common people to admire and idolize compelling young outlaws like Billy the Kid, an early theme that echoes 100 years later in the veneration and authority accorded urban gang leaders by their members. The proliferation and popularity of dime novels, which obsess Sippy as well, are direct outgrowths of public fascination with the outlaw gangs and their leaders. In the early twentieth century, after Sippy's brief return to Philadelphia and his move back to New Mexico, the medium chosen to mythologize the outlaw changes from the dime novel to the newly developed form of the motion picture. Sippy also mentions throughout his story the abiding interest that historians have in Billy and their reluctance to accept anything that diminishes the legend.

BIBLIOGRAPHY

Boorstin, Daniel. *The Americans: The National Experience.* New York: Vintage, 1965.

Bryan, Howard. *Robbers, Rogues, and Ruffians.* Santa Fe, NM: Clear Light Press, 1991.

Cawalti, John G. *The Six-Gun Mystique.* Bowling Green, OH: Bowling Green University Popular Press, 1971.

Drago, Harry Sinclair. *The Great Range Wars: Violence on the Grasslands.* New York: Dodd, Mead, 1970.

Grey, Zane. *Nevada: A Romance of the West.* New York: Harper and Brothers, 1928.

Hertzog, Peter. *Outlaws of New Mexico.* Santa Fe, NM: Sunstone Press, 1984.

Hollon, W. Eugene. *Frontier Violence: Another Look.* New York: Oxford University Press, 1974.

Keleher, William A. *Violence in Lincoln County 1969–1881.* Albuquerque: University of New Mexico Press, 1957.

L'Aloge, Bob. *Knights of the Sixgun*. Las Cruces, NM: Yucca Tree Press, 1991.

McMurtry, Larry. *Anything for Billy*. New York: Simon and Schuster, 1988.

Neider, Charles. *The Authentic Death of Henry Jones*. New York: Harper's, 1956.

Rasch, Philip. *Trailing Billy the Kid*. Stillwater, OK: Distributed by Western Publications, 1995.

Reynolds, William. *Trouble in New Mexico*. Bakersfield, CA: B. Reynolds, 1994.

Rosa, Joseph G., and Robin May. *Gun Law: A Study of Violence in the Wild West*. Chicago: Contemporary Books, 1977.

Simmons, Marc. *When Six-Guns Ruled*. Santa Fe, NM: Ancient City Press, 1990.

Tuska, John. *The Filming of the West*. New York: Doubleday, 1976.

Utley, Robert M. *Billy the Kid: A Short and Violent Life*. Lincoln: University of Nebraska Press, 1989.

———. *High Noon in Lincoln*. *Violence on the Western Frontier.* Albuquerque: University of New Mexico Press, 1987.

Watson, Frederick. *A Century of Gunmen: A Study in Lawlessness*. London: Ivor Nicholson and Watson, 1931.

Webb, Walter Prescott. *The Great Plains*. Lincoln: University of Nebraska Press, 1981.

West, John Oliver. "To Die like a Man: The 'Good' Outlaw Tradition in the American Southwest." Diss. University of Texas, 1964.

Wright, Will. *Sixguns and Society: A Structural Study of the Western*. Berkeley and Los Angeles: University of California Press, 1975.

6

The 1920s in Chicago: James T. Farrell's *Studs Lonigan* (1932)

FROM FREDERIC M. THRASHER, *THE GANG: A STUDY OF 1,313 GANGS IN CHICAGO.*

Chicago: University of Chicago Press, 1927.

IRISH SWASHBUCKLERS

Along one street on the West Side there were three names that stand out in the history of the earlier gangs: the Healeys, Shaneys, and Canaleys. There were between one hundred and one hundred fifty of them there from eighteen to twenty-eight years old, with headquarters in a certain saloon on a nearby corner. They had a baseball team and ran dances to raise money. They had fights with another notorious gang which had influential political connections. They carried on a war between 1906 and 1910, using sticks, stones, blackjacks, and saps as weapons. If a fellow of one bunch was trimmed by a member of another, he would have his revenge; he would come and get his gang and a street fight would result.... They were mostly loafers and some were criminals, hanging around the saloons and doing very little work. They had a stand-in with the politicians and four or five of them were always on the public payrolls. The use of firearms in their altercations was rare. [Interview with a politician who grew up in the area. 422].

A POOLROOM GANG

A Jewish girl eighteen years of age on her way home from work flirted with two young men and finally accepted a ride. Instead of driving her home, they stopped in front of a poolroom where soft drinks were served and coaxed her to come inside.

This was the hang-out of about seventeen Italian boys ranging in age from seventeen to twenty-one. The door was locked and the girl was attacked by six or seven of the group. The proprietor of the poolroom in the meantime called up the remainder of the gang, seventeen in all, and the girl was attacked by this number within an hour. The girl was three months in a hospital before she recovered. The men were sent to the Joliet penitentiary.

This is the type of poolroom gang that loafs consistently and whose members are always on the lookout for a way to make some easy change. They gamble and are out for any excitement. [Interview with a police matron. 138]

In the first two decades of the twentieth century, at a time when Monk Eastman was boss of an organized gang of thousands in New York City where gangs had flourished for a hundred years, informal gangs of Irish youth clustered together on their neighborhood streets of Chicago, Illinois. In 1932, James T. Farrell, a writer who had grown up in Chicago in the second and third decades of the twentieth century, saw into print the first two novels of his trilogy entitled *Studs Lonigan*. This amazing social history of national life during Prohibition and the Great Depression is the first fiction in America to chronicle the life of a young man whose gang shaped his values, became the center of his existence, and contributed to his demise at the early age of 33.

In Farrell's novel, one sees many of the universal traits shared by gangs throughout history: most prominent is the fierce ethnic and racial bigotry, the violence, the peer pressure, the sexual promiscuity and brutality, the drug and alcohol dependency, and the overwhelming need for a tough self-image and reputation. On the other hand, the gang depicted in *Studs Lonigan* is not an organized group, as were the New York gangs and those of the late twentieth century. Although there is a hierarchy of sorts, it is not formalized. Nor does the gang as a group resort, in organized fashion, to criminal activity to raise revenue.

Studs Lonigan consists of three novels. The first book, also entitled *Studs Lonigan*, begins in 1916 when Studs is 15 years old, in the summer after his 10th-grade graduation. These pages develop the fatal attraction that a rowdy, ne'er-do-well gang holds for him and the way he becomes entrapped, at several turning points in his life, by his own actions, inaction, and decisions with regard to the gang.

The second novel, *The Young Manhood of Studs Lonigan,* takes place from 1917 to 1929, bringing Studs to his late twenties. Studs and his gang continue to be, even well into their twenties, little more than irresponsible street toughs. The final novel, *Judgment Day,* first published in 1935, takes place in 1931, just after the onset of the Great Depression. In this final book, the members of Stud's gang have been dispersed. The last of the trilogy shows the unhappy consequences of Stud's boyhood decision to throw his lot in with the 58th Street gang rather than to finish his education and commit himself to the decent young woman he loves.

CONTEXT

Few novels, even including John Steinbeck's *Grapes of Wrath,* provide such a comprehensive picture of the nation's cultural history from 1916 to the early 1930s: its changing morality; its movies, music, baseball, football, and boxing engagements; its Prohibition culture of speakeasies, pool halls, and prostitution. It is also a meticulously detailed portrait of a single, unique midwestern city during these years. That city, Chicago, was a mix of imported cultures, the most numerous and oldest working-class group being Irish, the group to which Studs's family and friends belong. The defining institution in the lives of the Irish was the Roman Catholic Church, and the most authoritative figure was not the mayor or governor but the parish priest. The rituals and traditions of the church reinforced its subsidiary associations, like its schools, strengthening family and neighborhood ties.

For a nominal fee, Catholic children, even those from poor families, attended a church school where they were taught by nuns, many of whom were not known for their compassion or understanding of young people. Irish Catholic adults continued their ties with the church in organizations like the Order of Christopher, which Studs joins as an adult.

Changes of several kinds were rapidly beginning to erode the cohesive Irish neighborhoods, even as Studs's story begins. The church was losing touch with its youth in the Roaring Twenties, and it had less and less of an impact on moral behavior and little or no interest in the pressing issues of social reform. As the parish church began to lose its hold on the new generation, the old morality faded before new, more positive values developed to take its place.

Neighborhoods were beginning to break up as other ethnic groups moved in and the Irish, in sharp reaction, moved out. These groups, constantly referred to in obscene language marked by hatred and derision, were mainly African Americans, Eastern European Jews, and Poles. As the neighborhoods changed, the pure Irish character of the church also changed. For Danny O'Neill, Studs's childhood friend (generally regarded as a thinly veiled version of the author, Farrell), education, new associates in the university he attends, and a passionate interest in social justice replaced the old, narrow structures. But for many others, like Studs, nothing took the place of the crumbling homogeneity of the old society, and they found themselves ill-prepared to live in the real, wider world composed of a blend of many cultures and religions.

A further deterioration in values came on the heels of the passage of a law intended to promote morality. The prohibition of the sale of alcoholic beverages led to hypocrisy, gangsterism, smuggling, and speakeasies and houses of prostitution where "rot gut" was freely dispensed. Studs and his friends who remain adolescents in their reckless pursuit of fun and leisure were, along with the characters in the works of F. Scott Fitzgerald, typical of the temper of the age.

But the carefree life collapsed with the stock market in the late 1920s and early 1930s. The economic depression is the setting for *Judgment Day*, the last book in Farrell's trilogy. Although the 1920s was characterized by booming production and the booming stock market, wages had always remained low. By 1929, the widening gap between the supply of and demand for goods led to the wholesale collapse of businesses. As businesses closed, workers lost jobs. On top of that, the feeding frenzy on Wall Street had led many investors to buy on margin—that is, to borrow, from their brokers or banks, the money to invest in stocks. So, as businesses failed, investors found themselves with worthless stocks and huge debts. Banks began to close, having lent money to investors for now-worthless stocks and having invested heavily in the market themselves. As a result, millions of people lost their life savings because banks were not insured as they are required to be today. The fatal day in the stock market was October 29, 1929, named Black Tuesday, when 16 million shares of stock were sold. In 1931, bank customers lost $531,776,004. Out of a population of 125 million, 15 million people were unemployed in the 1930s, and an average of 5,000 people applied for every 100 job openings. Those who secured jobs were not paid a living wage. As people lost jobs, income, and savings or investments, they were unable to meet their mortgage or rent payments. Many came home at the end of a day's job hunting to find their belongings piled in the street.

This is the setting of *Judgment Day*.

Studs Lonigan (1932)

From the age of 15, when Studs graduates from St. Patrick's grammar school, he is a defiant tough who views his school as "a jailhouse," a place of boredom and intimidation. The nuns who teach there are little more than violent, physically abusive jailers. At his graduation, he momentarily thinks warmly of his school years, but quickly returns to his disgust with it and concludes that he was lonelier in school than anywhere else. Nothing he is taught interests him or is relevant to real life. The two things he knows for sure about himself are that he hates school and loves Lucy Scanlan, a schoolmate. Other than deciding to quit school, however, he seems to be mentally drifting, without goals or plans.

At 15, Studs is at a crossroad. He is still a member of the Indiana Street gang, a group of high-spirited boys, including Danny O'Neill, a basically decent bunch that has done fairly well at St. Patrick's parochial school. He also has as a friend Helen Shires, a tomboy with good sense and courage, with whom he can share his thoughts. Early in the summer, when Weary Reilley, the most despicable young thug in the neighborhood, attacks Helen, Studs beats him up, an incident he remembers with pride for the rest of his life. Studs's highest feelings are for Lucy, a decent young girl who brings out the best in him. In a key scene, as he sits in a park tree with Lucy, he feels mentally and spiritually lifted up, above the sordidness of the world and the vileness of his body, to something ethereal and good. Throughout the trilogy, the goodness of Lucy stands as an antithesis of the doomed world of Studs's gang.

Helen Shires warns him that the 58th Street gang, with which he has begun hanging out, is bad business. They "picked on Jews, and beat kids up," "thought every night was Hallowe'en" (166), considered all girls created for their personal sexual pleasure, and routinely and thoughtlessly committed petty crimes.

But Studs is attracted to the violent bullies, and his break with his old friends, including Helen Shires and Lucy, occurs, ironically, when he reacts nastily and hastily to neighborhood taunts that he is sweet on

Lucy. He is afraid that his caring for Lucy will be seen in the wrong light and will damage the tough image he is trying to create in the eyes of the gang. His position in the new 58th Street gang is secured when he beats up one of its leaders, Red Kelly, and a younger boy named Denny Doyle. Afterward, he has the promise of acceptance by the older toughs at Bathcellar's Billiard Parlor and Barber Shop. Although his parents think he is going to school throughout the fall of 1916 and the winter and spring of 1917, he has only attended a few days before dropping out. Instead he hangs out with the boys, who watch how he handles himself around those they consider undesirable and take him on his first visit to a prostitute. That experience, like all desires of the flesh, makes him ashamed, but he realizes there is no way of evading such encounters without losing face with his gang.

The Young Manhood of Studs Lonigan (1932)

The Young Manhood of Studs Lonigan, the second book in the trilogy, most fully develops the life of Studs Lonigan's gang, taking Studs from April of 1917 to New Year's Eve of 1929, from his 16th to his 28th year. When he is 16, World War I begins—the war in which Monk Eastman enjoyed fighting. Studs and his friends desperately want to join the army or navy to prove they are men. They desire not only to help defeat the enemy but to become heroes. Studs, who is often made uneasy about death and hell because of his sexuality, thinks that the war is not only a way to gain a reputation but to avoid being sent to hell for his sins: "you know, a soldier dying for his country don't have to worry about going to Hell" (15). But the gang members are too young to join the service and are ridiculed as babies in diapers by the recruiting sergeant.

The Young Manhood of Studs Lonigan documents night after night of gang members drinking themselves blind, going to houses of prostitution, bullying weaker kids and old people, and getting into fights. By their twenties, their habits as a gang have already begun to take a heavy toll on their health. Studs, at least, at 22, tries occasionally to go on the wagon. ("He didn't know why he had drunk so much of the world's liquor in his twenty-two and a half years" [201].) He also now knows that the education he passed up when he was 15 could have made all the difference in his life and even realizes that he has squandered his chance in order to have adventure on a local pool room.

After many years, Studs tries to rekindle his relationship with Lucy by taking her to a dance. But he feels uncomfortable with the college men and young working men he sees there and wishes that he were spending this time with his gang, where he feels he belongs. After the dance, he attempts unsuccessfully to persuade Lucy to let him make love to her, approaching her more like he would one of the strangers he has sex with than like the young woman he respects.

Despite the profligate life he leads with his friends, several of them join Studs in attending a church "mission," a time of religious revival. The lengthy mission sermon is a diatribe against sins of the flesh and radical politics. After the sermon, in an automatic response, Studs praises the sermon to his buddy as a "knock out." They regard it only as a warning to cads who would seduce their sisters, not as an admonishment of their own behavior. They also find in the sermon approval for having a socially progressive waiter fired from their favorite hangout. On Sunday night, following their attendance at the last day of the mission, the gang "got drunk and raised hell" and ended up "going to a can house"—a house of prostitution. "They went and had the girlies, and gypped them out of their pay" (428).

When Studs is in his late twenties, he returns to the old neighborhood several months after he and his family have moved to get away from the blacks, Jews, and Poles. As an adult, he still longs nostalgically for the good old days, when he had enjoyed acceptance and companionship there.

The barbaric actions that form the climax of the entire trilogy occur at the end of *The Young Manhood of Studs Lonigan* at a New Year's party, meant to be a reunion of the old gang, "in a suite of three rooms at a disreputable hotel on Grand Boulevard in the black belt" (395). All the men arrive drunk, carrying bottles of bootleg liquor. Gang members take their dates, some of them prostitutes, into the bedrooms for sex. They force whiskey down the throats of less cooperative girls, force their reluctant dates to have sex with their friends, several men having sex with one woman. The evening ends with the brutal beating and rape of a young girl by Weary Reilley, followed by his arrest by the police. Studs Lonigan spends the night in the dirty street, passed out from drink. The drunk Lonigan is described as having "once, as a boy, stood before Charley Bathcellar's poolroom thinking that some day, he would grow up to be strong, and tough, and the real stuff" (411).

Judgment Day (1935)

The third book of the trilogy, *Judgment Day,* takes place between 1927 and 1931. It opens, fittingly, with a funeral of one of the gang members. For this book discloses the damage done to Studs and many others in the gang by the life they had once enjoyed. Some of their members have escaped and built new lives as businessmen and politicians, but others, like Weary, are in prison. Some are invalids, at least one is in a mental institution, and some, like Shrimp Haggerty, are dead. Studs, at 28, still lives with his parents and is single and in poor health. He is ready to change his life, maybe even get married, but now his past lifestyle, his lack of education and training, and the economic depression closing in on the whole country all militate against his self-renewal. Studs's father is growing old, and his painting company, like so many other businesses, is going under. Studs can no longer depend on a job in the painting company. Indeed, now his father, mother, and younger siblings tentatively look to him for help. Suddenly, for the first time in his life, Studs's desire for a job is genuine and urgent. Unskilled and uneducated, he enters the job market at the worst possible moment in the nation's history. Moreover, with his lifelong tendency to choose the quick fix, he is easily conned by a friend into investing all his savings in a stock that becomes worthless in a matter of weeks.

To make matters worse, Studs's past way of living—the heavy drinking and smoking, cases of venereal disease, the fighting, the nights lying drunk in the cold, wet streets—have ruined his health.

When Catherine, the girl he asks to marry him, becomes pregnant, the stark realization strikes him that, with no prospects of a job, he will be responsible for a family. He insists that Catherine go swimming with him, hoping silently that the exertion will bring on an abortion. Instead, he faints in the water, probably of a mild heart attack. At the end of one of many more days looking for work unsuccessfully, he wanders around hopelessly in the rain. When he finally reaches the door of his home that night, he is desperately ill. This is the end of Studs Lonigan. He soon falls into a coma and dies.

Desires and Deceptions

Although the gang, unorganized as it is, is at the center of Studs Lonigan's life, he does not fit the usual profile of the gang member, as we have seen it unfold in New York City at the turn of the twentieth century and in the newspaper chronicles of the twenty-first century. Studs is not poor, does not live in a slum, and is not a recent immigrant trying to survive in a hostile environment. His family is comfortably situated, upstanding, religious, and generous to their children. There is no economic imperative that leads him to steal and deal to alleviate any financial suffering. His mother and father live primarily for their children, though they don't pretend to understand their rebellious oldest child, Studs.

But Studs is drawn to his gang, a lifelong group of close associates, for many of the same reasons that have always attracted youths to gangs—and with the same disastrous results. What strikes one in the story of Studs Lonigan are the nagging ironies that issue between what he searches for in the gang and what he actually finds there.

He is drawn to the 58th Street gang because it promises comradeship and acceptance. As surely as he can always find his mother in his home, he can always find his gang in the local pool hall or drugstore. The gang members become his family, young men with whom he has something in common, who also have haunting, inexpressible needs. Studs deludes himself that he understands them and they understand him as members of his family do not.

He is also attracted to the gang as an avenue to pleasure. The pleasure of daring hijinks, violent sports, and simply hanging out together inevitably involves tormenting and beating younger boys, the physically or mentally weak, and males they considered to be non-Irish interlopers. Their main pleasure and escape is through alcohol, and although the sale of liquor is illegal, someone in the gang can always find a bottle to share with the rest. The gang, which provides Studs with his first sexual encounter with a prostitute, can always organize a group visit to a "can" house. As long as the gang flourishes, Studs and the others freely seek pleasure within the moment, with no thought to any issues beyond their own self-gratification. But pleasure does not mean fulfillment for Studs. The gang, which promises adventure, so circumscribes his existence that he very rarely, during his entire life, ventures outside the six square blocks of his Chicago neighborhood. As an adult, he watches with great longing a movie of adventure in Alaska, never realizing how he has robbed himself of a larger life.

The overarching question of the trilogy involves manhood and independence, made manifest by the ironic title of the second book, *The Young Manhood of Studs Lonigan*. It is the desire to be a "macho man" rather than a boy, the need for a tough, manly self-image and a tough, manly reputation that attracts Studs to the gang in the first place. The young gang members want to be men: they hang around with older toughs and are introduced at an early age to illicit adult activities. But the key to independence and importance in the eyes of the larger world is education, which Studs has relinquished, substituting the gang for further schooling.

On the other hand, although members of Studs's gang want to be men, they are not interested in taking on adult responsibilities. They remain boys who live in their parents' homes well into their twenties, take money from their parents to live on, spend their time playing football and other sports. During and immediately after the war, Studs, like the others, is disinclined to look for a job that will bring him real independence. He only begins working when, at 17, he is hired as a painter by his father. Working is not one of the aspects of manhood in which most of his gang members have an interest. In fact, they positively and admittedly avoid work and ridicule those who are insufficiently clever to avoid working. When gang members are finally forced to go to work in their late teens, many continue into adulthood to see their jobs as temporary ways to find the money to spend on liquor and prostitutes, not as steps in careers or professions.

Nor are they interested in adult relationships with young women. While some members of the gang at least have girlfriends, Studs, in his late twenties, does not. Only a few members of the old gang marry and have families. These men still feel closer to their old buddies than they do to their wives. Studs is especially juvenile in his relationships with women. At one extreme, he still views Lucy as a pure, untouchable saint, and, at the other extreme, he continues to have brief sexual encounters with prostitutes and strangers.

This brings us to one of the most melancholy ironies in the life of Studs Lonigan: his eternal longing for Lucy and idealistic love rival Dante's love of Beatrice. The scene in the tree with Lucy, to which he returns so often in memory, deliberately echoes the innocence of Adam and Eve in the Garden of Eden. That leitmotif plays through Studs's brain constantly for the rest of his life. On his deathbed, he envisions Lucy Scanlan kneeling in the corner of his room.

Studs goes to the gang to dispel a nagging, existential loneliness and emptiness that he can not understand or express. One would expect that he could find spiritual succor in the religion that is the center of community life. But the irrelevancy and bankruptcy of the church is graphically shown in the chapters on the mission, in which Studs hears no word addressing his spiritual needs, no word to alleviate his aching spiritual poverty—only a diatribe of "thou-shalt-nots." In the chapter that follows a description of the mission, Danny O'Neill reveals much about the reasons for the hopeless search for meaning on the part of the youth of St. Patrick's. He suggests that the church is at least in part responsible for driving young men like Studs away and to self-destructive arenas. Danny, who is fast losing his religious faith, discloses that on the first day of the mission, he had gone to Father Shannon in a desperate and honest appeal for help. He asked, as a young college student whose religion is being challenged, if he could talk to the priest "about the faith" (369). The priest responded that he was too busy to talk to him and turned on his heel, leaving Danny alone. Danny concludes that the church is not only ignorant and superstitious, but that at bottom, it hates truth and honesty.

Danny, while disillusioned with the church, finds his meaning in intellectual inquiry and in working for social reform. But the case is different with Studs and his gang. The church has so reinforced their racial and class prejudices that such a healthy prospect—like working for the betterment of society—would never have occurred to them.

Perhaps one of the reasons for the irrelevancy of the church and for its inability to reach men like Studs lies in its refusal to concede that the body and physical urges are natural. On his deathbed, Studs imagines a priest telling him, "Remember, O Lonigan, that thou art dirty dust and like a dirty dog thou shalt return to dirtier dust" (194). But Studs knows and feels the irrefutable reality of his carnality, and the church's refusal to acknowledge this takes away from its credibility. It also leads Studs to give up on the possibility of his own goodness, even though he never loses his longing for the ideal of goodness in the person of Lucy Scanlan.

BIBLIOGRAPHY

Aaron, Daniel. *Writers on the Left*. New York: Harcourt, Brace and World, 1961.

Bogardus, Ralph F., and Fred Hobson. *Literature at the Barricades: The American Writer in the 1930s*. Tuscaloosa: The University of Alabama Press, 1982.

Branch, Edgar M. *James T. Farrell*. New York: Twayne Publishers, 1971.

Farrell, James T. *Studs Lonigan*. 1932, 1935. New York: The Vanguard Press, 1978.

Howe, Irving. *Politics and the Novel*. New York: Horizon Press, 1957.

Kazin, Alfred. *On Native Ground*. New York: Reynal and Hitchcock, 1942.

Walcutt, Charles C. *American Literary Naturalism*. Minneapolis: University of Minnesota Press, 1956.

———. *Seven Novelists in the American Naturalist Tradition*. Minneapolis: University of Minnesota Press, 1974.

7

Jewish Gangs in Brownsville, 1944–1945: Irving Schulman's *The Amboy Dukes* (1946)

FROM JENNA WEISSMAN JOSELIT, *OUR GANG: JEWISH CRIME AND THE NEW YORK JEWISH COMMUNITY, 1900–1940.*

Bloomington: Indiana University Press, 1983.

After graduating from eighth grade in 1920 [Abe] Reles became a delivery boy and worked at a succession of ill-paying jobs. While in his late teens, he became a pressman and worked for a printer. When his employer went bankrupt, Reles took to the streets and, as one enforcement agent put it, "chose to pass his leisure time, of which he had plenty," in a Sutter Avenue poolroom. The poolroom or poolhall was the common meeting ground for Brooklyn youth and the fringe element of society. One former Brownsville resident, himself a frequent poolroom visitor while an adolescent, recalled that his favored haunt, Label's poolroom, was a surrogate home. There he would socialize and gossip with his friends; it was also a place to find "someone to break a head, beat up a guy, break a strike, buy junk, set a fire, plan a robbery or muscle a pedlar." (151)

The Amboy Dukes by Irving Schulman, set in 1944–1945 during World War II, provides a perspective on Jewish gangs in Brownsville, New York, at the time one of the most dangerous neighborhoods in the United States. The novel graphically portrays issues that persist in the gang culture of most countries: the economic hardships that contribute to family breakdown and the difficulty of reversing the course of one's life once it has become involved with gangs.

THE TIME AND THE PLACE

The setting of *The Amboy Dukes* is Brownsville, one of several neighborhoods in Brooklyn, New York, across the East River from Manhattan. The area was settled in the late nineteenth and earlier twentieth centuries by Eastern European Jews, chiefly from Russia and Poland. By the 1930s, Brownsville had the largest concentration of Jews in the New York City area. Most were members of the working class. Many of the new arrivals plied their wares from pushcarts. By the 1930s, Brownsville residents primarily worked in construction, in the plumbing and electrical trades, or as salesmen, drivers, or shipping clerks. The young men and women coming of age in Brownsville in the 1930s and 1940s were largely native-born children of immigrants. Those who succeeded financially moved out of the neighborhood.

The character of Brownsville was shaped by the residents' common Jewish heritage. One of the most cohesive neighborhoods in the metropolitan area, it was also one of the most crowded. Synagogues, *shuls*, and a variety of Jewish agencies attempted to provide shelter and guidance for the youth of the area. In the 1940s, the Brooklyn District Office of the Jewish Boards of Guardians was located in Brownsville at Stone and Pitkin streets.

The Great Depression of the 1930s, which looms so large in the background of *The Amboy Dukes*, devastated the residents of Brownsville. Arthur Granit, who recorded his impressions of Brownsville in the Depression, writes of the Brownsville men who, having lost their jobs in Manhattan's garment district, became homebound and depressed, in the process losing the esteem of their wives and children as well as their own self-esteem. By 1932, the unemployed in the metropolitan area reached 750,000, and the weekly allowance for families from relief agencies was $2.39. Alter F. Landesman, in *Brownsville: The Birth, Development and Passing of a Jewish Community in New York*, stresses the impact of the Depression on the children of the unemployed:

> The long and severe depression affected both old and young. It depressed their minds and spirits, and robbed

many of them of their self-respect. It fell with particular severity on the young people. Instead of being presented with hope of a bright future, they were to behold long lines of unemployed men and women waiting outside the relief station on Pitkin Avenue and elsewhere. The popular song of the period was "Brother, Can You Spare a Dime?" and the apple and the apple vendor became a symbol of the times. Some people lost hope of ever finding a job, and thought of themselves as a lost generation. (312)

It was the outbreak of World War II in 1941, the year in which *The Amboy Dukes* opens, that ended the massive, ruinous unemployment in the United States. Workers, male and female, were now desperately needed in every sector, but particularly in the defense industry. Brooklyn, with its East River harbors, became one of the centers of manufacturing and shipping for the war industry. It housed the headquarters of the world's largest port of embarkation, and its navy yard was the largest in the world. Nearby were shipyards in the Erie Basin, on Staten Island, and in Kearney, New Jersey, which were all in need of employees. With Brooklyn's large port, it attracted numerous factories that manufactured goods for both the war effort and domestic consumption. Workers throughout the United States flocked to Brooklyn and other centers of industry to find jobs, but the war had brought house construction to a virtual halt, making it difficult in such areas to find any housing at all, thus the impossibility of the Goldfarbs being able to leave the slums in *The Amboy Dukes*. Other circumstances during the war kept Frank's family and others from seeing their way out of poverty. Frank's parents finally are able to secure enough money to put food on the table, but they bring home too much to qualify for public housing. Wages rose very little during the war years. Frank's mother makes 65 cents an hour packing ammunition. There was a new minimum-wage law, but the minimum wage was set at 25 cents an hour. The War Labor Board placed limits on wage increases, and unions were forbidden by the government from negotiating for better wages and conditions, yet there were more "wild cat" strikes in 1944, the year of the novel's main action, than at any previous time in American history. Taxes increased and many essential and nonessential goods were in short supply and rationed.

Near the beginning and near the end of *The Amboy Dukes,* Frank and especially his little sister Alice note the enormous contrast between their own squalid neighborhood in Brownsville and the lives of the wealthy Manhattanites they observe on their afternoon outings. It is true that during the war, although employment was available, the gulf between rich and poor grew even wider as business profits enjoyed by the few soared. In 1941, for instance, three-fourths of the military contracts in the United States were held by only 56 corporations. From 1940 to 1946, textile mill profits grew 600 percent, but wages for textile workers rose only 36 percent.

The economic situation during the Depression of the 1930s and during the war had a ruinous effect on the cohesiveness and influence of the traditional family and traditional Jewish values. To have any prospects of escaping the slums or educating their children, both mother and father had to labor long hours outside the home, working nights and weekends to receive overtime. As a consequence, the children, like those in the Goldfarb family, had to fend for themselves at a time when they needed guidance and support. The fathers' inability to support their families adequately in the 1930s and 1940s eroded their authority and ability to influence and control their children. And the need to secure a bare living superseded and eroded the old values that resided in the synagogue and family.

Although in the early days of the twentieth century, the family and community in Brownsville had been able to guide children toward upright, successful lives, the 1930s and 1940s saw the rise of juvenile delinquency and gangs. As Alter F. Landesman writes in *Brownsville*, "To boys who live under such conditions, few prospects are as exciting and inviting as truancy, gang warfare, vandalism, and theft" (333). Most of the delinquency in Brownsville was attributable to the children of immigrants and not to immigrants themselves. These children were most often charged with peddling, begging, disorderly conduct, malicious mischief, ungovernable behavior, stealing, burglary, truancy, violation of the railroad law, and desertion of home. Some of the gangs began as "defense" groups, formed to protect pushcart peddlers from attack by hoodlums. The defense groups then evolved into outlaws themselves. The reason most often given for a boy's delinquency was that he let himself be influenced by bad company or gangs. In *Our Gang: Jewish Crime and the New York Jewish Community, 1900–1940*, Jenna Weissman Joselit describes the pervasiveness and activity of gangs in the Jewish community in the Lower East Side of Manhattan and elsewhere in the area:

> [T]he area "bristled" with gangs. Some were little more than temporary if "rough schools of experience" for Amer-

ican Jewish youngsters entranced by the hi-jinks of life on the street. Others, though, were far more pernicious. Lacking what one concerned reformer called "healthy outlets," the youthful residents of the Lower East Side drifted to the streets, where, forming small groups, they played ball, flirted with girls, and occasionally engaged in acts of petty thievery; virtually every street, recalled one former gang member nostalgically, had its own gang.... Another veteran gang member put it this way: "It was the exceptional, almost abnormal boy who did not join the gang. The gang was romance, adventure, had the zest of banditry, the thrill of camp life, and the lure of hero worship." Parents and teachers worried that their young charges would become "street bums" and later graduate into the ranks of more hardened criminals. (26)

Contributing to the general hooliganism among the young in Brownsville was the rise of large crime syndicates. Such organizations developed throughout the country, but Brownsville became a center of organized crime. A notorious group called the Combination, sometimes referred to as Murder, Inc., began as a Brownsville youth gang whose activities were stealing fruit from carts and merchandise from trucks, and extorting payments from individuals and businesses. Joselit points out that the career of Abe Reles, one of the most notorious Jewish gangsters, began in a Brownsville youth gang.

As the gang became more bloodthirsty and organized, it terrorized the populace. In the 1940s, it was responsible for 24 murders. It was well known that the adult mobsters, in grooming young men for their organization, encouraged and protected youth gangs.

FRANK GOLDFARB AND THE AMBOY DUKES

The many gangs of Brownsville, Brooklyn, in the early 1940s included the Bristol Friends, the Herzl Street Boys, and the Amboy Dukes. In other areas nearby, gangs could be found coming in occasionally from East New York, Sutter Avenue, and Williamsburg. All these gangs were made up of the children of Jewish immigrants. There was little animosity between these various neighborhood gangs, which often had alliances and dances together. But other ethnic boys, like the two members of the Puerto Rican gang the Sharpsters, discovered in Amboy Duke territory, were chased from the area, sometimes lucky to escape with their lives. The Jewish gangs rented their own clubhouses and, in addition, hung out in local pool halls, candy stores, drugstores, barbershops, and restaurants. They assumed a gang uniform consisting of suits with three-button jackets, pegged and pleated pants, and long key chains to go with their slicked-back, ducktail hairstyles.

The gang members' chief occupations were making fast easy money through petty crimes, like selling counterfeit gasoline coupons. They anticipated the day when they would graduate to become big-time mobsters, who made money on the numbers, slot machines, and the black market. They took their pleasure in prostitutes brought into their clubhouses, smoking marijuana, drinking, picking up girls, going to movies, and having the occasional dance.

Violence was a regular part of their culture. They wore large rings that could cut like weapons; they knew how to make their own guns; and they kept stores of knives and brass knuckles. When they were angered, their technique was to kick their opponent in the ankle, hit him in the groin, and kick him in the kidneys and head.

In Schulman's tale, the attractive, exciting Amboy Dukes capture Frank Goldfarb's attention before he is even into his teens. One of the Dukes takes Frank under his wing and introduces him to reefers when he is 13 years old. Two years later, Frank has become one of the gang's most valuable members. Soon he has adopted their attitude and expression: narrow hard eyes and sneering lips. His fellow club members include Black Bennie, a classmate at the vocational school, and Crazy Sachs, a violent gang member who has a job but in his spare time likes to knife his opponents and refuse to pay for the services of prostitutes and the bands who are hired by the Dukes.

When Frank isn't hanging out in the clubhouse, which is coming to be less and less satisfying to him, he is taking care of his sister Alice, double-dating with Black Bennie, and playing hooky from vocational school. He also learns from Stan Alberg, the community-center director, that there is less and less money to develop the kinds of programs that would appeal to boys and keep them out of gangs.

The initiating circumstance in Frank's story is his and Bennie's drunken confrontation with a teacher who has expelled them; this incident will spell his doom. Bennie, to save Frank from a brutal beating by the teacher, hits the teacher over the head and shoots him dead. For the rest of his short life, Frank is hounded by the police and makes vain attempts to escape from Bennie, who has come to distrust him; the Dukes, all of whose members have been implicated in the crime; and Crazy Sachs, whom Frank deliberately and recklessly taunts.

Despite wanting to withdraw from the gang, Frank makes several foolhardy and dangerous decisions that seal his fate. On one occasion, Crazy makes a date with Fanny, a foolish 12-year-old whose family lives in the same block as Crazy's and Frank's families, and on whom Crazy has a mad crush. Frank convinces the girl to go away with him instead of keeping her date with Crazy. Frank then taunts Crazy with what he has done. Moreover, Frank gives the girl a ticket to the big gang dance, which is expected to turn into a violent melee. Crazy's rage at the girl leads him to beat and rape her at the dance.

After Frank's peaceful trip to Fifth Avenue with his sister Alice, Stan Alberg, the community director, can only watch while the world closes in on Frank—as his family, gang, neighbors, and the police come to see the responsibility he bears for Fanny's brutal rape and the murder of his teacher Mr. Bannon. His death comes fittingly at the hands of one of the gang members, Crazy Sachs, who throws Frank to his death from the top of their tenement building.

"THE VIOLENCE THAT HAS ITS BIRTH IN MISERY" (32)

Frank Goldfarb, member in good standing of the Amboy Dukes, is a graphic example of how poverty breeds gangs. In looking back to his boyhood, he remembers how his father lost his job during the Depression and then remained unemployed because he refused to work in a nonunion shop. He remembers the ignominy of depending on relief, food stamps, clothing tickets, and having to beg continually for money to eke by. He remembers the disgrace of having to beg his rich uncle for the money to buy his bar mitzvah suit. He also remembers the constant arguments between his parents brought on by their lack of money. This physical and emotional wasteland is what first drives Frank to the street gangs. When Frank is a boy, having lost respect for his father, he looks to the older boys in the gang for role models. And his aim is to please and impress the gang leaders rather than his father and mother, who haven't the time or understanding to deal with him.

By 1942, both his parents have jobs in the booming wartime economy and, with overtime, are able to look forward to climbing out of poverty, but the bitterness and recriminations of the Depression years still hang like black clouds over the marriage and the children. Moreover, though they have the money now to buy essentials, the lack of housing keeps them trapped in the depressing tenements of Brownsville. Time and again, they look for housing without success. This situation and the fact that he has little respect for his father or teachers lead him continually to his fellow gang members, who provide him with many means of escape: prostitutes, alcohol, and marijuana.

It is not just material poverty that has driven Frank into a street gang; it is spiritual poverty as well—the utter lack of warmth and beauty in his life in the slums. As Frank's story gets underway in April 1944, he takes his little sister Alice on a bus ride from Brooklyn, down Riverside Drive, as they make their way to the Radio City Music Hall in Manhattan. Both are impressed with the immense difference between the lives of the poor in Brownsville and the lives of the wealthy along Riverside Drive.

> The buildings rose story after story, strong and proud of the wealth housed in their duplex apartments, with wood-burning fireplaces in the libraries, parlors, and master bedrooms. Blue and black limousines stood at attention along the curbs, and sitting smartly in the drivers' seats were the uniformed chauffeurs waiting patiently for the occupants of the apartments to descend to the street and to be driven to the churches and other places of smart assembly. (8)

Alice is enchanted with the Rolls-Royces, fancy beribboned poodles, and women in expensive coats. But the sight of Riverside Drive embitters Frank against the society that has placed them in "a stinking, rotten tenement of carrio brick in a putrescent neighborhood, where he had known nothing but the despair that was attendant upon hopelessness and an enervating poverty" (11).

Near the end of Frank's story, he and Alice again take a bus ride and a walk into the city. Alice basks in the beauty of the gardens along Fifth Avenue, then the stylish shops overflowing with luxurious clothes and housewares, but this time Alice's reaction is different, her early eagerness on their first trip now having turned to melancholy. And Frank recalls his own single experience as a boy with the "glories that money could purchase" when, at camp for two weeks, his spiritual hunger had been fed by the beauties of nature. But "the mold of the slum tenements and the years of public charity had cast Frank true to form: sullen, suspicious, bitter, cruel, uncaring" (251).

TRAPPED

Frank's is a typical and heartrending story of a young man who, having become a member of a gang, finds it impossible to leave the gang behind, even after he has seen something of the truth of his situation. Even from the first of Frank's story in 1944, on the morning after he had taken Alice to the Radio City Music Hall, he begins to draw away from the gang psychologically. He goes down to the gang's clubhouse, but declines the services of the prostitute on call, wishing, once he gets there, that he hadn't come at all. His change of heart comes in part from his anger over Crazy Sach's indecent gesture toward Alice, and the beating he gives Crazy creates the first split between him and the young boys who are supposed to be closer than brothers. Despite Frank's protests, a seed of doubt about the gang is planted when Stan Alberg at the community center tells him that he should "ditch" the Amboy Dukes while he can and get rid of his homemade gun. This makes an impression on Frank, who has to acknowledge secretly that the actions of Crazy in cutting a young boy has made him dislike being a Duke. Stan's suggestion also causes Frank to decide to get rid of his gun. But the murder of Mr. Bannon, while it causes Frank to give up alcohol and reefers, forces him to postpone any plans to split with the gang. He is already entrapped. And persuading Fanny to two-time Crazy makes the trap tighter.

When Benny's murder of Mr. Bannon gets the whole gang in trouble, the Dukes ostracize both Benny and Frank, giving Frank hope that he can eventually make his break with the gang. But for a time, to protect himself from the gang and from Benny, he goes along with their orders to sell tickets to the dance. At the dance, at the very moment he has a chance to leave both the dance and the gang, his pride will not let the Dukes drive him out, and he stays, deciding, as he tells Stan, that he will be through with the gang after that one night. But his plans have to change when the leader of the Dukes tells him that he knows that Frank and Benny killed Mr. Bannon. Frank leaves the dance knowing there is no chance of leaving the gang now. Stan, after observing the brutal fight between Frank and his parents, finally admits defeat, believing that Frank is not wise or strong enough to get out of his situation and break with the Dukes. He will, Stan rightly predicts, die violently. Frank makes a final attempt to extricate himself with a call to the police station, but it is too late.

BIBLIOGRAPHY

Bird, Caroline. *The Invisible Scar.* New York: Longman, 1966.
Granit, Arthur. *The Time of Peaches.* New York: Abelard-Schuman, 1959.
Green, Gerald. *The Last Angry Man.* New York: Scribners, 1956.

Joselit, Jenna Weissman. *Our Gang: Jewish Crime and the New York Jewish Community, 1900–1940*. Bloomington: Indiana University Press, 1983.

Kazin, Alfred. *Starting Out in the Thirties*. Boston: Little, Brown, 1962.

Landesman, Alter F. *Brownsville: The Birth, Development and Passing of a Jewish Community in New York*. New York: Bloch Publishing, 1969.

Perrett, Geoffrey. *Days of Sadness. Years of Triumph: The American People, 1939–1945*. New York: Coward, McCann and Geoghegan, 1973.

Schulman, Irving. *The Amboy Dukes*. 1946. New York: Buccaneer Books, 1947.

Turkus, Burton B., and Sid Feder. *Murder, Inc., the Story of "The Syndicate."* New York: Farrar, Straus and Young, 1951.

8

1940s in Harlem: Richard Wright's *Rite of Passage* (1978)

FROM HOWARD ZINN, "OR DOES IT EXPLODE?"

A People's History of the United States, 1492–Present.
New York: Harper Perennial, 1995.

The black revolt of the 1950s and 1960s—North and South—came as a surprise. But perhaps it should not have. The memory of oppressed people is one thing that cannot be taken away, and for such people, with such memories, revolt is always an inch below the surface. For blacks in the United States, there was the memory of slavery, and after that of segregation, lynching, humiliation. And it was not just a memory but a living presence—part of the daily lives of blacks in generation after generation. (434)

FROM BERNICE ROBINSON, "DON'T WORRY, I'LL BE ON THE TRAIN TOMORROW."

Refuse to Stand Silently By. *Ed. Eliot Wigginton. New York: Doubleday, 1992.*

Finally I realized that I wasn't going to be able, with my education, to find anything to do in Charleston except to work seven days a week as a domestic making a dollar a day. So about 1936, I left my daughter with Momma and moved back to New York to a job in the factories in the garment industry.

. . .

Maybe for two months straight, you are working real hard and steady to get the winter clothes out, and then it slows off because you've gotten everything ready for the winter season. Then it slows until they start making the spring goods. I had to *know* that I was going to have money coming in every week, because I was sending money home to take care of my daughter, and I had to take care of myself. (182)

. . .

And all this time I had been worried about getting my daughter back and sending her to a good school, so finally, even though my parents didn't want me to, I moved back to New York, took the civil service exam again, was sent to work in the Internal Revenue Service, and I got my daughter back. (184)

Richard Wright's *Rite of Passage*, set in the 1940s, lays bare the universal domino effect of poverty, dislocation, desperation, and family disintegration that leads inevitably to a gang culture.

HARLEM

Wright's story does not develop in any detail the issues of poverty and racial discrimination in the neighborhood in New York City called Harlem, home to the largest concentration of African Americans in the United States. Yet his major concerns, the disintegration of the family and the subsequent rise of violent youth gangs, derive directly from the social and economic problems of the novelette's context.

The hardships of poor African Americans in the first decades of the twentieth century were both economic and cultural. Segregation, discrimination, and lack of opportunity had left them with little hope in the southern United States. Legally they could be and were denied all but the lowest-level jobs: maids, cooks, field hands, and garbage men. If a community had no school designed specifically for African Americans, strict segregation kept them illiterate. Segregation laws closed avenues, not only to opportunity, but to equal justice.

While a few people were enjoying the general euphoria of the Roaring Twenties, black and white farmhands alike in the South found it impossible to find work. These years saw a rise in poor white hatred of blacks, in competition with them for the few jobs available, leading to even greater intimidation, violence, and more lynching.

Given the situation in the South after the Civil War, African Americans had begun migrating and continued throughout the first half of the twentieth century to relocate to northern cities. With the poverty and dangers increasing in the South in the 1920s and 1930s, many more African Americans left behind the places they had once called home and many of their older and extended family to find better lives in places like Harlem. At the age of 19, Richard Wright, born and reared in the South, himself migrated north to Chicago and eventually, as an adult, moved to Harlem, where he became interested in the plight of young black men who were drawn into gangs. By 1941, the population of Harlem had grown to six times its inhabitants in 1925.

In the 1920s and 1930s, Harlem became famous for its exotic night spots, a playground for talented, innovative African American musicians and the white people who had the money to amuse themselves there. Certainly, some African Americans found conditions better in the urban North, but Harlem was not by any means the answer to the prayers of most who moved there. Even in the Roaring Twenties, only 10 percent of the nation's population prospered, and 2 million residents of New York City lived in tenements where for decades 233 persons were packed into each acre of land. By the 1940s, 10,000 families in Harlem still lived in tenements. Disease, especially tuberculosis, was rampant.

Wallace Thurman, one writer who lived in Harlem in the 1920s, made the following observation about what many had regarded as the Promised Land:

> The people seen on Fifth Avenue are either sad or nasty looking. The women seem to be drudges or drunkards, the men pugnacious and loud—petty thieves and vicious parasites. The children are pitiful specimens of ugliness and dirt. The tenement houses in the vicinity are darkened dungheaps, festering with poverty-stricken and crime-ridden step-children of nature.... Evil faces leer at you from doorways and windows. Brutish men elbow you out of their way, dreary looking women scowl at and curse children playing on the sidewalk. This is Harlem's Fifth Avenue. (in Anderson 144)

Another writer, Hope R. Stevens, observed the following:

> To lawyers who frequent the inferior courts where the com-
> plaints against landlords are processed, it is a matter of con-
> stant wonder that the filthy backyards and area ways and the
> dark, rat-infested tenements in which so many of our work-
> ing people live, seem to continue unchanged in their condi-
> tion, year after year. (Clarke 110)

And George F. Brown enlarges on the housing problems of Harlem
by observing: "It is not a rare sight to see an evicted family's belongings callously dumped on the sidewalks somewhere in Harlem from
rat-infested firetraps that in other areas would be condemned as unfit
for human habitation" (Clarke 198). In 1931, evictions from homes
and farms occurred throughout the country. In Harlem alone at that
time, there were from 10 to 20 evictions a day.

The New Deal, while it improved the lives of many people, did little to help the African Americans who had chosen to move to Harlem.
Even in the North, they still faced segregation in education, services,
medical care, shops, and restaurants. Throughout the 1930s and
1940s, twice as many patients died in Harlem Hospital as died in the
white hospitals in New York City. Most discouraging, however,
African Americans still suffered from job discrimination. In 1930, of
Harlem's 200,000 adults, half were unemployed. Half of the women
working in Harlem worked as domestics as they had done in the
South. As the poor of all races did, throughout the country in the
1930s, many black men and women were able to get jobs only by
gathering on street corners to wait for employers to come by, look
them over, and maybe give them a job for the day. The residents of
Harlem called these gatherings "slave markets."

Beneath the laughter and the music was an economic hopelessness
and spiritual despair that brought about the collapse of the family and
bred massive youth-gang-generated crime, with which the over-
whelmed justice and social services systems could not possibly cope.
African Americans constituted only about one-fifth of the total population of Manhattan, yet they made up more than one-half of the juvenile offenders.

A particularly heartless policy on the part of authorities charged
with the welfare of children is used by Wright as the initiating incident
in *Rite of Passage:* this was the practice of automatically wrenching foster children from their foster homes after a few years had elapsed,
whether or not the situation was an advantageous one. Wright was
able to document case after case in which a child was forced out of a

loving foster home where he had lived for five or six years and reassigned to a different family or to an institution. Johnny's case has evidently fallen through the bureaucratic cracks because he has remained with the Gibbs family for 16 years, believing himself to be their natural son. The suggestion is that authorities are more intent on enforcing an impersonal and ill-conceived policy than they are in considering the welfare of the individual child. Wright knew from experience with the homeless juveniles of Harlem that many of them, to escape the system and its institutions, took to the streets to form gangs like the one Johnny joins.

THE PASSAGE

Fifteen-year-old Johnny Gibbs's harsh awakening takes place in the course of one day. Although he lives in the bleak tenements of Harlem, Johnny is a fairly happy innocent who performs well in school, is highly regarded by his teacher, is supported by a loving mother, and is content in a family that also includes a father, sister, and brother. The switchblade knife he sees out of the corner of his eye outside school on his way home is only a hint of the violence that has not yet touched his life. And the bleak slums are scarcely a distraction for the boy who looks forward to a bowl of his mother's comfort food at the end of the school day.

Within minutes after walking through his front door, however, his world turns upside down, transforming Johnny from a trusting child into a desperate outcast. His mother and sister are compelled to tell him that, though he has lived with them as a son and brother since infancy, he is not really a biological member of the family. He is a foster child whom social services have now decided, according to some senseless, heartless policy, to take away from his family and place in another foster home. He now realizes that his meager belongings, which he had puzzled about seeing in the hallway of the apartment building on his way in from school, have been placed there because both he and they have been removed from the family. Neither Johnny's brother nor his father is there when he is told that he must leave. Nor are they there to say goodbye when the new foster family arrives to pick him up shortly after he has learned his fate. Johnny, stunned, turns on his passively grieving mother and flees the house.

He wanders aimlessly, taking a train to an area far from his neighborhood near Times Square, where he believes he will not be apprehended. Perhaps not having eaten a meal all day (his mother's food had lost its appeal in being delivered at the same time her maternity had been taken away), he commits the first of what the reader expects will be many crimes. After prying open the lock from a stand, he steals peanuts and candy bars.

An overwhelming desire seizes him to talk to someone, anyone, but the shock he has undergone has left him uncertain, unstable, not knowing where and who he is or where to turn. Some of his memories and present encounters with older people—the policeman, his teacher, the man who allows him to slip through the turnstile—suggest evidence of goodwill in the world, but the trauma Johnny has recently experienced has left him distrustful. He realizes that at any moment he could be discovered, taken by social services, perhaps even placed in an institution.

Nonetheless, he seems to have no choice but to return to Harlem, where he seeks out his friend Billy. When Billy drags his feet in extending understanding and help, Johnny's desperation leads him to threaten to kill Billy if he betrays him. Billy reluctantly conveys to Johnny the stark truth he has heard from the evening's conversation in Johnny's house after he ran away. Johnny's birth is the result of a single sexual encounter between strangers. Immediately afterward, his biological father had vanished without a trace and his mother, a schizophrenic, had been institutionalized.

It is Billy, his own family torn apart by alcoholism, who holds out the only hope for Johnny. There is a small gang of youthful outlaws who might be persuaded to take him into their pseudofamily and, in effect, see that he has shelter, food, and the means of survival that the Gibbs family had once provided.

The gang to which Billy leads him has a practice of convening in the furnace room of the school's basement at dusk. The members—Treetop, Stinkie, and their leader, Baldy—are initially as suspicious of Johnny as he has been of everyone else since his fall into knowledge. Finally, "The Moochers," made up of boys like himself who have been displaced by the foster-child system, take him in. It is a different culture for Johnny. These boys lack homes, parents, and schooling. They have to scrounge for food and shelter. They are never without dangerous knives and guns. And they make their way in the world by committing petty crimes and holdups, usually for a man who pays them for their loot and gives them a place to stay. Johnny soon finds that in the commission of their crimes they have engaged in sadism and murder.

Although Johnny is physically thin and ignorant of the ways of the street, his desperation has made him an animal. Within a few hours of his introduction to the Moochers, he provokes an attack from Baldy and then brutally beats him in what is not only his initiation into the gang but his assumption of its leadership. The young boy, who earlier in the day had basked in his teacher's approval and looked forward to little more than a bowl of food in his mother's kitchen, has become what the Moochers name him—the Jackal.

Late in the evening, the gang proceeds with its usual night of crime. They head to the ironically named Morningside Park—not a place of light and children's play but a place of danger where dark crimes are committed by gang members. Their routine begins as usual: one of the gang approaches a mark and politely asks directions, while the others creep up behind to strangle the victim, strip him of his money and valuables, and remove and run away with his trousers and shoes. On this, his first night of crime, Johnny either sees or imagines that he sees a woman stand beside their elderly victim, yelling "You boys! You boys!" She continues to haunt him into the early hours of the morning.

The gang proceeds from the robbery in the park to the building occupied by a thief and fence called Gink, who takes their proceeds, pays them each $50, and gives them food, shelter, and safety. As a gang member of a few hours, Johnny is very successful but sick at heart, unaccustomed to the violence and sickened by Baldy's mindless murder and cruelty. What Johnny wants is something he has lost inevitably— a true home and family, its devotion, and the comfort and care of a mother. The gang cannot replace those things. Despite his revulsion with the life he has experienced this evening, the future seems to hold little else for Johnny Gibbs.

FAMILY AND GANG

Richard Wright wrote his novel at a time when he was intensely interested in the tragedy that had unfolded in Harlem's African American families. He was deeply concerned with the way in which family disintegration had driven young black men into violent criminal gangs. In writing *Rite of Passage,* as he tried to focus on the psychological dimensions of the problem, Wright consulted with psychologists. As he studied the work of psychiatrist Dr. Louis Wertham, he helped the doctor establish the first psychiatric clinic in Harlem. Wright also supported the Wiltwych School in the Catskills, established for troubled boys. Both these organizations acknowledged, as did Wright, that the problems of young delinquents would not be solved without social change.

Not only was the prevalence of gangs evidence of wasted human lives, but they had a perpetual ruinous effect on the populace they terrorized. The root causes were centuries of degradation, discrimination, and poverty. In the African American's displacement to Harlem, hopelessness and self-abasement were grimly validated.

The African American family had been outlawed during slavery, literally ripped apart when members were bought and sold. In the diaspora that occurred in the decades following the Emancipation, the family unit was sundered again as, seeking a way out of poverty, one parent or both parents left behind children, grandparents, extended family members, and a caring culture. Once in the urban centers, the African American family seemed to be exhausted by economic necessity, anxiety, and the disruption of family tradition. Traditional values evaporated for those without hope and with nothing to lose. Johnny's birth as a result of a one-night stand and his father's immediate disappearance illustrate the point. In Harlem, there was a large population of orphans and single-mother households. When fathers did live with their families, they made themselves absent, by either working of necessity from dawn to dusk, by drinking and carousing as a means of escape, or by literally running away. Johnny's biological father has never been in the picture, and his foster father seems remote, even absent at this critical moment in Johnny's life.

The loss of the father in African American families, including Johnny's, results in a psychology that encourages gangs. The most obvious reason is the lack of a paternal role model to show young boys what it means to be a man. Paternal guidance and discipline are lacking in their lives. So these young men fill the vacuums in their lives, not with caring fathers and grandfathers, but with uncles and brothers who are gang members. They turn not to educational or religious leaders but to gang leaders. They remain perpetual boys whose games have become violent. Their behavior is not refined by the nuclear family that traditionally socializes the child, teaching him to care for and be responsible for others, first within the family itself and then, beyond that, in the community. Instead, the young man, like Johnny, learns that the gang values physical force, duplicity, self-gratification, and freedom from responsibility.

Family disintegration has also resulted in Johnny's loss of identity. After 16 years of believing he knows who he is and that he has a place in a family, he comes to the realization that he literally does not know who he is. His real father has no name and no face. His real mother, suffering from acute mental illness, probably doesn't even know who

she is. The people he has called mother and father for 16 years are im-
postors. So Johnny formulates his own new identity as a gang member
and a gang leader because he thinks he has no other choice.

Yet that choice, we are led to believe, will leave him with a poverty
of the soul that only a caring family could have prevented. As Johnny
mulls over his day, he realizes that no "voice would call him home, re-
prove him with love, chastise him with devotion, or place a cool soft
hand upon his brow when he was fevered with doubt and indecision"
(115). For all the gang's words about friendship and loyalty, finally
Johnny knows that each of the boys in the gang is alone and is on his
own.

Johnny is also driven to gang life by what he sees as betrayal by the
people he regarded as his family. His mother, typically the center of
strength of the family, collapses before the dictates of the authorities
and makes no attempt to challenge them in order to keep the child she
has reared since infancy. From her own lack of self-worth and hopelessness, we are led to believe, she gives in without an objection. From
that moment, he comes to regard his family as a fraud. Even the love
and comfort he thought he had experienced there was a shallow ve-
neer that disintegrated with the notice from the authorities. This leads
Johnny and the other gang members, who have had similar experiences, to such a profound distrust that they sever their human ties.
They are now all jackals.

BIBLIOGRAPHY

Anderson, Jervis. *This Was Harlem: A Cultural Portrait, 1900–1950*. New
    York: Farrar, Straus and Giroux, 1981.
Clarke, John Henrik, ed. *Harlem: A Community in Transition*. New York:
    The Citadel Press, 1964.
Davis, Charles T. *Richard Wright: A Primary Bibliography*. Boston: G. K.
    Hall, 1982.
Fabre, Michel. *The Unfinished Quest of Richard Wright*. Urbana: University
    of Illinois, 1993.
Felgar, Robert. *Student Companion to Richard Wright*. Westport, CT:
    Greenwood Press, 2000.
———. *Understanding Richard Wright's Black Boy*. Westport, CT: Green-
    wood Press, 1998.
Fishburn, Katherine. *Richard Wright's Hero*. Metuchen, NJ: Scarecrow
    Press, 1977.
Gayle, Addison. *Richard Wright*. Garden City, NY: Anchor Press, 1980.

Kinnamon, Kenneth. *A Richard Wright Bibliography.* Westport, CT: Green-
    wood Press, 1988.
Mitchell, Hayley, ed. *Readings on* Black Boy. Westport, CT: Greenwood
    Press, 2000.
Webb, Constance. *Richard Wright: A Biography.* New York: Putnam, 1968.
Wright, Richard. "Almos' a Man." *Learning in Focus.* Northbrook, IL:
    Coronet Films and Video, 1985.
———. *Black Boy.* New York: Harper and Row, 1945.
———. *Rite of Passage.* 1978. New York: HarperCollins, 1994.

9

Nazis and Gangs: William Golding's *Lord of the Flies* (1954)

FROM WILLIAM L. SHIRER, *THE NIGHTMARE YEARS.*

Boston: Little, Brown, 1984.

As he worked toward the inevitable climax of his discourse, the natural voice would reassert itself, the tone rising in scale, and, as the words came tumbling out in a torrent, it would become shrill and he would begin to shriek hysterically and reach, as one Irish correspondent irreverently put it, an orgasm of sound and fury, followed by an ecstasy such as I had never seen in a speaker, and which the awed listeners seemed to fully share.

He appeared able to swing his German hearers into any mood he wished. He could stir up a burning hate, as when he spoke of the Bolsheviks and the Jews, and later on, of those who stood in his way: the Czechs at the time of the Sudeten crises, the Poles just before he attacked them. I shall never forget how he shrieked at the Jews, in a paroxysm of hysteria, calling them animals, barbarians, pygmies, and threatening them with utter destruction—a threat he would make good. (128–29)

FROM STEPHEN E. AMBROSE, *CITIZEN SOLDIERS.*

New York: Simon and Schuster, 1997.

[Captain Belton] Cooper came to a warehouse, where German civilians, old men, women, and children were plundering. "The crowd was ravenous; they were pushing and shoving. They paid absolutely no attention to the poor pitiful wretches lying in the streets." Further on, "we passed three large stacks of what appeared to be wastepaper and garbage piled in rows six feet high and 400 feet long. The stench was overwhelming and as I looked I noticed that parts of the stack were moving. To my absolute horror, it dawned on me that these stacks contained the bodies of naked human beings. A few were still alive and they were writhing in the excrement and human waste. (462)

. . .

Later that day an awful black, acrid smoke appeared. It came from one of the outlying camps of the Dachau system. When the Americans approached, the SS officer in charge had ordered the remaining 4,000 slave laborers destroyed. The guards had nailed shut the doors and windows of the wooden barracks, hosed down the building with gasoline, and set them on fire. The prisoners had been cremated alive. (464)

In *Lord of the Flies,* William Golding's classic novel, youth gangs are compared to Germany's fascist gangs in the 1930s and 1940s, under the leadership of Adolph Hitler. The point Golding intends to make, however, is that Nazism is not just a phenomenon isolated to World War II Germany; beneath the surface, we are all capable of atrocities. Our natural instincts, allowed free rein by any outlaw gang, are kept under control by civilized laws. *Lord of the Flies,* the story of a group of boys marooned on a desert island, uses the development of youth gangs to comment on the human character in general and the rise of the Nazis in particular. It raises the following issue with regard to gangs: Our human nature inclines us to allow brute force, violence, and animalism to triumph over reason and civilization, to sacrifice humaneness and democracy to cruelty and tyranny. Once in motion, barbarism tends to escalate.

THE SETTING

Despite the novel's references to nuclear war, which could only have occurred at the *close* of World War II, the action of the novel seems to be based on events that occurred in the middle of the war, when England was attacked by German bombers, eventually killing an estimated 30,000 people and injuring 50,000. During this time, English children were evacuated from urban areas under attack. Most were taken by train to safer areas in rural England. Some were sent by ship to other countries. Not all arrived safely at their destinations. The fate of the boys in *Lord of the Flies* echoes the sinking of the *City of Benares,* when some 80 British children perished on their way to safety.

Other relevant events include the rise of Hitler and his Gestapo and Hitler Youth, the atrocities committed during the war, and the post-war disillusionment that led many thinkers, like Golding, to speculate on the human—not just German—capacity for evil.

THE RISE OF ADOLPH HITLER

In 1926, after eight post–World War I years of reform and repression, Adolph Hitler, a strangely charismatic politician, became the leader of the Nazi Party. He quickly amassed a following of storm troopers who were not taken seriously by the general populous. They were regarded as little more than Hitler's personal gang of toughs who strutted around in their brown uniforms. But these "Brown Shirts" engaged in the nasty business of physically attacking Jews, Communists, and homosexuals. In a divided country ravaged by economic disaster, Hitler soon became chancellor and immediately saw the Enabling Act passed into law, giving him absolute authority. He carried a riding whip with him on all occasions to convey his power, and used loud, yelling tantrums to terrorize his staff. To rally Germans to his cause, he instituted assemblies at Nuremberg, great emotional pageants of German military power and song. One of those causes was the building of concentration camps to incarcerate all manner of citizens who were the object of Hitler's hate.

His policies were carried out by a Nazi Party gang called the Gestapo and the SS, the secret police. To create a constant source of enthusiastic followers ready to do his dirty work, Hitler used blatant propaganda to seduce German young people. He was not interested in schooling German youth in the classics and sciences; what he wanted was a national outlaw gang of fearless toughs. The weak, he wrote, must be destroyed, and the strong must become cruel, violent, and arrogant. As early as 1932, his "Hitler Youth" numbered 100,000. In 1939, the fuhrer decreed that *all* youth had to join the movement. At the height of his power, the Hitler Youth had grown to

10 million and recruited boys and girls as young as 6. They were schooled primarily in Nazi propaganda and soldiering. At the age of 18, the boys either joined the government-controlled labor service or the army.

Even to the end of the 1930s, after Jews had been deprived of citizenship, civil rights, and property, most Germans, if not enthusiastic about Hitler, allowed him a free hand in exchange for an improved economy. Scholars have consistently debated the matter of how much the ordinary German people knew about the atrocities being ordered by the Nazis. It is difficult to imagine that citizens in urban areas had no knowledge of the extent to which Jews were being rounded up and shipped out in cattle cars and hard to imagine that people living within sight of the death camps had no hint of the cruelties being carried out there.

THE ATROCITIES OF WORLD WAR II

So-called unauthorized concentration camps were set up in Germany by the Brown Shirts in the early 1930s to incarcerate "undesirables," including Jews, gypsies, and some Slavs. These were brutal work camps into which the inmates were herded like cattle and worked or starved to death. Some 30 major camps of a similar nature became authorized by the Nazi government and eventually housed approximately one million slaves. One of the worst practices of the camps was sadistic medical experimentation. At one camp, Oranienburg, 100 inmates were gassed to death to furnish skeletons for the Institute for Practical Research in Military Science.

The most notorious segment of the concentration camps was built for extermination, that is, murder of undesirables. Three million people, some 12,000 a day, were killed in the Auschwitz camp alone. It was not until 1945, with the Allied liberation of the camps, that the rest of the world knew the extent of these horrors.

Although these were the most notorious atrocities of the war, other countries exterminated civilians, notably during the Japanese rape of Nanking, in which 42,000 civilians were massacred; the Allied bombing of Dresden, in which about 35,000 civilians died; and the American bombing of Hiroshima, where 240,000 died, and Nagasaki, where 23,753 died.

These events led many thinkers, like Golding, to speculate on the human capacity for evil.

THE RISE OF A PRIMITIVE YOUTH GANG

In the opening of *Lord of the Flies,* two young boys, Ralph and Piggy, find themselves on a deserted island after the crash of an airplane carrying them to safety. Ralph, who will shortly assume leadership of the group, and Piggy, his chief supporter, shed their clothes and find an enormous conch shell that, at Piggy's suggestion, they blow to summon other survivors of the crash. Among the boys who appear on the beach are a bunch of "little'uns" around 6 years old. There were also twins named Eric and Sam and a group of black-clad choir boys, who march onto the beach under the direction of a red-haired boy named Jack Merridew. Among the choir boys is Roger, who will later prove to be a sadist, and Simon, a gentle, sensitive child, derided by the others.

Ralph, who is in possession of the conch, a symbol of democratic law, is voted the leader of the whole group, while Jack is in charge of the choir boys, whom he designates as hunters. The group works together at first, claiming the island as their territory and meeting in assembly when the conch is blown.

A foreshadowing of evil is introduced when a small boy reports that he has seen a snake-like beast, an evil specter that hovers over the island. Some mistake a corpse in a parachute for the beast; Jack and his hunters perceive it as an evil god to which they must make sacrifices. But Simon, the insightful boy, senses that the beast is within every boy on the island.

The gang of boys soon begins to separate into two factions with opposite concerns. Ralph urges his followers to keep a fire burning so they can be rescued by a passing ship, to respect parliamentary law, to build shelters and preserve water, and to bathe everyday and keep their environment clean. Jack, on the other hand, is not bound by civilization, hunts for the sadistic fun of the kill, and is only interested in the fire as a means to cook meat.

Piggy is the unwilling Prometheus figure whose eyeglasses are the only means for starting a fire. So Piggy, the derided scapegoat, guards the only instruments of civilization—the spectacles that make fire and the conch that represents parliamentary law.

Jack begins securing greater control when he paints his face before leading the hunt, creating a mask that seems to release all his animalistic urges and is a sign of his swift decline into barbarism. He also develops a mesmerizing bloodthirsty chant to encourage cruel joy in the hunt: "Kill the pig. Cut her throat. Spill her blood" (62). Meanwhile, his choir boys, who have been left in control of the fire, let it go out in order to hunt. Their dereliction of duty comes at a bad moment, when a ship sails within sight. In the confrontation that this lapse provokes, Jack attacks Piggy, breaking one of the lenses in the precious glasses.

The antagonism between Jack and Ralph finally erupts, dividing the boys into two opposing gangs. Jack, without the restraints imposed by Ralph, falls further into savagery, along with the sadistic Roger, who tortures a pig until Jack slits its throat. At this point, Jack decides to begin leaving the head of the pig to appease the mythical beast.

As the others feast on the pig and continue to quarrel, Simon, who has begun to hallucinate, sees swarms of flies attacking the pig's head and supposes that the Lord of the Flies ridicules him for his good-hearted generosity and naïveté, which will lead to his defeat in this situation. On the way home from his encounter with the Lord of the Flies (a universal symbol of the devil), Simon finds the corpse of the parachutist and prepares to tell the others that they have mistaken the parachute for the beast. But as he approaches the feast with the parachute, Jack and his gang mistake him for the beast and kill him.

After this incident, Ralph and Piggy find that all but a few boys have joined Jack's gang. Jack imposes his own rules on the group. He ties up and beats Wilfred, secures the borders of his territory to keep out all but his own gang, prepares for a gang war against Ralph, and incorporates more and more primitive rituals to identify his gang. When Jack's fire for cooking meat goes out, his gang raids Ralph's community to steal Piggy's glasses in order to start a new fire.

In the fray that breaks out when Ralph and his few remaining supporters attempt to retrieve Piggy's glasses, Roger inadvertently kills Piggy. Jack has the twins in the group arrested and tortures them for information about Ralph, who has escaped just in time. Ralph finds that their plan is to hunt him down, decapitate him like a pig, and put his head on a stick.

In Jack's gang's thoroughgoing search for Ralph, he sets the whole island on fire to smoke him out. In the middle of the hunt, Ralph stumbles upon a naval officer who has come ashore from his ship. All the remaining savages emerge from the brush and, in the presence of their rescuer, become sobbing little boys again.

GANG ISSUES AND *LORD OF THE FLIES*

Jack's savage tribe is a youth gang that shares many characteristics with the youth gangs of today. The boys are lured to Jack by danger, adventure, and good times. He also uses the promise of desirable goods, in this case, the meat of the pigs, to attract a following. He exerts peer pressure to secure his power. Shortly after he has established his sizable gang, he becomes territorial, intent on protecting his turf from outsiders like Ralph and Piggy. And he uses rituals, ceremonies, and war paint to add a mesmerizing element that secures his gang's loyalty. The chief characteristic that emerges from the novel is the triumph of violence and brutality over laws of humane behavior. From the first, Jack rejects the more lawful, gentler aspect of civilization that Piggy and Ralph hope somewhat naïvely to hold on to. Like the contemporary street gang that operates outside law and order, Jack's gang reverts to animalistic "tooth and claw" behavior. Also, consistent with contemporary gangs, Jack, as leader, dismisses representative government to become a tyrant.

Set outside civilized society, the gang reverts to cruelties ranging from throwing sand and rocks at their comrades to torturing and planning to kill their rival.

Lord of the Flies ultimately shows the inevitability of gang savagery when individuals are placed outside societal controls. It contradicts the message of Jean-Jacques Rousseau and Ralph Waldo Emerson that children are innocent until they are corrupted by society. Golding paints a verbal picture of an innate darkness—a beast—at the heart of every human, a beast that is kept at bay only by society. We see the beast emerging not only on the island where the boys are stranded but in the youth gangs that arise in squalid slums or in environments where morality has been eroded and law has become irrelevant or anathema.

Through the novel, Golding draws a clear connection between youth gangs and Adolph Hitler's Germany. Indeed, it is scarcely surprising that many of the gangs throughout the world in the late twentieth and early twenty-first centuries have been neofascist, singling out as their enemies groups of people they regard as scapegoats, whether they be Jewish or homosexual.

Hannah Vogt, in writing of "Life in the Third Reich," says that Hitler abhorred the legal system above all other things. Jack parallels Hitler in this disregard of law.

Like Hitler, Jack is able to wield violent power and commit atrocities because other boys, like Ralph, refuse to acknowledge the inherent danger in his personality. Even Piggy, like the undesirables throughout Europe who became scapegoats, is not sufficiently aware of the danger he is in. He, like they, believes he has a chance of surviving a confrontation with Jack, believes that the democratic instincts of those in Jack's gang will eventually bring them around when the conch is blown. Holding to similar beliefs about Hitler and his gangs, many Jews remained in Germany after their civil liberties had been revoked.

Like Hitler, Jack and other gang leaders use pageantry, secret codes, ceremonies, and distinctive appearance to cement their power. For Hitler's and other gangs throughout history, it was the uniform, the bizarre dress. For Jack, it is the war paint that releases his followers from their inhibitions. Both use mantras to hypnotize their followers. Hitler had only to mount a podium and harangue his audience with the evils of the Jewish people, having trained them to respond with a rousing "Heil Hitler." Jack has only to repeat the bloodthirsty chant, "Kill the pig! Cut his throat! Spill his blood!"

In this way, Golding equates youth gangs with the most notorious leader and mass killer of the twentieth century.

BIBLIOGRAPHY

Babb, S. Howard. *The Novels of William Golding*. Columbus: Ohio State University Press, 1970.

Baker, James R. *Critical Essays on William Golding*. Boston: G. K. Hall, 1988.

Boyd, S. J. *The Novels of William Golding*. 2nd ed. New York: Harvester, 1988.

Dick, Bernard F. *William Golding*. Rev. ed. Boston: Twayne Publishers, 1987.

Dickson, L. L. *The Modern Allegories of William Golding*. Tampa: University of South Florida Press, 1990.

Friedman, Lawrence S. *William Golding*. New York: Continuum, 1993.

Gindin, James. *William Golding*. New York: St. Martin's Press, 1988.

Golding, William. *Lord of the Flies*. 1954. New York: Wideview/Perigee Books, 1955.

Hodson, Leighton. *William Golding*. Edinburgh, UK: Oliver and Boyd, 1969.

Kinkead-Weekes, Mark, and Ian Gregor. *William Golding: A Critical Study*. New York: Harcourt, Brace and World, 1967.

Olsen, Kirstin. *Understanding* Lord of the Flies: *A Student Casebook to Issues, Sources, and Historical Documents*. Westport, CT: Greenwood Press, 2000.

Page, Norman, ed. *William Golding: Novels, 1954–67*. London: Macmillan, 1985.

Reilly, Patrick. Lord of the Flies: *Fathers and Sons*. New York: Twayne Publishers, 1992.

Vogt, Hannah. "Life in the Third Reich." *Hitler and Nazi Germany*. Ed. Robert G. Waite. New York: Holt, Rinehart and Winston, 1965.

Whitley, John S. *Golding:* Lord of the Flies. London: Edward Arnold, 1970.

10

A Girl Gang in the 1950s: Joyce Carol Oates's *Foxfire* (1993)

FROM MARY G. HARRIS, *CHOLAS: LATINO GIRLS AND GANGS.*

New York: AMS Press, 1988.

Reselda: A lot of girls do come from families that are messed up. A lot of girls like they ain't got back up in their families. If they get into a gang they got more back up. They've got more girls to really hang around with. More girls to hustle with, and pull this and pull that, and maybe get money. They come from low families, a lot of them. Of families that are messed up. They ain't got too much love in the family. So they don't care what's going on. If their family don't care, she don't care. In the family they don't really sit down and get to understand each other. And she don't care. Nothing's going right in her house so what should she care about what's going on out there. She'll do whatever she has to do. So it won't be hard for her to decide to join a gang. She'll just go out and do it. (154)

FROM MEDA CHESNEY-LIND, RANDALL G. SHELDEN, AND KAREN A. JOE, "GIRLS, DELINQUENCY, AND GANG MEMBERSHIP."

Gangs in America. Ed. C. Ronald Huff. London: Thousand Oaks, 1996.

Media portrayals of young women suggest that they, like their male counterparts, are increasingly involved in violence and gang activities....

Let us turn first to the question of girls' violence. A review of girls' arrests for violent crime for the last decade (1984–1993) initially seems to support the notion that girls are engaged in more violent crime.... These increases certainly sound substantial, but on closer inspection they become considerably less dramatic....

[S]erious crimes of violence represent a very small proportion of all girls' delinquency, and that figure has remained essentially unchanged. Only 2.3% of girls' arrests in 1984 were for serious violent crimes....

Detailed comparisons drawn from..."supplemental homicide reports" also indicated that, in comparison to boys' homicides, girls who killed were more likely to use a knife than a gun and to murder someone as a result of conflict rather than in the commission of a crime....

Self-report data trends in youthful involvement in violent offenses also fail to show the dramatic changes found in official statistics.... These data revealed significant *decreases* in girls' involvement in felony assaults, minor assault, and hard drugs, and no change in a wide range of other delinquent behaviors—including felony theft, minor theft, and index delinquency....

Although many questions can be raised about the actual significance of differences between official and self-report data, careful analyses of these data cast doubt on the media construction of the hyperviolent girl. (189–90)

Foxfire: Confessions of a Girl Gang, by Joyce Carol Oates, weaves social theory into the story of a girl gang. The gang's leader, Legs, puts together her own experiences with the learned discussions she has with Father Theriault, a defrocked Catholic priest. The questions the gang raises with regard to revolution and charity are as old as human ethics. If the socioeconomic structure of capitalist society is unjust, just how far should one go in defiance of the system?

BACKGROUND: GIRL GANGS, THE 1950S, AND FIDEL CASTRO

Stereotypically, the 1950s was a time of economic prosperity that allowed many American families to enjoy the fruits of new technology and live comfortably on one salary brought home by the husband/father. The material comfort that many experienced in the decade fostered a kind of complacent conservatism that favored unfettered

capitalism. Tradition and authority had "come through" on the promise to preserve the good life, and capitalism deserved to be left to rule
undisturbed. The great fear of those in authority was that Communism, perhaps even the Soviet Union itself, which was toppling power
bases in Eastern Europe, would creep into the United States through
left-wing politics and labor unions. So the decade was characterized by
government attempts to silence dissent. Measures taken in the 1940s
to check the spread of Communism picked up speed in the 1950s: the
Smith Act allowed the government to bring to trial anyone suspected
of planning the violent overthrow of the government; the House
Committee on Un-American Activities, operating on both state and
national levels, could subpoena anyone who was suspected of subversion; the Taft-Hartley Act made it illegal for union members to join
the Communist Party; and loyalty-review boards forbade those suspected of subversion from working in government or education. In
October of 1954, 2,600 civil service workers were dismissed as a result
of the Communist Control Act.

The 1950s were characterized not only by prosperity and political
conservatism but by a particular vision of the American family, pro-
mulgated on film and in advertisements. This idealized family con-
sisted of a working father, a stay-at-home mother, and two children.
However, as Luis Rodriguez writes in *Always Running:* "Family can
only exist among those who can afford one" (250). This is also the argument that emerges from Joyce Carol Oates's *Foxfire.* The poor
could not afford the kind of family idealized in the 1950s. Economic
distress in the poor end of Hammond has produced mental collapse,
alcoholism, drug abuse, physical illness, and moral decay—taking its
toll on the family unit and its individuals. Maddy's mother, her sole
support, ends up in a mental institution, leaving Maddy at the mercy
of relatives. Legs's mother has died of kidney failure brought about by
drug use. When her father brings his girlfriends into the house, social
services takes Legs out. By the time she is released from detention, her
father has left town without telling anyone where he is going. Rita's
father is an alcoholic wife beater, and when Rita's brothers rape her,
her mother turns on Rita in terror.

Foxfire shows the reader the underside of the 1950s. Here is an
urban community of the laboring poor who, like the rural poor, had
seen little improvement in their lives in the 1950s. It was they who
were hit hardest when advances in technology began replacing workers and when in the late 1950s the economy slowed down, resulting
in the closing of businesses, cutbacks, and layoffs. Cases of hardship,

which Foxfire alleviates with its charity fund, are typical of the under-side of 1950s society.

One of the results of 1950s capitalism was a society of inequities. The millionaire businessmen like Whitney Kellogg, with his posh house and bulging closets, live on one side of the hill in Hammond, and on the other side of the hill, a few streets away, the Foxfire girls and their families live in slums and attend for a brief time the worst schools in the district. Corporate earnings were booming in the 1950s. In February of 1950, General Motors recorded a profit of $656,434,232, the largest earnings ever by a U.S. corporation. In 1951, AT&T reported a record one million stockholders. The upper-and middle-class children who shared in the prosperity of the decade could look forward to playing sports, taking music lessons, going to camp in summer, graduating from high school, and going on to col-lege. They could, as Maddy says, "aspire to the head of General Mo-tors—General Mills—AT&T—U.S. Steel" (6). But for the Foxfire girls and their friends, the handwriting is already on the wall—having to drop out of school to struggle forever in low-wage jobs, always liv-ing close to the bone.

So it comes as no surprise that not all Americans were as eager to defend the status quo as was a government backed by corporate Amer-ica. Many American workers, like those in the poor section of Ham-mond, were unionized. Significant strikes marked the decade. A strike of steel workers in April of 1952 caused the government to take over the steel mills. In 1953, the administration stepped in to prevent a dockworkers' strike. A twelve-hour walk-out of steel workers occurred in 1955, and 1956 saw a 156-day strike by Westinghouse Electric Corporation employees. When union members were ineffective, it was not for want of faith in solidarity but because government regulation was designed to weaken the unions.

Beneath the surface conservatism were those, like Father Theriault and Legs, who hoped for revolutionary changes in the country and those whose lives were ruined in the witch hunts of the 1950s. Legs's dream of revolution would not be realized in the United States, but it would be realized in Cuba.

In 1952, as Legs, with Father Theriault's help, was noticing the in-equities and injustice in the system, Juan Batista returned to Cuba from exile and seized power through a military coup. He established an absolute military dictatorship, canceling the constitution and exe-cuting hundreds who opposed him. Cuba had long belonged to the sugar producers and, under Batista, their earnings grew at the rate of hundreds of millions of dollars. Their millions of dollars did not go to the state to improve the country but went, rather, into their private estates. At the same time, prices rose and the poor became poorer.

In 1953, when the action of *Foxfire* was beginning, Fidel Castro emerged as a revolutionary leader of the opposition to Batista. Not until 1959 did Castro prevail over Batista and the sugar producers. One of his first reforms was to limit the profits of the wealthy and to redistribute massive estates. As Castro's government seized estates and nationalized vast U.S. holdings in Cuba, it also reduced rents and established health-care and literacy programs. In April of 1961, the United States made an abortive attempt to invade Cuba via the Bay of Pigs, and in December of the same year, Castro declared himself to be a Communist.

Foxfire in many ways is a paradigm of labor unions, reformers, and revolutionaries in the 1950s. In their pursuit of reform, these outlaws in solidarity are pushed over the edge. Decency and humaneness fall by the wayside when they choose to reform society by means of violent revolution.

As a paradigm containing references to political theory, the fictional Foxfire gang of the 1950s might appear at first to bear only scant resemblance to the girl gangs that first gained visibility in the 1980s.

Important early studies of gangs like Frederick Thrasher's 1927 *The Gang* and W. F. Whyte's 1943 *Street Corner Society* found that girls were involved in gang activity only as the property of male gang members, or were in "sister gangs," complimentary to male gangs. Not until the 1980s did significant numbers of independent girl gangs emerge. Unlike the Foxfires, the girl gangs of the late-twentieth and early-twenty-first centuries are overwhelmingly young women of color, highly territorial, as violent as their male counterparts, and invariably involved with sex and all sorts of narcotics, especially crack cocaine.

But similarities between real girl gangs and Foxfire are in evidence. African American gangs of the 1960s, including sister gangs, took political positions with the Black Power and Black Nationalist movements, much as Legs did with Communism. And like Foxfire, young women in real gangs speak of a sisterhood that both helps and protects them, especially from sexual abuse by older men.

FOXFIRE: 1952–1956

The girl gang named Foxfire is memorialized by its recording secretary, Madeline Faith Wirtz, called Maddy, who, 33 years after the gang's demise, puts together the narrative from the notebook she kept during the gang's 4-year history. In the story, Maddy writes of herself in third person, perhaps to ensure her equal footing with other members of the gang and to suggest that she is not shaping the story she records. Maddy, who was a member of Foxfire from age 13 to 17, stresses that Foxfire never operated from an urge to do evil for evil's sake or for revenge. She also emphasizes that the last disastrous days of Foxfire embraced actions that all its members regretted.

The setting of her story is Fairfax Avenue in Hammond, New York. It is a working-class neighborhood called Lowertown, a place plagued by poverty, alcoholism, and family disintegration, where most of the young men and women are school dropouts, having either flunked out or been expelled. A high percentage of the young men are in correctional facilities.

The gang called Foxfire is born in November of 1952, after Margaret Ann Sadovsky, called "Legs," runs away from her grandmother's home in Plattsville where she has been placed when the authorities determine that her own home, where her father lives with his girlfriend, is unfit for a young girl. Maddy's family situation is not much better than Legs's. Her father was killed in a war, and her mother is rapidly becoming so mentally incompetent that before the year is out her mother will be taken by an ambulance to an institution, and Maddy will be forced to live with unsympathetic relatives. When Legs finds her way from her grandmother's to Maddy's house in Hammond, she begins toying with the idea of a gang, which would be formed to extend help to girls, just as Maddy had readily agreed to help Legs. The first members of the gang are Legs, their leader; Goldie Siefried, their first lieutenant; Lana Macguire; Rita Hagen; and Maddy, their recorder. On New Year's Day of 1953, the birth of the gang and their initiation into it, in sharp contrast to initiation into boy gangs, is a riotous but nonviolent affair lit by candlelight, toasted with whiskey, and secured by a ceremonial dance, the tattoo of a flame, the mingling of their blood, and an oath. They vow themselves to loyalty, secrecy, courage, and constancy. Legs also believes that the group should work in sympathy for the "Revolution of the Proletariat." Part of the gang's promise, the reader learns later in the narrative, is always to put loyalty to Foxfire first by avoiding romantic involvement with boys.

A series of events reinforces Legs's conviction that the girls do need an organization to help one another effectively. The first involves Elizabeth "Rita" Hagen, a fat child, prone to weeping uncontrollably, who is tormented and eventually sexually abused by her older brothers and viciously berated by her mother afterward. Rita, who is mentally slow, is also publicly tormented in class by her math teacher, Mr. Buttinger, who forces her to stay in after class, where day after day he repeatedly "accidentally" brushes her breasts in reaching across her to correct the mistakes she has made on the blackboard. The first action of Foxfire occurs in January of 1953, when Mr. Buttinger drives his car through town, not knowing that it has been painted with words identifying him as a repulsive "Dirty Old Man" and with the words, "Foxfire Revenge! Foxfire Revenge!" When Buttinger is finally forced to leave Hammond, Legs gloats that they have effectively "killed" him.

In a second instance, the gang comes to the rescue of another of its members. This time it is Maddy Wirtz, who is attempting to buy a used typewriter from her uncle. Not only does he keep raising the price each time she comes in with the money; now he tries to exact sexual favors in exchange for the typewriter. When Maddy returns to his shop again, he exposes himself to her, and Foxfire intervenes, beating him unconscious and taking the typewriter with them.

A third instance occurs when Goldie, a devout animal lover, notices that a local pet shop is keeping its dogs in cages that have become much too small for them. The dogs are forced to lie in their food and are unable to stand up. Foxfire repeatedly reasons with and warns the owners of the pet store. When nothing is done, they take their cues from the union activity in their working-class neighborhood. They put together graphic picket signs, which they parade in front of the store. This gets the store negative publicity in the paper, prompts a visit from the Society for the Prevention of Cruelty to Animals, and forces the owners to sell their animals cheap and close the store.

Some of the girls' other Robin Hood–type activities include establishing a charity fund for people who are down and out. After a series of murders in the area, they bond more closely together against "They, Them, Others," by which they mean primarily male sexual predators. Foxfire gets into trouble with the law on a night when Lana and Violet are menaced by a male gang. When Bud Petko lays hands on one of the girls, Goldie beats him up and Legs appears on the scene brandishing a switchblade knife. A furious principal comes on the scene to expel them all. The evening ends with the gang's wild ride in a car Legs has stolen. With the police right behind them, Legs races ahead in the stolen car and crashes it. Although the girls are injured, all of them are alive. But Legs, who unconvincingly claims she only borrowed the car, is sent to Red Bank State Correctional Facility for Girls.

Defiant and betrayed by her father's testimony, Legs's detention sentence gets longer and longer. She is threatened, beaten (her eye is almost gouged out), and thrown repeatedly into an inhumane hold, ominously referred to by matrons and fellow inmates as "The Room." Legs takes a long time in coming to the conclusion that, despite what she sees as injustice, she needs to refine her behavior if she wants to survive. When she is released on June 1, 1955, she tells Maddy that men aren't the only enemies—women and girls can be enemies too. While she had been incarcerated, her state of mind had been made worse by a visit from her father, who told her for the first time that her mother had tried unsuccessfully to abort her and had died later of drug-induced kidney damage. Relations between father and daughter have gotten so bad that he moves away from Hammond while she is in prison without telling her where he has gone. Legs angers members of the gang by inviting two black girls to the celebration following her release.

In the summer of 1955, Legs independently takes what she sees as a necessary action for justice. Roaming around in the performance of her job with the Parks and Recreation Service, she discovers a remote house with an iron bar attached. Behind it, a physically stunted, mentally retarded woman called Yetta has a dog collar around her neck and is chained to a clothesline. When Legs returns at night to find out about the woman, she finds her chained to a bed, where she is raped by one man after another, having been prostituted by her brother. Legs first approaches the brother to demand that he stop treating his sister worse than an animal. When this fails, she returns, not knowing exactly what she will do. The words of her mentor, the renegade priest, come back to her, insisting that we must act to alleviate pain. She takes kerosene from the barn behind the house, pours it around the outside of the house, lights it, and watches the house go up in flames.

A turning point in the demise of Foxfire comes when finances begin to loom far too ominously in their lives. Most important, there is Legs's father's sick baby to care for and shelter to provide for themselves. The idea of "hooking" comes about when Legs, dressed as a boy, goes to apply for a job. When the boss makes a pass at her during the interview, she scrapes him with her knife and demands all his cash and his watch. In the winter of 1955–1956, similar hooking scams enable them to have just enough money to live on. But they fall short of one of the main Foxfire aims—to help those in need. The success of these scams and mounting financial distress inspires Legs with the idea of a million-dollar scam—kidnapping a rich person for ransom. She stresses to the others that no one will be hurt. They will take their victim back alive, whether or not the ransom is paid. This is insufficient assurance for Maddy, who is subsequently exiled from the house and gang for refusing to cooperate.

Legs's victim will be the wealthy father of a young woman who has befriended her in order to convert her. Having promised Legs and Violet jobs, the target, Whitney Kellogg, asks that they meet him in the parking lot behind his branch office. Smelling of whiskey, he gives them a tour and then asks them to come with him to an "inn" outside of town so that they can get to know each other better. But just as they are walking to his car, the other girls in the gang swoop down on them, bind and blindfold him, and put him in the trunk of his car. Crammed into the back of the car, he decides that God loves him and that he will not cooperate in any way. This foils their plan, since he will not agree to pay them or to speak to his wife on the telephone. Finally, after several days, while Legs and 15-year-old V.V. are trying to move him upstairs, he kicks out at Legs, knocking her down and causing her to drop her gun. In the ensuing fray, V.V. accidentally shoots him in the shoulder. Legs orders the girls out and calls an ambulance. Goldie, Lana, and V.V. refuse to leave, demanding to go in the car with her, driving north toward Canada. At the end of a nine-mile chase to escape a patrolman, the car careens off a bridge, and the car and the girls disappear. Goldie and Lana are eventually found and serve time in prison. But V.V. and Legs are never discovered.

Maddy, who had been exiled from Foxfire at the time of the kidnapping, finishes high school and gets a scholarship to the University of Iowa. Now 50 years old and working as an astronomer's assistant in New Mexico, she has returned to Hammond a few times over the years to read old newspapers and court transcripts in an attempt to find out what happened in the final days of Foxfire. On one trip, she runs into Rita, the fat girl Foxfire had rescued from her brothers and her teacher so many years before. Rita tells her that Goldie and Lana are now out of prison and are getting on with their lives. Then she brings out an old newspaper with a picture of Fidel Castro taken shortly after the Bay of Pigs. Among the crowd, almost at the edge of the photograph, is Legs.

Maddy looks back on Foxfire before the disastrous last year. She remembers that she used to think she loved the stars because they provided permanence. But then she learned that stars change and that the starlight we see is something from the past, just reaching us from stars that have long been extinct. It is the past that we see. The implication is that transcribing the notebook is like looking at a star—Foxfire is over, but its light still reaches Maddy.

A REVOLUTIONARY WORLD VIEW

The explicit political undercurrents in *Foxfire: Confessions of a Girl Gang* are some of the strongest to appear in any gang novel. Most gang novels claim that gangs grow out of not only economic but also spiritual poverty. But Legs, in *Foxfire,* consistently puts forward a specific political philosophy identifiable as communism. Ironically, the exuberant risk taker has been strongly influenced in her life by two sisters of charity and a radical priest, Father Theriault, thrown out of the church because of his alcoholism. Like them, Legs no longer finds her place in the institution of the church itself. Like them, she has become convinced that the teachings of Jesus lead inevitably to socialism and communism. Father Theriault reveals dark secrets about the Vatican entertaining Adolph Hitler. The priest also speaks of "the Revolution...the one that's on its way" (541). Father Theriault told her about the many revolutions throughout history that laid foundations for the revolution to come. He excoriates the church for its accumulation of wealth, militancy, intolerance, and tyranny. Then, Maddy records his impressions of a Socialist Party congress in New York City, "where with thousands of men and women his brothers and sisters his comrades he'd stood to sing the 'Internationale,' and in an instant he'd known God as every heart in that gathering beat in unison with every other" (55).

The radicalism of the Foxfire girls is shaped by the poverty that limits them and has broken their miserable families. It is also influenced by the working-class mentality and the unions in which the residents find some hope for improved working conditions. The girls don't need a mentor to tell them their reality is despair and that the message of the congressman who speaks to their school is a patronizing fantasy:

> We so resented that asshole up there talking talking talking taking up the entire assembly expecting us to believe there isn't a special creation of God, or of man, to which we didn't belong, here at the shabby end of Hammond in the worst damn public school in the district, we didn't belong and never would. (7)

Even as a 13-year-old girl, Legs has developed strong political biases that will shape the gang she envisions. She finds contradictions in the glorification of spies during wartime and the demonization and hunting down of spies in peacetime, in the Red-Baiting Fifties. She comes to believe that World War II had been a time when "a very few devious men" held "power over the lives and deaths of millions" (35). Her hatred of the greediness of those in power has led her to make heroes of Jesse James and Billy the Kid. So she envisions Foxfire as a minisociety, embodying the socialism that she hopes will someday reshape society as a whole. Into the Foxfire oath, she places the following words, combining the words of Jesus with the Communist Manifesto: "I swear to think always of your sisters as you would they would think of you... in the Revolution of the Proletariat that is imminent in the Apocalypse" (39). As Foxfire becomes bolder, Legs often quotes Father Theriault: "The oppressed of the Earth, rising, make their own law" (83).

The first major strategic move Foxfire undertakes to change the way society works is the attempt to reason with the pet-store owners; the second is the picketing of the store, replicating a form of action well known in the union town of Hammond. The members of Foxfire gain surprising sympathy for their actions, and unionized laborers will not cross their picket lines to shop at the Giffords' pet store. Then, on Halloween, they paint protest messages on the windows of what they consider to be the worst, most exploitative representatives of capitalism among the town's businesses.

Legs tells them that the "basis of human life is charity, which means love for people you don't always know" (96). In turning this idea into action, she establishes Foxfire Charity, a fund to which she generously contributes, urging her sisters to contribute as well. The money goes to an old woman whose daughter beats her and steals her social security checks, to a crippled army veteran, to a pregnant girl whose family has thrown her out, to old Father Theriault, and to others. Yet, quoting Father Theriault, she declares that after the Revolution, no one will have to depend on charity.

Even though Legs has suffered what seems to be almost unbearable pain at the hands of matrons and other inmates in detention, when she emerges, she endorses Father Theriault's philosophy that the evil in individuals, even those who have brutalized her in detention, is caused by society, by capitalism, and the necessity, she says, to sell ourselves.

In 1955, when the girls have to go out to find serious work and pay for a place to stay, what they see around them is the larger picture of the town's decay. It is a city in decline. Its slaughterhouses have long been closed; men and women are being laid off at some of its once-thriving factories; and desperate and despondent workers picket other factories. Meanwhile, the pollution caused by the factories permeates the soil and air. This dismal scene and the urgency of their own financial needs lead them to take up the scams they call hooking. As Maddy sits in the bus station waiting for a mark, she thinks of one of Foxfire's mottoes that Legs has given them: "MONEY IS MEANT TO CHANGE HANDS!" And then, "From each according to her abilities, to each according to her need" (238).

When Legs is invited to the wealthy Kellogg house, her class animosity grows, especially on her second visit, as she is shown the fine, carved furniture and beautifully embroidered linens and tapestries.

> Legs was disoriented for an instant, overcome with an inexplicable rage. *How the fine handiwork of the poor, the exhaustion and depletion of their souls, slave-labor, wage-slave-labor, ends up ineluctably in the possession of the rich.* (267–68)

She forces entry into the Kellogg's private bedroom suite and goes berserk—stunned by the luxuries—perfumes, clothes, linens, hats. Whitney Kellogg naturally becomes her victim when he berates the girls that the reason "some rise to the top and some do not" is because God helps those who help themselves (253).

One can almost predict that Legs will end up living in postrevolutionary, Communist Cuba, perhaps in the inner circle of Fidel Castro.

Her life raises the problem of just how far in the righting of wrongs, just how far in the defense of the defenseless, one can go in all decency? It is the question that has arisen in every revolution in human history, the Cuban revolution included. Despite the message of Mahatma Gandhi, violence seems to be inevitable to break the hold of absolute power over the poor and disinherited. But, the revolutionary too often becomes the monster that he or she despises. Where, then, does one draw the line?

BIBLIOGRAPHY

Burleigh, Edith N. *The Delinquent Girl: A Study of the Parole in Massachusetts.* New York: New York School of Social Work, 1923.

Campbell, Anne. *Girls in the Gang.* New York: Basil Blackwell, 1984.

Chesney-Lind, Meda. *Girls, Delinquency, and Juvenile Justice.* Pacific Grove, CA: Brooks/Cole Publishers, 1992.

Fleisher, Mark S. *Dead-End Kids: Gang Girls and the Boys They Know.* Madison: University of Wisconsin Press, 1998.

Hansen, Kitty. *Rebels in the Streets.* Englewood Cliffs, NJ: Prentice-Hall, 1964.

Oates, Joyce Carol. *Foxfire: Confessions of a Girl Gang.* 1993. New York: Plume, 1994.

Rodriguez, Luis. *Always Running.* 1993. New York: Simon & Schuster, 1994.

Sikes, Gini. *8 Ball Chicks.* New York: Anchor Books, 1997.

Taylor, Carl S. *Girls, Gangs, Women and Drugs.* East Lansing: Michigan State University Press, 1993.

Thrasher, Frederick. *The Gang.* 1927. Chicago: University of Chicago Press, 1960.

Trese, Leo John. *101 Delinquent Girls.* Notre Dame, IN: Fides Publishing, 1962.

Whyte, W. F. *Street Corner Society.* 1943. Chicago: University of Chicago Press, 1993.

11

Gangs in the 1960s: S. E. Hinton's *The Outsiders* (1967)

What future could there have been for Riff or Bernardo? None that she could see. In the warped years of their youth they had seen, witnessed, found joy and participated in enough violences to age a dozen men. They loved nothing and destroyed everything, although they protested that it was one thing only that they hated—each other. So she pitied Riff as she pitied her brother, and would have willingly, at that moment, given her life for either of them.

But to what purpose? That they might kill other men? Eventually they had to die: in a bar or outside a poolroom, at some dance or in the back seat of an automobile, along a lonely stretch of highway or on some tenement roof. But not in bed. For boys like Riff and Bernardo preyed upon each other and were in turn preyed upon by every man and woman who could cater to and find profit in their violence. If they had to grow a little older, they would never grow wiser. (109–10)

The Outsiders, a popular young-adult novel written by S. E. Hinton when she was 16 years old, is a narrative of conflict and qualified reconciliation between gangs of poor boys and rich boys in the American Southwest in the 1960s. The novel dramatizes the fundamental differences in the socioeconomic level, temperament, appearance, and type of activities of the two rival gangs. It also stresses the effect of family life, particularly on the lower-class gang members, and the extent to which the gang itself constitutes a family. The last topic to be considered in discussing gangs in the novel is the extent to which its portrait of gang life and its message of reconciliation are less than realistic, compared to other representations of gangs in novels and memoirs of the same era.

THE SETTING

Although the setting for *The Outsiders* is roughly the mid-1960s (Hinton entered high school in 1963), the novel has more of a 1950s flavor because few of the concerns of the 1960s are mentioned. The Vietnam War, the Civil Rights movement, Women's Liberation, the sexual revolution, and the blossoming drug culture form no part of this narrative. Nor does the novel address the issues that created and perpetuated the social warfare between rich and poor kids, which is at the heart of the novel. Its purview is the local scene, removed from the turbulent national and international forces that shaped the 1960s, reminding the reader more of the personal rebellion of the Beats, the rise of rock and roll and Elvis Presley, and the popular movies of the 1950s: *Blackboard Jungle* (1955), *The Wild One* (1953), and *Rebel Without a Cause* (1955).

THE NARRATIVE

The Outsiders is a first-person narrative told by Ponyboy Curtis, who, at 14 years old, is the youngest member of the gang of working-class boys called the Greasers. Since the death of his parents, he is being reared by his 16-year-old brother, Sodapop, and his 20-year-old brother, Darry. Other Greasers who play major roles in the story are Johnny Cade, the next-youngest greaser, who has been severely beaten and traumatized by the rival gang called the Socs; Dallas or Dally, the most hardened Greaser, who was first arrested at the age of 10; and Two-Bit, who hangs out frequently at the Curtis home. Bob Sheldon and his friend Randy Adderson are two Socs who play major roles in the novel. The only two girls to make appearances in the novel are Cherry Valance and Marcia, associates of the Socs who become friendly with Ponyboy, Two-Bit, and Dallas.

The initiating circumstance is a chance meeting of several Greasers with Socs's girlfriends Cherry and Marcia at a drive-in movie—an encounter that enrages the Socs. Later that same evening, when Ponyboy's older brother Darry slaps him, the young boy runs away to a park, where he finds his friend Johnny. Soon, as a result of their earlier conversation with Marcia and Cherry, the resentful, drunk Socs drive up in their cars and are on the point of drowning Ponyboy in a fountain. When Ponyboy regains consciousness, he finds that Johnny, in order to save him from drowning and save himself from another brutal beating, has killed the Soc named Bob with his knife.

The tough Dally helps the two young boys to leave town and seek refuge in an abandoned church. They live for five days on baloney and cigarettes, Dally comes to check on them, and Johnny decides that they should go back and turn themselves in. But, as they prepare to leave, they notice that the church is on fire and learn that young children are trapped in the burning building. In their attempt to rescue the children, Dally and Johnny are hurt, Johnny fatally. The boys become local heroes and two Socs, Cherry Valance and Randy Adderson, agree to testify that Johnny killed Bob in self-defense. The more imminent danger is that Ponyboy and perhaps his brother Sodapop will be taken by social services to a home for boys.

In the inevitable gang rumble that ensues, the Greasers cause the Socs to retreat, but not before Ponyboy has been brutally beaten. After the rumble, he and Dally rush to the hospital where Johnny is said to be dying. The third death occurs when Dally, distraught by Johnny's death, raises his unloaded pistol as police are attempting to arrest him, and is shot.

The trauma of Johnny's and Dally's deaths and the wounds Ponyboy has received in the rumble send him into a severe physical and emotional decline. A court hearing concludes with Ponyboy's acquittal of any involvement in Bob's death and in his being allowed to continue living at home with his brothers. Nevertheless, he denies that Johnny is dead, loses all interest in his schoolwork, and sees his relationships with other individuals fall apart. A letter from Johnny that falls from their treasured copy of *Gone with the Wind* is a turning point. Ponyboy decides to begin his recuperation by writing his stories of Bob, Johnny, and Dallas in a theme for his high-school English teacher.

A CONTRAST OF GANGS

Readers who have read other accounts of gangs in the 1950s and 1960s will note differences between these and the gangs in *The Outsiders*. For instance, most gangs of the 1960s were highly organized and hierarchical. They had a recognized leader, systems of initiation, and group-planned goals and activities, most of an illegal nature. The Greasers and Socs have no such organization. They have no gang leaders, no levels of importance. Their illegal activities are conducted on the spur of the moment, sometimes by only one gang member, sometimes by a group, but never as part of an overarching plan. Most youth gangs come from the ranks of the very poor, but in *The Outsiders* (as well as in *The Chocolate War*), one gang is made up of the sons of the wealthy. In urban areas, gangs usually form along racial or national lines: African Americans, Hispanics, Chinese, Italians, or Irish. Each group battles others of different cultures. In this novel, however, all the gangs are made up of Caucasians. The divisions are economic, the animosity existing between the very rich and the very poor.

THE GREASERS AND THE SOCS

Difference in economic status alone is not the only thing that separates the Greasers from the Socs. Both gangs engage in illegal activities, but while the Socs like to wreck houses and to attack smaller kids and Greasers in general, Greasers are chiefly known for petty thievery—stealing hubcaps and shoplifting. A few of the tougher, older Greasers, like Dally, have also been known to hold up gas stations.

Partly as a result of the nature of the Socs's crimes and partly because of their social standing, they rarely go to jail for their criminal activity. Greasers, on the other hand, are jailed frequently—Dally even at the age of 10.

Like Sodapop, Greasers frequently have to drop out of high school to work at menial jobs and rarely go to college, but Socs are expected to go to college and often become community leaders.

Each group is easily recognized by the way its members dress and wear their hair. The Socs are characterized by their short haircuts, white shirts, and madras jackets. The Greasers sport blue jeans, T-shirts with the tails hanging out, and leather jackets. But their real badge of honor, from which their name comes, is their slicked-back long hair. When Johnny insists that he and Ponyboy cut their hair in the church in which they are hiding, Ponyboy thinks, "Our hair labeled us Greasers, too—it was our trademark. The one thing we were proud of" (71).

The other physical difference between the Socs and the Greasers is that the Socs drive fashionable cars—Mustangs and Corvairs. Ponyboy thinks that the real difference in character between the Socs and Greasers is that the Socs don't feel anything, while the Greasers feel too intensely.

The economic situation of the Greasers also exacerbates family tensions. The only family problem apparent among the Socs is the tendency of Bob's family to spoil rather than discipline and guide him when he gets in trouble. Randy tells Ponyboy, "He kept trying to make someone say 'No' and they never did. They never did. That was what he wanted" (116). The death of Ponyboy's parents brings a premature end to the boyhood of his older brothers. While he is proud of his two older brothers, the death of his parents leaves him empty and sad. In marked contrast to Bob's parents, Darry imposes strict discipline, causing Ponyboy to think his brother doesn't really love or like him. Darry slaps him for coming in too late and talking back to him, and the two brothers are constantly fighting until the middle brother convinces them how deeply their fighting is hurting him.

Johnny's home is devoid of affection or consideration. His parents are monsters. His father beats him mercilessly, and his mother either ignores him or yells at him. He frequently spends the night either at the house of one of his friends or in a vacant lot. Still, Johnny is "bewildered" that his parents haven't inquired about him for the five days he has been missing. When his mother appears at the hospital to visit him on his deathbed, Johnny refuses to see her. As he predicted, all she can refer to is "all the trouble his father and I've gone to raise him," leading Two-Bit to reply to her, "No wonder he hates your guts" (123). Dally's parents are scarcely different. When he comes to the church to replenish Ponyboy and Johnny's supplies, he remarks, "Shoot, my old man don't give a hang whether I'm in jail or dead in a car wreck or drunk in the gutter" (88).

FRIENDSHIP

In *The Outsiders*, the friendship among the Greasers is a major theme. "We are almost as close as brothers," Ponyboy declares (3). We see his brother and other Greasers rescuing Ponyboy from a severe beating at the hands of the Socs and Johnny killing a boy, in large measure to save Ponyboy's life. All the Greasers adopt Johnny and give him the material and psychological support he never gets at home. "If it hadn't been for the gang, Johnny would never have known what love and affection are" (12). The Curtis boys frequently come home to find other Greasers in their house. Dally, who is always under police surveillance and frequently in jail, risks his freedom to help the two younger boys, and later saves Johnny and Ponyboy from getting trapped in the burning building, getting himself injured in the process. The grief, which the Soc attack on Johnny and Ponyboy has led to, causes the other Greasers to take part in the rumble. And the close ties of affection to Johnny cause Dally to, in effect, commit suicide when Johnny dies. Johnny's and Dally's deaths cause Ponyboy to have a nervous breakdown.

RECONCILIATION

Despite the Socs disdain for the Greasers and their repeated brutal attacks on them, Ponyboy gradually comes to question the wisdom of fighting and to believe that the Socs include decent boys who are very much like himself.

Randy, one of the first characters to question the wisdom of fighting, seeks out Ponyboy to tell him that, because of his sorrow over Bob's death and his admiration for Ponyboy and Johnny, he will not take part in the rumble that will pit all Greasers against all Socs. "I'd fight," he says, "if I thought it'd do any good" (117).

Perhaps this encounter leads Ponyboy to ask both his brothers why they like to fight. He concludes after conducting his "survey":

> Soda fought for fun, Steve for hatred, Darry for pride, and Two-Bit for conformity. Why do I fight? I thought, and couldn't think of any real good reason. There isn't any real good reason for fighting except self-defense. (137)

Johnny's message on his deathbed, "Useless...fighting's no good" (148), reinforces Ponyboy's disillusionment with violence.

Ponyboy's encounter with Cherry and Marcia leads him to the unheard-of suspicion that he has had the wrong idea in classing all Socs as rotten. "It seemed funny to me that Socs—if these girls were any example—were just like us" (37). Then, when he and Johnny came home as heroes for rescuing the little children from the fire, some of the Socs, namely Randy, take a different attitude toward the two of them. When Randy calls on him, Ponyboy tells him that one can't pigeonhole people into groups. "Maybe you would have done the same thing, maybe a friend of yours wouldn't have. It's the individual" (115). After his conversation with Randy, Ponyboy again concludes, "Socs were just guys after all. Things were rough all over, but it was better that way. That way you could tell the other guy was human too" (118).

Even during the rumble, Ponyboy, seeing Darry and his former friend circle in preparation for the fight, Ponyboy thinks, "They shouldn't hate each other...I don't hate the Socs any more...they shouldn't hate" (143). After the rumble, Ponyboy, flipping through his brother's yearbook, finds a picture of Bob, the Soc Johnny had stabbed. He remembers what his friends had said about Bob, and wondered about him as an individual, not as a Soc. As he is wondering, Randy comes in for a second visit because he cares what happens to Ponyboy. During the visit, he confides in Ponyboy as if he is his best friend.

Cherry, like Randy, has a change of heart about the Greasers, agreeing to spy for them and, even though she loved Bob, later testifying, as did Randy, that Bob was drunk and enraged, and that Johnny stabbed him in self-defense.

SYMBOLS AND LITERARY REFERENCES

The most important symbol in the novel, the sunset, represents the possible links between the Socs and the Greasers: the Socs might be rich and the Greasers poor, but they can both see and enjoy the sunset. Ponyboy and Cherry had talked about sunsets when they first met at the drive-in movie, when he first wondered if Socs and Greasers were essentially alike. Later, just before the rumble, Ponyboy calls to Cherry, "Hey...can you see the sunset real good from the West Side?" and tells her one can also see the sunset from the East Side, his side of town (129–30).

Appreciating the sunset is emblematic of a childlike sensitivity to beauty and gentleness, something that Bob and Dally had lost long ago. Johnny appreciates Ponyboy's tendency to look at a sunset as if it is new in nature. It is this sentiment, expressed in Johnny's letter to Ponyboy and Dally, that turns Ponyboy from his self-destructive decline.

Three literary works are especially important in the novel: Margaret Mitchell's *Gone with the Wind,* Robert Frost's poem, "Nothing Gold Can Stay," and Charles Dickens's *Great Expectations.* Johnny is transfixed by the gallantry of nineteenth-century southern gentlemen, ignoring the slavery, class snobbery, and meaningless violence that characterized them. As an orphan misunderstood even by his family, Ponyboy sees himself in Pip of *Great Expectations*. In Frost's poem, Ponyboy and Johnny see a lament for lost innocence.

THE QUESTION OF REALISM

The Outsiders was one of the first young-adult books that dealt with the question of contemporary gangs, and it was criticized at the time for portraying behavior inappropriate for young readers. Yet the novel's portrayal of gangs is scarcely realistic, compared to other gang novels such as *Lord of the Flies* and *The Chocolate War*. Despite the three deaths in the novel, it exhibits little of the true brutal ugliness of gangs. There is in the novel, for example, no hint of the obscene or sacrilegious language of gangs, words that, admittedly, would have blocked the approval of the novel for study in the classroom. The problem of drugs is nonexistent in the novel, and alcohol abuse seems to be underrepresented, being an issue only in connection with the Socs' arrival at the fountain when Johnny stabs Bob. Gang violence, including the rumble, beatings, and the deaths of Bob and Dally, is insufficiently graphic to represent the reality of gang activity or to elicit alarm on the part of the reader. Guns in these Southwest gangs are also, surprisingly, a rarity. And the blatant, brutal sexuality that characterized youth gangs dating back to the turn of the twentieth century is not even suggested in *The Outsiders*. The camaraderie of gang members creates an idealistic picture that gains the reader's admiration, but it ignores the truth that throughout history the chief victims of gangs are their own members. *The Outsiders* has often been touted as the first in a wave of New Realism in young-adult fiction. Yet, though the novel is set in an area that has long been rich in ethnicity, no African American, Native American, Mexican, or Mexican American characters appear.

The Outsiders is still considered Hinton's greatest success, but her later work, *That Was Then, This Is Now,* a sequel about gang life in Tulsa in which Ponyboy appears as a minor character, a novella entitled *Rumble Fish*, and a novel, *Tex*, are more realistic pictures of gang life in the Southwest.

The strength of the novel is not its realism, but rather its idealism. The reader can readily identify with Ponyboy's sensitivity, the pain he feels for his lost friends and his parents, and his refusal to condemn his enemies as a group. Through Ponyboy, the reader is given hope that even the most traumatized individual need not be brutalized and that reconciliation is always possible.

BIBLIOGRAPHY

Daly, Jay. *Presenting S. E. Hinton.* Boston: Twayne Publishers, 1989.

Hinton, S. E. *The Outsiders.* 1967. New York: Puffin Books, 1997.

Lenz, Millicent, and Ramona Mahood, eds. *Young Adult Literature.* Chicago: American Library Association, 1980.

Loer, Stephanie. "Bringing Realism to Teen-Age Fiction." *Boston Globe* 31 August 1988: 65.

Mills, Randall K. "The Novels of S. E. Hinton: Springboard to Personal Growth for Adolescents." *Adolescence,* Fall 1987: 641.

Peck, Richard. "In the Country of Teenage Fiction." *American Libraries,* April 1973: 204.

Seay, Ellen A. "Opulence to Decadence: *The Outsiders* and *Less than Zero.*" *English Journal,* October 1987: 69.

Stanek, Lou Willett. *A Teacher's Guide to the Paperback Editions of the Novels of S. E. Hinton.* New York: Dell, 1980.

Sutherland, Zena. *The Best in Children's Books.* Chicago: University of Chicago Press, 1973.

12

Vietnam and Civil Rights: Pat Conroy's *The Lords of Discipline* (1980)

FROM "DISCUSSANT: ELIZABETH HOLTZMAN" IN *WATERGATE AND AFTERWARD: THE LEGACY OF RICHARD M. NIXON.*

Ed. Leon Friedman and William F. Lavantrosser. Westport, CT: Greenwood Press, 1992.

I would like to focus here on something that I consider to be one of the failings of the impeachment process. And that is the failure to come to grips with one of the most serious abuses of executive power in the Nixon administration which, in my judgment, was the bombing of Cambodia, the use of American troops and the risking of their lives, the killing of people in a neutral country through the process of lying and deception of the Congress and of the American public. This article—proposed Article IV—was not approved. This failure raised very, very serious questions about our constitutional system of government. Many people do not know very much about that article and the background behind it, but I think its relevance for today is especially clear.

The facts show that shortly after the Nixon administration took power, the president authorized the bombing of Cambodia. It was a neutral country that was not at war with us at the time. In order to conceal this bombing from the United States Congress, the Joint Chiefs of Staff were ordered to, and in fact did keep, two sets of books. A false set of records was submitted to the United States Congress to deceive them. Oddly, the Cambodians knew they were being bombed, the North Vietnamese knew Cambodia was being bombed, the Vietcong knew about it, the Russians knew about it, the Chinese knew about it. But the United States Congress did not know, and neither did the American people.

Considering the significance of the war-making power itself—whether or not Congress would have acquiesced had it been told, whether or not the American public would have approved had it been told—the fact that this awesome power to commit American troops and authorize them to take the lives of other people in a country with which we were not at war was exercised by deceiving Congress and the American people about it, was in my opinion, a very gross abuse of power. It was a very serious undermining of our democratic system, which functions on a basis of public accountability. (222)

(Elizabeth Holtzman, senator from New York, sat on the committee to determine whether Richard Nixon should be impeached.)

FROM SEPTIMA CLARK AND BERNICE ROBINSON, "FINDING YOUR WAY BACK HOME."

Refuse to Stand Silently By. *Ed. Eliot Wigginton. New York: Doubleday, 1991.*

It was Judge Waring, for example, who ruled that blacks should be allowed to vote in the primary elections—one of the most important decisions made in our behalf.

They were a very unpopular family with most of white Charleston. I don't know what the whites hated worst about them—the things they stood for, or the fact that the judge had married a Yankee. . . .

In January of 1968, when the judge was buried, there were two hundred blacks and about twelve whites at the funeral. A man who had done so much . . . (237–38)

. . .

At the end of that summer, I went back to teaching. It was during that school year that the law was passed by the state legislature that no city or state employee could be a member of the NAACP. That meant none of the teachers could be members, and there were 726 of us black teachers who were. . . . All forty-two who admitted being members were dismissed, and I've never been able to teach in South Carolina since. (241–42)

FROM SEPTIMA CLARK, "I PAID MY OWN WAY TO OSLO."

Refuse to Stand Silently By. *Ed. Eliot Wigginton. New York: Doubleday, 1991.*

[On registering African Americans to vote in the 1960s]

[But] we had lots of opposition. Andy Young was badly beaten in Tallahassee, Florida, going down there to try to recruit the people. That was in the latter part of '61. (241)

· · ·

Five members of our group got beaten for going into the white side of a bus station in Tupelo, Mississippi. It came to trial in Oxford, and everyone was so frightened that when we had recess, not even the black restaurant would sell us a meal. (241)

· · ·

Those people in Mississippi were something. In Grenada, a white fellow took a fifteen-year-old boy that was working with me and threw him on the ground and broke his leg in three places. We had to carry him all the way to Clarksdale to a hospital. (242)

━━━━━━━━━━━━━━━━━━━━━━━━━━━━━━━━━━━━━━━

Pat Conroy based *The Lords of Discipline,* the story of a secret gang at a military institute, on his experiences in the 1960s as a student at The Citadel, a state military college located in Charleston, South Carolina. The novel addresses many topics universally true of gang experience: hazing and initiation; violence; the cultivation of fear through intimidation or bullying; psychological and physical cruelty; intolerance of physical weakness, eccentricity, individualism, and difference; the importance of brute physical strength over other attributes; and the value placed on order and tradition at all costs. Conroy shows the relation of these typical gang attitudes and practices to other matters that do not come as frequently into play in gang literature: segregation, social elitism and exclusion, and institutional militarism.

THE CONTEXT

The setting of the narrative's action is the mid-1960s, but the plantation system of the American South, the Civil War, World War II, the Korean War, the cold war, and the racial segregation of the first half of the twentieth century are histories that constantly impinge upon the present.

The narrator reminds the reader that the Citadel, fictionalized as the Carolina Military Institute could exist only in Charleston, South Carolina. Charleston was a stronghold of slavery, the epitome of the Old South, and the seat of genteel aristocratic life in America. The Institute itself was established to protect the community after a slave rebellion threatened the tranquility of the upper class. Charleston was one of the first and most prominent cities to lead the South to secession from the United States, and the first shot of the Civil War was fired off its coast at Fort Sumter. Both the city and the Institute continue to be plantations with rigid social hierarchies, antebellum traditions, and a reluctance to accept social change of any kind, particularly desegregation. Charleston's refined cruelty and the Institute's crude cruelties shaped one another and are still mutually supportive. Both the city and the Institute are tyrannical in their need for order. Both are inhospitable to the stranger, the outcast, the eccentric, and the rebel against the old order. In Charleston, the lower-class Irish narrator, Will MacLean, feels a kinship with the Indian chief Osceola, imprisoned on Sullivan's Island, off the coast of Charleston; with Edgar Allen Poe, who spent some time on the islands around Charleston and was later expelled from West Point; and with Tom Pearce, the first African American to be accepted by the Institute—all outsiders like himself.

The deep background of the novel includes World War II, in which Will's father and many other graduates of the Institute, including its president, had distinguished themselves. The military and World War II permeate Will's childhood, through his father's education at the same military institute and his father's valor at Iwo Jima. World War II is responsible for further brutalizing not only his father, who earned the Navy Cross at Iwo Jima, but also his son, whom he beats savagely and psychologically abuses.

The Institute has been molded by the men who rose to high rank in World War II and by the militarism that evolved in the cold war years of the 1950s, when military power was kept in high readiness to combat what was perceived as the threat of the Soviet Union and world

Communism. Both Democrat and Republican congressmen supported the military expansion, using the country's nuclear buildup to intimidate the USSR and to help overthrow what were considered to be leftist regimes throughout the world.

The military mentality in the United States was heightened between 1950 and 1953, when the country was involved in the "Korean Conflict," incited by Communist North Korea and supported by Joseph Stalin and Mao Tse Tung in its attempts to overthrow South Korea. In the course of this war, 53,000 American men were killed and 142,000 were wounded.

Looming large in the background of Will MacLean's years at the Institute are three other events discussed in the introduction of the 1960s: the Civil Rights struggle to desegregate education, the Vietnam War that began with the Gulf of Tonkin Resolution passed by Congress in Will's second year at the Institute, and the widespread resistance to that war throughout the 1960s.

ONE CADET'S WAR AGAINST THE GANG

The gang that rules life at the Institute is a secret organization known as the Ten. Its membership and even its very existence are faint rumors rather than proven facts. For one-third of the novel, the reader only has vague hints of this elite group composed of 10 seniors and of alumni from previous years—all of whom secretly control the campus and wield power in the state. Not until the last third of the novel is the gang unveiled, but they are part and parcel of the values, attitudes, and practices of the Institute, the city of Charleston, and the country's larger military system.

The first-person narration is divided into four parts: part 1 is Will MacLean's return as a senior in the late summer of 1967 to Carolina Military Institute; part 2 is his flashback to his freshman year; part 3 is the winter of his senior year; and part 4 is the spring before his graduation.

Part 1

Part 1 is entitled "The Cadre," in reference to an elite group of upperclassmen, chosen from the highest-ranking cadets, to train first-year students. The selection of the Cadre reflects the values of the military and the military institute. Those awarded this choice post are campus leaders, militarily astute, ambitious, with a high sense of duty

and devotion to the system. Conspicuously missing from this list of attributes are academic excellence, intelligence, and character. Scarcely
Cadre material, Will is known as a wit, an English major, a liberal, and
a basketball player. Even in his senior year he is sloppy, rebellious, and
still a private, but since he has been chosen as vice chairman of the
Honor Court, he must arrive early with the members of the Cadre to
speak to the freshmen about Honor Court expectations.

As Will greets various friends, he learns that the Institute is to take
a momentous step in admitting its first African American student, a
move set in motion by *Brown v. Board of Education*, which compelled
the desegregation of public schools supported by state or federal funding. In this brutal environment, Will looks up to two adults. One is
Colonel Thomas Berrineau, a rough man affectionately called "Bear,"
who, as the commandant of cadets is known for looking out for the
best interest of his "lambs." It is he who elicits Will's help in making
sure that Tom Pearce, the new African American recruit, is not run
out of school by racist cadets and alumni. At this August meeting with
Bear, Will has his first inkling that a secret gang, known as the Ten,
operates on campus and that their chief current mission is to ensure
that Pearce will leave the Institute. The young black man has already
received a threatening letter from the Ten.

Will's other surrogate parent is Abigail St. Croix, the mother of his
roommate Tradd. Abigail gives him the key to the fine St. Croix house
and introduces him to the graces of South of Broad Street high society. Abigail's husband, Commerce, a wealthy businessman who is also
fond of Will, confesses to him that he has been for years an inveterate
keeper of journals, many of them about the Institute, of which he is a
graduate.

Will has two roommates in addition to Tradd. Mark Santoro and
Dante Pignetti, otherwise known as Pig, are tough, working-class
Northerners. Tradd is known as a somewhat effete Charleston aristo-
crat with scant interest in girls; Pig is known for battling anyone
whom he believes may be dishonoring his fiancée, Theresa. The four
roommates are passionately devoted to one another. They share all
things equally. To challenge one of them is to challenge all four.

Until the semester starts, Will spends most of his free time with
Abigail and Tradd. On his way home one evening, he meets a young
woman named Annie Kate. He soon discovers that she must hide herself away on nearby Sullivan's Island because she is pregnant by a
young man who has rejected her. Nevertheless, he begins to spend his
weekends with her.

Before the rest of the students arrive, Will has an audience with "the General," president of the Institute, who lectures him on honor and the system, including "the Walk of Shame," a practice to which Will objects. But the Walk of Shame, an old military tradition, is one of the general's innovations, of which he is very proud. This rule forces a cadet expelled for an honors violation to walk out the gate between rows of his classmates who turn their backs on him and vow never again to speak his name.

Shortly after delivering his honors-board speech to the freshmen, Will finds two cadets, a junior and a senior, tormenting a fat freshman in the usual way by screaming deafening obscenities in his ear and by making him do push-ups and hold his rifle at arm's length until he collapses. Will stops the hazing and, in front of the two upperclassmen, tells the crying freshman named Poteete that one of the men harassing him had also cried miserably two years earlier, and Will had come to his rescue. In a private interview with Poteete, Will insists that if Poteete wants to survive, he must stop crying when upperclassmen taunt him. Some weeks later, however, Poteete tries to leap to his death from a balcony, deliriously suggesting that, after having been taken to "the house," he can no longer carry on. Will and his roommates rescue Poteete, but the next day, he hangs himself in the infirmary. Will, distraught over Poteete's suicide, continues to mull over the mention of being taken to a house.

Part 2

Part 2, entitled "The Taming," is a flashback to Will's freshman year. He remembers his paralyzing fear after verbal and physical attacks, especially during Hell Night. Primarily, however, he remembers the young men who did not survive the taming and left, like his first roommate, Harvey Clearwater, who just disappeared one night. The Cadre selects boys whom they deem to be unworthy of the Institute, most of them weak in some way or different from the ideal cadet. During the taming, the Cadre uses every psychological and physical means to force the misfits to leave. Boys with phobias are tortured with exposure to the very things of which they are terrified. Bobby Bentley, a cadet who urinates on himself when he is being screamed at, continues to remain even after being cruelly mortified repeatedly. Eventually, his classmates rally a show of sympathy for him, but the next day, he too mysteriously disappears. Two of the more sadistic members of the Cadre decide to break (and succeed in breaking) Will in his freshman year by forcing him to perform feats of impossible endurance, making him get down on all fours to lick their shoes, and kicking him in the stomach. Finally, he is rescued by members of the basketball team, of which he also is a member, and his roommates who join him in exacting revenge on his attackers.

Part 3

Part 3, "The Wearing of the Ring," returns the action to Will's senior year. At the St. Croix house, he listens to Tradd's father, Commerce, read from his journals about his life long ago at the Institute. The high point of the year for most of the seniors is the ceremony in which they receive their rings. But Will's pride in his ring is undermined by learning that the African American plebe, Tom Pearce, is having trouble, and that one of the plebes who has suddenly left campus had a 10 painted on his door. Will, who is subsequently asked by the Bear to find out something about the Ten, quizzes Professor Reynolds, his English teacher and author of a history of the Institute. Reynolds tells Will that he could never verify the existence of the Ten, despite circumstantial evidence that it had operated on campus for many years. Reynolds also tells him that rumor has it that the Ten will never allow a woman or a black person to graduate from the Institute.

Two positive events occur in the tension-filled winter of Will's senior year. His friendship with Annie Kate turns into a love affair, and he agrees to be the father of her child. And his basketball team wins their final game. But the thrill of love and victory are diminished by his secret talk with Tom Pearce at the yacht basin after the game. Pearce reveals that he has received repeated warnings to leave the Institute and that a mysterious letter writer has threatened "to take him for a ride" if he doesn't leave, leaving Will determined to find the notorious house. Pearce has also left several notes for Will that never reached him. Someone, they conclude, is betraying them.

Part 4

The first story in part 4, called "The Ten," is about Annie Kate. Will takes her to the hospital when she goes into labor, but the child he has agreed to call his own is born dead. The next week, upon visiting her home, he finds that she has determined to forget, even deny, the previous nine torturous months, including her friendship and love affair with Will.

Professor Reynolds arranges another meeting with Will to reveal that at one time he did have proof of the existence of the Ten—in a letter he acquired from the widow of one of its members. But after Reynolds turned in the manuscript of his history of the Institute, the material was expunged, and when he returned home from his trip to object to the excising of the material, the incriminating letter had been stolen from his house.

Will, Mark, and Pig then go to Columbia, South Carolina, to look up Bobby Bentley. He tells them how the Ten had driven him to a house where he was broken and agreed to leave the Institute. Bentley also directs them to Dan Molligen, whose voice Bentley had recently recognized as one of the masked men who tortured him. Pig, Mark, and Will kidnap Molligen and tie him to a railroad track no longer in use, threatening to leave him there. So Molligen confesses that he is a member of the Ten and that the house is the plantation of General Durrell, the president of the Institute.

As Pearce feared, the Ten kidnap him in April, and Will follows them to the house, where he witnesses their torturing of Pearce and intercedes to save Pearce's life. In the aftermath, one of the Ten, Cain Gilbreath, who has been Will's friend, catches up with the escaping Will and begins beating him until his roommates, Mark and Pig, come to the rescue. Later, when Will confronts Cain, Cain tells him that Pearce will be allowed to remain at the Institute, that the Bear is part of the Ten, and that Will, Mark, and Pig are in grave danger.

Just before graduation, Pig is caught by the Cadre just as he is about to siphon gas out of Will's car. After the Honor Court finds him guilty of dishonesty, he is automatically expelled and has to go through the Walk of Shame. Immediately afterward, he kills himself by walking in front of a train. Will, mourning deeply for Pig, vows revenge. The Institute's campaign to eliminate Mark and Will begins as the campus leaders suddenly begin assigning them so many demerits that they will be unable to graduate. But Bear gets them off by assigning them enough special merit points to offset the demerits. He also proves to Will that he is not one of the Ten, as Cain had claimed.

At the last parade of the year, honoring those soon to graduate, Mark spots Tradd's father, Commerce, standing on the platform with his arm around Dan Molligen. So while the St. Croixes are out of town for the weekend, Mark and Will enter their house and find Commerce's journals, in which are recorded all the names, throughout the years, of the members of the Ten. These include the Institute's president, Commerce, and Tradd. They also find in the journals that

Tradd is the father of Annie Kate's baby and that Abigail had set up Will to take care of the pregnant Annie Kate and agree to be father to her child.

The president decides to expel Will and Mark and refuse to let them graduate, but he backs down when the two young men threaten to expose the names of the Ten to the newspapers. Before graduation, Will has one more confrontation—with Abigail and Tradd, who, as a member of the Ten, has betrayed his friends, even bearing responsibility for Pig's death.

At graduation, Will publicly defies the tradition insisting that the name of one who goes through the Walk of Shame be forgotten: as the general grudgingly hands him his diploma, Will says, "Dante Pignetti...Dante Pignetti, my roommate, sir" (498).

DISCOVERING THE TEN

Will first gets a hint of the Ten during his freshman year when a senior tells him that a secret organization called the Ten had probably stepped in to get rid of Bentley when it became evident that the Cadre was not successful in doing it. It is not until his senior year that the Ten begins to surface again, this time in connection with Poteete, who says that "they" took him to the house and that he "couldn't stand what they were doing" to him. He says, "They treated me worse than if I was an animal" (117). After Poteete is dead, Will is bothered by Poteete's comments, which he cannot understand. He next gets a hint of the Ten from Bear, who tells him in confidence that the number 10 is on the door of the room of one of the plebes who left campus suddenly. Will learns from his professor that the Ten is the highest honor an Institute cadet can hope for and that each vows to keep the organization secret, even from their wives and children. Their purpose is to uphold the traditions of the Institute as they see them. For seniors who have been chosen by the Ten, this means seeing that no one deemed by the Ten unworthy of the ring graduates from the Institute. Thus, when the taming fails to discourage an undesirable, the Ten steps in to run him off.

Membership in the Ten is chosen on the basis of leadership, academic standing, military ability, loyalty, and physical strength. Reynolds also implies that there have always been rumors that the tactics of the Ten include torture. The existence of the Ten is confirmed for Will when Tom Pearce indicates that a cadet had drawn a 10 on his back after telling him that he would be taken for a ride off campus. It is the disgraced Bentley, however, who first details the Ten's practices: he was bound, gagged, and thrown into the trunk of a car; a masked man with a bayonet threatened to castrate him; he was forced to drink water until he vomited; they had poured gasoline on him and thrown matches toward him until, from terror, he had given in. Will sees with his own eyes even worse torture when they send an electrical shock through a clamp attached to Pearce's penis.

MORE THAN ONE GANG

Tradd, a secret member of the Ten, deceives himself into thinking that the Institute stands for order, discipline, tradition, and honor, when, actually, neither the Institute nor the gang called the Ten that it spawns is orderly, disciplined, or honorable, and the traditions it upholds are those of the most brutal plantation slave drivers. The Ten is the secret gang that intimidates through terror, but it is not the only gang in the novel. It is merely the most secretive of several gangs. The Cadre itself is an official, institutional gang that brutalizes the freshman, its excesses only slightly less heinous than the tactics used by the Ten. As Will comes to see it, the whole institution and the military establishment are part of a brutal gang, addicted to power, physical force, and violence. As in *The Chocolate War,* the most powerful man in the institution lends his house to these atrocities and collaborates with the torturers.

The Ten and the Institute differ from the typical gang in that they have little interest in petty crimes for the generation of revenue and in the fact that they are made up of middle- and upper-class whites instead of lower-class minorities. But in other ways, the Ten and the Institute reflect typical gang behavior: the rigid hierarchy, even the use of uniforms; the rites and ceremonies; the brutal initiations; and the graffiti-like signs used to intimidate.

The Ten, the Cadre, and the Institute itself are not only identified with the brutalities of the plantation system, they are identified with the Vietnam War. The very problems that arose with regard to Vietnam in the 1960s are raised at the Institute and on the islands surrounding Charleston. They include the issue of race, the rumor of massacre and torture, and the divided loyalties arising from doubts about the war. Will's response to Vietnam parallels his response to the Institute and the military itself. The tendency of the Institute to use gang-like physical force and violence parallels the same U.S. tendency in its dealings with Vietnam. Will first learns about Vietnam when he enters the Institute as a freshman. Then, the idealism with which he views the Institute is echoed in his dreams of dying heroically in Vietnam for his country. Will's disillusionment with the Institute occurs simultaneously with his growing sentiment against the Vietnam War, a matter he frequently argues with Cain. The military in Vietnam seem little different from the actions of the Ten, their secrecy the same. Daily, during his senior year, he hears of former cadets, men he has known, dying in Vietnam. And the sacrifices that the Institute exacts from young misfits are somehow tied up in his mind with the sacrifices exacted by the country's military from soldiers in Vietnam.

Will finds that speaking his mind and writing speeches, poems, and editorials critical of the Institute and the military have given him a reputation for disloyalty, kept him a private for four years, and made him an outsider. The degree to which he has gone to save Pearce and unmask the Ten has put him in danger. It is a reenactment of the divided loyalties evident throughout the country over the war. On both planes—narrowly in the Institute and, more broadly, throughout the country—those who either disapproved of or had little enthusiasm for the injustices being perpetrated (whether in the Vietnam War or at the Institute) were reluctant to be disloyal to the group and its leaders.

Secrecy and retribution are the supreme weapons of the gang of the Ten and the Institute itself, which tries to enact vengeance on those it considers to be disloyal to the cause. And secrecy and retribution are also the weapons used by the military and law enforcement against those who objected to the Vietnam War.

BIBLIOGRAPHY

Atkinson, Rick. *The Long Gray Line*. Boston: Houghton Mifflin, 1989.

Burns, Landon C. *Pat Conroy*. Westport, CT: Greenwood Press, 1996.

Conroy, Pat. *The Boo*. Vernona, VA: McClure Press, 1970.

———— *The Great Santini*. New York: Bantam Books, 1987.

————. *The Lords of Discipline*. 1980. New York: Bantam Books, 1994.

————. *My Losing Season*. New York: Nan A. Talese/Doubleday, 2002.

Crews, Harry. "The Passage to Manhood." Rev. of *The Lords of Discipline*, by Pat Conroy. *New York Times Book Review*, 7 December 1980.

Rose, Frank. "The Martial Spirit and the Masculine Mystique." Rev. of *The Lords of Discipline,* by Pat Conroy. *Washington Post Book World,* 19 October 1980.

Truscott, Lucian K. *Dress Gray.* Garden City, NY: Doubleday, 1978.

Wertsch, Mary Edwards. *Military Brats.* New York: Harmony Books, 1991.

Willingham, Calder. *End as a Man.* New York: Vanguard Press, 1947.

13

Prep Schools and Watergate: Robert Cormier's *The Chocolate War* (1974)

FROM DAVID R. SIMON, "WATERGATE AND THE NIXON PRESIDENCY: A COMPARATIVE IDEOLOGICAL ANALYSIS."

Watergate and Afterward: The Legacy of Richard M. Nixon. Ed. Leon Friedman and William F. Levantrosser. Westport, CT: Greenwood Press, 1992.

The Watergate scandal that toppled the Nixon Presidency involved virtually every type of political deviance. These included (1) excessive secrecy, lying, "dirty campaign tricks," political repression, and violations of civil rights, (2) "the fix"—accepting campaign contributions in return for personal favors, (3) acts that resulted in personal financial gain for the politicos involved, and (4) possible violations of the president's warmaking powers. These divisions are arbitrary; they are meant only to categorize what in reality are many interrelated acts of either questionable ethical conduct or outright criminality (e.g., bribery, perjury, obstruction of justice, forgery, burglary, and possible income tax code violations, to list some of the most frequently mentioned. (1)

FROM ALAN F. WESTIN, "INFORMATION, DISSENT, AND POLITICAL POWER: WATERGATE REVISITED."

Watergate and Afterward: The Legacy of Richard M. Nixon. Ed. Leon Friedman and William F. Levantrosser. Westport, CT: Greenwood Press, 1992.

White House officials up to the president approved and furthered a chain of illegal conduct from the break-in at Dr. Lewis Fielding's office to the Watergate Complex break-in. They approved decisions to go ahead with illegal wiretapping; illegal dirty tricks in election campaigns; illegal use of campaign funds; illegal cover-up of the "Dita Beard" affair; the attempts to misuse Internal Revenue Service (IRS) funds to punish political enemies; false reporting of the secret bombings on Cambodia; and then the whole chain of lies, deception, shredding of official papers, and obstruction of justice that became the "cover-up." (57–58)

The most distressing message of Robert Cormier's frequently read and often-censored young adult novel, *The Chocolate War*, is that people retain authority and control through cruelty and greed. To secure their positions of power, the Trinity school administration and the highly organized gang of bullies called the Vigils who run the school collaborate to exploit and terrorize the rest of the school faculty and students.

CONTEXT: THE CIVIL RIGHTS STRUGGLE

The Civil Rights movement, the Vietnam War, and the Watergate political scandal left their marks on the era preceding publication of *The Chocolate War* and on the writing of the novel itself. The behavior of federal and local leaders in this era was characterized by corruption and duplicity, similar to the actions of Brother Leon and the Vigils in Cormier's novel. Resistance to corrupt authority also characterized the age and is seen in the novel in the person of Jerry Renault.

BULLIES INSIDE AND OUTSIDE THE LAW

The Chocolate War, which shares with *The Lord of the Flies* the theme of the reversion to barbarism on the part of young boys under the influence of a gang leader, argues that not all gangs are the products of poverty and slums. The setting of the book and the territory of the gang known as the Vigils is a struggling Catholic prep school in New England. Few scenes occur off the school's campus. The gang is run by several students: Obie, its secretary; John Carter, its president; Emile Janza, its muscle; and most powerful, Archie Costello, its "Assigner." Even though the main Chocolate War, itself, involves selling merchandise, the Vigils are unlike typical gangs in that their main reason for being is not stealing merchandise and selling drugs: their main activity is terrorizing those around them. They exercise their power by making a heartless game of intimidating their classmates and teachers. Their chief activity is concocting dangerous and humiliating assignments for younger students to carry out. Although Archie is known for his psychological cruelties, Carter and Janza are also physically brutal to those smaller or weaker than they are.

The Vigils are only able to keep up their terrorism because the school administration, in the figure of Deputy Headmaster Brother Leon, enables them to. Brother Leon goes beyond just protecting the Vigils; he uses them to further his own ends. This is seen primarily in his enlistment of their help in selling 20,000 boxes of chocolates. Little of the cruelty perpetrated by the Vigils escapes Brother Leon, even though the gang is supposed to be a secret, forbidden organization. Archie rubs Leon's nose in the fact that Leon is asking for help from an unscrupulous gang by mentioning the gang by name: "The Vigils will help" (29).

One of the major characters who is not a gang member is Roland Goubert, called Goober, whom the gang forces to loosen every desk, table, and chair screw in Brother Eugene's classroom. After all the contents of the room crash down during a lesson, Brother Eugene has a nervous breakdown, and Goober eventually withdraws from all school activity, including the football team on which he had shown much promise. The major focus of the novel is Goober's friend, Jerry Renault, who is haunted by his mother's recent death, by what he perceives as his own uninteresting life, and by his failure to have a girlfriend. It is he who launches the Chocolate War. Even though the gang has pledged to help Brother Leon with the chocolate sales, Archie loves to cause trouble and forces Jerry to refuse to sell chocolates for 10 days just to make life uncomfortable for Jerry and enrage Brother Leon. After the 10 days are up, the gang orders Jerry to reverse himself and begin selling chocolates, but Jerry decides to defy both gang and Brother Leon by continuing to refuse to sell chocolates. At first, other students express sympathy for Jerry's antiauthoritarian stance, as Archie and Brother Leon had feared they would. Chocolate sales begin to plummet, and a sign briefly appears on the school bulletin board: "Screw the Chocolates and Screw the Vigils" (183). One might hope at this moment that Jerry will be the inadvertent leader in overthrowing the gang and Brother Leon as well. But such is not the case.

Archie's shrewd manipulation and Brother Leon's encouragement of the gang soon turns things around. The gang launches a blitz of terror against Jerry. He is attacked from behind at football practice. His locker is vandalized, including his poster of a man alone on a beach above a quote from T. S. Eliot's "The Love Song of J. Alfred Prufrock": "Do I dare disturb the universe?" He and his father receive crank calls at all hours of the day and night. His homework is stolen, and someone trips him on the stairs.

At the same time, the Vigils and Brother Leon, by manipulating sales figures, public relations, and mob psychology, make it seem that the sale is a huge success. The gang members are ordered to sell chocolates in any way they can. They descend on factories to make sales and they intimidate weak individuals into buying. Then they and Brother Leon make the figures show that all students are making sales, when, in fact, this is not so. In this way, the administration and the gang whip up the student body into a frenzy of school spirit and turn sentiment against Jerry. Archie sends Janza, the gang enforcer, to beat up Jerry. Instead of doing the dirty work himself, Janza enlists the help of a group of neighborhood toughs to attack Jerry.

The final horror is a raffle and boxing match, engineered by Archie to destroy Jerry and cement his own power as leader of the Vigils. With Brother Leon's cooperation, it is held without adult supervision. Jerry, a skinny boy, is put into the boxing ring with the sadistic Janza. The boys in the audience have been whipped up into a riotous fever against Jerry and the rules have been concocted to ensure his defeat. With the spectators screaming, "Kill him, kill him" (254), reminiscent of the gang's chants in *Lord of the Flies,* Janza lands an excess of 16 punches, and Jerry collapses with a broken jaw and internal injuries.

Meanwhile, Brother Leon has been sitting silently in the darkness on the hill above the ring, watching the whole slaughter. As Archie explains to one of his lieutenants afterward:

> I tipped him off.... I figured he would enjoy himself. And I also figured if he was here and part of the proceedings, he'd also be protection for us if anything went wrong. (262)

THE GANG'S ABUSE OF POWER

The story of the Vigils' abuse of power is characterized by the following:

- The use of force, especially psychological violence, to terrorize those around them.

- The complete lack of compassion or humane instincts within the gang leadership and on the part of Brother Leon. Archie refuses to show sympathy to Jerry, even when Obie tells him that Jerry's mother has recently died. The subhuman lack of compassion is especially illustrated by the planned brutality of the boxing match and Archie's and Leon's total lack of concern for Jerry, whose injuries may well be fatal.
- The rivalry between gang members. Three of the gang leaders—Obie, the gang secretary; Carter, the gang president; and Janza—despise Archie and at some point challenge his position. On his part, Archie is disdainful of all the other gang members, whom he regards as weak or stupid.
- The parallels between gang cruelty and the greater establishment of which it is a part. Brother Leon is as much of a psychological terrorist as is the cold-blooded Archie Costello and his gang. For no apparent reason, he humiliates a boy named Bailey to the point of tears and then blames his bad behavior on the class, calling them idiots. He uses the threat of an F to blackmail a straight-A student for information and cooperation. He falsifies and misuses the school's funds and then places the burden of recouping the money on the boys, who are perpetually required to take on the role of hustlers. A student named Caroni, who is being blackmailed by Brother Leon, asks himself if teachers are as villainous as they are portrayed in the movies and in books.
- The partnership between the power structure and the gang. In exchange for being allowed free rein to bully their classmates, the gang keeps order and gives Brother Leon help in selling chocolates. Brother Leon goes to the extreme of ordering Archie to "take care of" Jerry in order to save the sale, telling him, "If the sale goes down the drain, you and The Vigils also go down the drain" (165).
- The fearful silence on the part of decent people, which further enables abuses. The boys who are initially sympathetic with Jerry learn to remain quiet, to back down, or allow themselves to be manipulated by Archie and Leon into hatred of Jerry. One sympathetic faculty member is driven to a nervous breakdown. Another faculty member, after hearing Leon's jovial and decisive dismissal of the gang's cruel boxing match ("Boys will be boys" [261]), slinks out as the ambulance takes Jerry away, knowing that, in his own best interest, he should say no more about the horror that the gang has perpetrated, even

though he knows that Leon is misusing funds and the gang and Archie are out of control.

CHOCOLATE WAR/VIETNAM WAR

Just as William Golding used a comparison of Jack's youth gang and Nazi Germany as a commentary on the evils of both, so Robert Cormier used the parallels between the Chocolate War and the Vietnam War to expose the abuses of power in both situations. Like Brother Leon, who has created a fiscal deficit that he must make good, both Presidents Johnson and Nixon found themselves involved in a war from which they could not extricate themselves without, they believed, compromising their power and reputations. As Leon condones the cruelties of the gang because, he duplicitously states, it had to be done for the good of Trinity, so Johnson and Nixon tell the people of the United States that the atrocities and sacrifices of life in Vietnam are necessary for the good of the country.

Like the peaceful protesters of the Vietnam War, Jerry Renault challenges the authority of Leon and the gang, both of whom he and the other boys despise and know to be unethical. Many demonstrators, like Jerry, acted as they did with great reluctance but determination.

As Brother Leon uses the gang's talent for intimidation to sell more chocolates, President Nixon, in particular, used law-enforcement agencies in an attempt to neutralize antiwar sentiment.

PRESIDENT NIXON AND BROTHER LEON

Although the presidential impeachment hearings, including the disclosure of the culpable contents of the White House tapes, did not occur until after *The Chocolate War* went to press, throughout 1973, the year before the novel's publication, the country was embroiled in the monumental case of the misuse of power on the part of the administration. The Watergate scandal resonates in Robert Cormier's novel. For example, the gang maintains secret files on everyone in the school, reminding the reader of the enemies list that the Nixon administration maintained and the extensive files compiled by the FBI on those who expressed opposition to Nixon's policies. Brother Leon's use of the gang for shady purposes is a reminder of President Nixon's use of illegal operatives to break into offices, his use of the FBI and director Patrick Grey to destroy evidence in the Watergate break-in, and his use of the CIA to spy on American citizens. The gang's dirty tricks in disrupting class with jigs and destroying a class-room by loosening all the screws are reminiscent of the political dirty tricks in the Nixon campaign. Brian, whom Brother Leon has chosen as treasurer for the chocolate sales and who discovers that Leon has cooked the financial books, is suggestive of White House lawyer John Dean and Nixon campaign manager Jeb Magruder, who both began to suspect that illegal activities were afoot but were at first too timid to refuse to cooperate. Janza is a reminder of Gordon Liddy, the blundering and hot-headed White House operative who had no com-punction about illegal activities and admitted later that he had con-templated killing Jack Anderson, a newspaper columnist critical of the president.

THE GANG, HUMAN NATURE, AND SOCIETY

The novel's picture of the human situation in general and the plight of young people bullied by gangs in particular is deeply cynical, pro-foundly pessimistic. By contrast, *Lord of the Flies* implies that civili-zation and reason offer some relief from the ravages of human cruelty and barbarism. But in *The Chocolate War,* civilization and reason are enlisted in the cause of unrelieved exploitation and brutality. Even what should be regarded as the loftiest arm of civilization, the church, is corrupt, inhumane, and exploitative.

Characters attest to the weakness and depravity of human nature and society. Caroni, the straight-A student who is blackmailed by Brother Leon, sees little to contradict his impression that life is rotten and that no one is to be trusted. Archie sums up the view of human nature offered by the novel when he tells Carter: "You see, Carter, people are two things: greedy and cruel. . . . The cruel part—watching two guys hitting each other, maybe hurting each other" (241). And Carter resents Archie most of all because he makes everybody feel "dirty, contaminated, polluted" (241).

The novel ends in utter hopelessness as the most evil forces win hands down. Even though the other gang members challenge Archie's power, even though he has perpetrated a horror with the boxing match and allowed it to get out of control, sending Jerry to the hos-pital with perhaps fatal injuries, he still continues in power. Not only is evil not punished, but none of the boys, especially Archie, seems moved by remorse or guilt.

The message the novel conveys is that those who challenge corrup-tion in the system will be obliterated.

BIBLIOGRAPHY

Burress, Lee. *Battle of the Books.* Metuchen, NJ: Scarecrow Press, 1989.

Campbell, Patricia J. *Presenting Robert Cormier.* Boston: Twayne Publishers, 1985.

Cormier, Robert. *The Chocolate War.* 1974. New York: Dell, 2000.

Donelson, Kenneth L. *Literature for Today's Young Adults.* Glenview, IL: Scott Foresman, 1985.

Gallagher, Mary Elizabeth. *Young Adult Literature.* Haverford, PA: Catholic Library Association, 1991.

Walker, Elinor. *Doors to More Mature Reading.* Chicago: American Library Association, 1964.

14

Family Disintegration in the 1980s: Walter Dean Myers's *Scorpions* (1988)

FROM LARRY WATTS, "THE CODE OF THE STREETS: AN INTERVIEW WITH A FORMER GANG MEMBER."

Understanding Adventures of Huckleberry Finn. By Claudia Durst Johnson. Westport, CT: Greenwood Press, 1996.

Watts: What attracted you to a gang? You hinted at it earlier, but expand on that a little bit more.

Ted: I guess—my family—I didn't have—I wasn't raised with brothers and sisters, even though I had half brothers and sisters in other states. But I didn't interact with them. Basically, all my "brothers" were people who stayed around me, people who were tight-knit, got close. And a lot of them—I was the kind of guy that hung with older people, people not my age. And they accepted me because I didn't talk too much, and I was a little mature for my age. You see a gang hanging together. You walk to school or something like that, and you see them hanging in the halls. They give each other the secret handshake and are standing up with each other, and, you know, it was just like—wow!— this is unity; this is something. This is something interesting. This is something I have in common, you know, and you see them throwing gang signs and at parties and always together. And just groups of people. And I guess it was different. It was something I hadn't seen. (201)

. . .

Watts: Security. There are different kinds of security—emotional, financial, family?

Ted: You've named all three. Perfectly. Financial, family—I mean you
can get in a gang, and something happens to you, somebody
wants to fight you, somebody wants to stick you up, somebody
wants to steal your things, and you've got your gang to back you
up. And chances are—you're in a gang, people won't mess with
you, because they know they have all the gang to deal with. Family—because—because—when I need something, I can go to
one of my members before I can go to somebody that's not affil-
iated with a particular gang. (203)

Richard Wright's *Rite of Passage* and Walter Dean Myers's novel
Scorpions are separated by more than 50 years, but the two novels
about African American gangs in Harlem tell us that very little in the
lives of young men has improved over the period that embraces many
social and economic reforms and much legal progress with regard to
race discrimination. At the center of both works are sensitive, intelligent young boys approaching manhood in a matriarchal household
within the Harlem ghetto. The trials of both boys emanate from the
collapse of the family, the absence of older males (in both cases the father and older brother), and the emotional attachment to the mar-
tyred mother. In both cases, the young boys become involved with
violent neighborhood youth gangs, not from attraction but from desperation. In *Scorpions,* Jamal is subject to numerous pressures, foremost the need to raise money for his brother's appeal of a case that has
sent him to prison for armed robbery and murder. Jamal's natural talents and his cherished friendship are both sacrificed in the process.

The picture of gangs in this novel is not from the viewpoint of an
established gang member, but rather from a non–gang member whose
life is disrupted by gangs and whose brother is a gang leader.

THE SETTING

The life of the young black man in Harlem was even more hopeless
in the late 1970s than it had been four decades earlier. After World
War II, many of the great leaders of Harlem had died, and black families who achieved middle-class status moved out of the neighbor-

hood. The poor, living in slums, were left behind, without the leadership they once had and without examples of achievement to give them hope. Economic destitution, homelessness, and social disorder, including crime and violence, became a grimly accepted way of life. By the 1970s, gangs had long since begun to rule and terrorize Harlem.

Gang delinquency among African American boys continued to exceed that of other minorities. While African Americans constituted 12 percent of the total population, they made up 25 percent of the total delinquents.

The number of families without fathers increased dramatically throughout the population in the 40 years that separates Richard Wright's *Rite of Passage* from *Scorpions*. The census for 1960 indicates that 22.7 percent of all families in the United States with children 18 years of age or under were without fathers. And the greatest increase came in African American communities like Harlem. The 1972 census showed that 1 of every 3 black families had an absent father, as compared with 1 in 10 for white families. Indeed, by the 1980s, there was little expectation in urban slums that the father be a constant presence within the family; and many mothers, concerned that their sons learn to be "men," reluctantly accepted the idea that they would turn to gangs for instruction in becoming physically tough, hard, aggressive, assertive, and violent. Sociologist Walter Miller writes: "Most boys from female-based households at a fairly early age adopt as their primary reference group and learning milieu a set of peers raised under similar circumstances" (219).

Sociologist Ray A. Tennyson observes that in the 1960s there was a "direct relation between adult male absence and gang membership" (52). By the 1970s, the approximate setting of *Scorpions*, 30 to 60 percent of delinquent boys came from fatherless families.

In *Crime and Delinquency*, Martin R. Haskell and Lewis Yablonsky present an argument for the correlation between poverty, family disorder, and gang membership:

> In the modern disorganized slum, the violent gang has been for many Negro youths their only source of identity, status, and emotional satisfaction. Ill-trained to participate with any degree of success in the dominant white middle-class world...they construct their own community. They set goals that are achievable; they build an empire, partly real and partly fantasy, that helps them live through the confusion of adolescence. (522)

Sociological studies have also addressed the role that schools, like Jamal's, inadvertently play in pushing underprivileged African Americans toward gangs. Boys from the ghettoes often exhibit characteristics (like talking loudly) that are unacceptable to middle-class society. Yet school officials and teachers are too ready to label such behavior as bad and the students who exhibit such behavior as troublemakers. As in Jamal's case, the authorities, while seeming to be well meaning, are too quick to label and rid the school of such students. The school's label often shapes the boy's self-image as a delinquent who would be more at home in a gang (Haskell and Yablonsky 487).

HEAVY PRESSURES ON A 12-YEAR-OLD

The central focus of *Scorpions* is a 12-year-old boy named Jamal Hicks. He lives with his hard-working mother and his young sister. His older brother, the former leader of the gang called the Scorpions, is serving a jail sentence for robbery and murder. His father, who has deserted the family, makes only one brief appearance in the course of the story.

Jamal's close, devoted friend is a wise and decent Puerto Rican boy named Otto, whose own father has moved back to Puerto Rico, leaving him with his grandmother. Other of Jamal's relationships outside the family are not so happy and supportive. There is Dwayne, a schoolmate physically bigger than Jamal who forces him into fights, and Mack, a 17-year-old dangerous associate of Jamal's brother, Randy. Angel, Indian, Blood, and Terry are 14-, 15-, and 16-year-old members of the Scorpions.

School officials are other important characters in Jamal's life: his principal, Mr. Davidson; his teachers, Mrs. Rich, Mr. Hunter, Miss Brown, and Mrs. Mitchell; and the school nurse, Mrs. Roberts.

One important character, who never makes an actual appearance, is one of the strongest presences in the narrative and hangs over the story like a black cloud. This is Jamal's older brother, Randy. Randy's actions before the novel's opening create perpetual agony for the family members and lead to the tragic catastrophe. At the time the story opens, Randy has been tried, convicted, and sentenced for the robbing and killing of a store clerk. Before his arrest, he has been leader of the gang called the Scorpions, whose main business has been running crack cocaine for drug dealers.

As the one-time "man of the house," Randy's character and influence are baleful and negative. Though he is obviously guilty of the murder he has tried to pin on his friend Willie, he refuses to acquiesce to his jail sentence and refuses to be satisfied with the services of a public defender, which would have alleviated the economic strain on his hard-strapped family. Instead, he burdens them with the cost of an appeal—first $500, then $2,000. To further cement his position in the Scorpions, Randy places his 12-year-old brother, Jamal, in harm's way by insisting that Jamal contact Mack.

Jamal's mother, who holds the family together with part-time jobs, is obsessed with getting the money to appeal her oldest son's case and possibly free him from prison, especially after Randy is knifed and has to be hospitalized. Perhaps because Randy is her eldest and in trouble, she neglects Jamal and his sister, Sassy, in order to visit Randy. On the first night of the story, her two younger children remain home alone until midnight while she visits Randy. Mama also places Jamal in peril in order to free Randy. She conveys Randy's message to Jamal, asking his little brother to contact Mack, a Scorpion and sadistic repeat offender who has just gotten out of prison for breaking a man's arm. Mama first tells Jamal to leave Mack and the Scorpions alone, but when Jamal agrees that he should not and will not contact the gang, she reverses herself and says, "Maybe you should, if Randy think somebody might bother you" (13). She also, perhaps inadvertently, places an enormous pressure on Jamal to help her come up with the money for Randy's appeal. Jamal, who finally has little sympathy with his gang-leader brother, is distressed by his mother's physical and psychological decline in the wake of her son's arrest.

Like the absent Randy, the Scorpions also profoundly influence the course of events, though Jamal never officially joins them, never engages in gang activities, never meets with them as a group, nor considers their members his friends. Yet his brother and his brother's friend, Mack, pronounce 12-year-old Jamal the leader of the Scorpions because, with Randy in prison, the Scorpions have split into factions, with no leadership, no organization, and no "business."

Jamal's impulse to help his mother with the money she needs for Randy's appeal leads him to nominally and briefly join the Scorpions. Mack reasons that a 12-year-old like Jamal could not be forced to testify in case one of the gang members got in trouble and that Jamal needs to "hold" the gang leadership for his brother Randy. His mother's anguish also leads him to accept the gun that Mack gives him. Both decisions destroy Jamal's promise for a better life through the use of his talents and a public-school education. They also destroy the one consistent force for good in his life—his friend Tito.

Tito is like a good angel—a decent and devoted friend urging Jamal to keep away from Mack and the gang, urging him to get rid of the gun, suggesting that he work to get money rather than negotiate with the Scorpions, giving Jamal his jacket to shield him from the cold, and taking the gun that Mack has forced on Jamal to his own home to keep Jamal from trouble. Finally, Tito jeopardizes his own life to save Jamal from being killed by the Scorpions.

Jamal has to confront pressures at school as well as at home. His teachers and principal don't strike one as incompetent or mean-spirited, but neither are they insightful or sensitive in dealing with the fragile Jamal. A different approach to him may have made all the difference in his young life. For no discernible reason, his principal labels him a bad student of undesirable influence, predicting that he will soon be tossed out of school. Even Miss Brown, a teacher he likes, seems unaware of his talent for drawing and disappoints him by not asking him to help paint the scenery for the school play.

Jamal has Mack's gun nearby in his second fight with the school bully, Dwayne. When Dwayne is in the process of beating him senseless, Jamal pulls out the gun and announces that he is the leader of the Scorpions. Although he scares Dwayne away, proving to himself the power of the gun, he is tortured by fears that the police will come after him. His fears are not sufficient to cause him to get rid of the gun, however, because he feels that it will protect him from the dangers around him. Sociologists Haskell and Yablonsky quote one gang member as saying, "A knife or a gun makes you ten feet tall" (525).

The job he takes to get money for Randy's appeal is short-lived when the Scorpions show up at his place of employment to threaten him. Instead of returning the gun to Mack as he'd planned, Jamal decides to bargain with the Scorpions: he will relinquish his claim to leadership if they come up with the $2,000 for Randy's appeal.

Meanwhile, the school principal, who had insisted on talking to Jamal's mother after Dwayne's allegation that Jamal had a gun, changes his mind and sends Jamal to the school nurse for medication. But, days later, Jamal's failure to do his homework is a last straw that leads the principal to recommend that he be transferred to a school for troubled boys. The sympathetic school nurse informs him, however, that there are ways he can get around the transfer.

Protecting his mother and himself from a school interview is good news, but it is followed by bad news. Mama's employer will not lend her the money for Randy's appeal.

On their way to meet the Scorpions in the crime-infested park, Jamal tells Tito that he has decided to resign from the Scorpions. If the tough gang members in the park decide to beat him up, he'll just take it without a struggle. But after a threatening conversation, Angel and the Indian don't just give Jamal a beating; they pull out a knife to kill him. This forces the gentle Tito to shoot Jamal's attackers with Mack's gun, which has been placed in his care. Only as they flee home do they throw away the gun.

Tito, who believes that his shooting of the two boys has angered God, thus guaranteeing that he will be sent to hell, becomes so physically ill that he can't eat or leave his house. Finally, he feels he has to tell his grandmother what happened. Together, they go to the police, who advise him, since the shooting was in self-defense, to return to Puerto Rico with his father.

Losing Tito is the hardest blow of all to Jamal, for he realizes that he is not just losing a companion but a rare person whose love, unlike that of his family, is positively productive of good and is supportive rather than burdensome. As Tito leaves, taking with him the portrait Jamal has drawn of him, Jamal anticipates having to be sufficiently hard to survive in this grim, hopeless environment.

A number of images scattered throughout the narrative enhance our understanding of Jamal's position with regard to his family, neighborhood, and the Scorpions. There is a small dog that menaces a woman at a bus stop, reminding us of the animalistic members of the Scorpions who terrorize the neighborhood. Large pigeons bully a tiny sparrow, reminding us of the way Dwayne, Indian, and Angel bully the smaller Jamal. The roaches that Jamal finds in the corn flakes and sees skittering across the floor are, Sassy thinks, an inevitable plague and mark on the poor. In contrast are two images of hope. One is the beautiful yacht in the harbor that Tito longs for as a way of escape from the poverty and oppression of the neighborhood. The other for Jamal is his ability to escape through his art, especially returning again and again to draw his Chinese neighbor's beautiful garden.

LETTING "THE BAD MESS UP THE GOOD"

Of all the men he encounters, only the Reverend Biggs appears to be a wise and decent male role model. He tells Mama after Randy has been knifed by a fellow prisoner, "The important thing here is that, as much as your heart is with your boy in the hospital, you got to hold

your family here together too. We can't let the bad mess up the good"
(153).

The good in Jamal's life is his great love and concern for his
mother; his talent for drawing, which is such a comfort to him; and his
good friend Tito. But, as Reverend Biggs warns, the bad *is* allowed to
mess up the good. A bad economic situation seems to have allowed
the bad to first threaten the good in the life of the family when their
father lost his job and became drunken and abusive, forcing Mama to
take Sassy and Jamal, and move out. Though Jamal has no great love
for his father and believes there is no excuse for his desertion of the
family, he can understand how his father felt. Lack of money continues to plague the family as Mama works herself into her grave, as
Randy joins the Scorpions in their illegal means to get money, and as
the family searches unsuccessfully for the money to help Randy. Jamal
is even tormented by his classmates because his clothes are cheap.

Randy realizes that his father's irresponsibility and shoddy values
have left the family weakened:

> At first Daddy used to come around a lot. Half the time he
> had been drinking. After a while he came around less and
> less. Jamal felt the same about his father as he did about
> Randy. They were both gone, and each of them had taken a
> little piece of Mama with them that they didn't bring back.
> (88)

His father calls Jamal a mama's boy and scolds the 12-year-old for not
being more of a man and not getting a job to get his gang-leader
brother out of jail. Jamal retorts, with reference to Randy's imprisonment and his father's desertion, "I'm the only man here, ain't I?"
(96).

Randy is another instance of the bad messing up the good. With no
male role model and a greater need for money in a one-parent family
that has financial troubles, Randy has turned to crime and the gang.
Jamal thinks over all the times Randy has gotten into trouble and
Mama has had to bail him out. In an unguarded moment, he blurts
out to Sassy his hope that Randy *never* gets out.

The gang and the gun are also forces for evil that threaten to "mess
up the good." It is to Jamal's credit that he doesn't take his father,
Randy, or the gang members for role models, even when his brother
calculatingly sets him up with the Scorpions, who cause him to lose his
job and try to kill him. But Jamal's independence in this regard

doesn't protect him. He is a physically small 12-year-old in an environment of dangers impossible to avoid. So, at one point he approaches the gang, as Randy and his mother have suggested, seeking protection. One small part of him yearns to carry the gun that has gotten him and Tito into so much trouble. For the gun means protection and power, when his size and his poverty place him at risk.

BIBLIOGRAPHY

Anderson, Jervis. *This Was Harlem: A Cultural Portrait, 1900–1950*. New York: Farrar, Straus, 1982.

Bishop, Rudine Sims. *Presenting Walter Dean Myers*. Boston: Twayne Publishers, 1990.

Haskell, Martin R., and Lewis Yablonsky. *Crime and Delinquency*. Chicago: Rand McNally College Publishing, 1974.

Miller, Walter. "Implications of Urban Lower Class Culture for Social Work." *Social Service Review* 33 (September 1959): 219–36.

Myers, Walter Dean. *Scorpions*. 1988. New York: HarperCollins, 1990.

15

1960s Los Angeles: Frank Bonham's *Durango Street* (1965)

FROM BOB HERBERT, "WHERE FEAR RULES THE STREET."

New York Times, 9 June 2003.

The three men were middle-aged and dressed as if they had just come from church. One pointed toward a tiny makeshift shrine of flickering candles and wilting flowers that had been placed at the curb in front of a rundown house on Budlong Avenue in South Los Angeles, a vast expanse of neighborhoods that has had its name changed from South Central in a futile effort to improve its image.

South L.A. is still a viciously destructive place. Some neighborhoods are so dangerous that residents are reluctant to leave their homes, even in the daytime. The neat residential streets and the palm trees are deceptive. The owner of a fast-food restaurant told me, "Out here, you're always in danger." (31)

Frank Bonham's *Durango Street* is the story of a young African American gang member in the perilous slums outside a large California metropolis in the early 1960s. The narrative of young Rufus Henry enlarges on the irrefutable necessity for young men in urban slums to join gangs as a means of self-protection. The story also presents the efficacy of intervention in gang life by social workers like George Nishinaka and the Group Service Council, to whom the novel is dedicated.

SOUTH CENTRAL: THE LOS ANGELES GANG SCENE

Bonham's novel was published in 1965, before the California area he depicts had been turned into a battlefield by large arsenals of assault weapons and crack cocaine. Rufus Henry's gang, the Moors, and their rivals seem almost tame compared with the heavily armed gang members of the 1990s, who are required to kill as part of their initiation and promotion through the ranks of the gang.

Some things, however, have remained constant from the time of Richard Wright's *Rite of Passage* to Kody Scott's *The Monster.* One is the desperation from which gangs emerge in the slums. Rufus Henry lives in a place hemmed in by grimy factories, interstate highways, concrete riverbeds, and railroad tracks—all having displaced trees and grass and cut off the sun and sky from the housing projects and collapsing slum houses around the area. The businesses that serve the area are a few dingy cafes, bars, and stores, run by surly, suspicious managers. A poor, depressing storefront church stands in the middle. The houses in Rufus's neighborhood are unpainted and rickety, the steps and porches warped and rotten. Garbage and trash have piled up between the houses and in the street.

The other constant in the gang scene is the one-parent household, run by a woman abandoned by her husband, a woman who must work hard at several low-wage jobs to hold the family together. Typically, she is both desperate and resigned to her sons' self-destructive lives on the streets.

Implicit in the picture is the difficulty of breaking the cycle of gang-related violence within the family. In the Henry household, Rufus's young brother Curtis confides that he will soon be joining a gang. Even in the mid-1960s, breaking away from a gang was a problem. The gang called the Moors entraps its members by reminding them, even from the start, that they will be beaten in when they join the gang and beaten out should they decide to leave it.

Even within a single neighborhood, like the one called the Flats, several gangs operate in deadly rivalry with one another over territory. Each gang has an ethnic identity: the Moors, the Bloods, and the Gassers are African American, and the Aztecs are Mexican. Gang members not only hurt members of rival gangs, but members of their own gang. And innocent people, like Rufus's little sister, get caught and harmed in the process.

Although the town in this fiction is named Coast City, it bears a close resemblance to Los Angeles, being described as a "big-city jungle" located in California (15). The Flats, where Rufus lives, is an out-lying neighborhood of hopeless poverty dominated by the Durango Housing Project. The fictional neighborhood is very like an infamous 16-square-mile area of Los Angeles called South Central, where race riots occurred in the year of the novel's publication. South Central, like the Flats, is understood to lie within and underneath several free-ways and streets: the Long Beach Freeway defines its eastern border; the Santa Ana and Santa Monica freeways its northern border; the San Diego Freeway and Crenshaw Boulevard its southern border.

Today, South Central's residents are African American, white, His-panic, and Asian, but in 1965, they were largely African American. In the 1960s, nearly half of the city's population lived below the poverty line. Unemployment was far greater than the national average. Among teenagers, it was especially high. These conditions have only worsened over the years. Census figures, for instance, reveal that in 1989, 100 percent of those over 16 in many South Central areas had not worked a single day in the year.

In the preface of *Do or Die,* a book about South Central in the late 1980s, Leon Bing describes the area as he first found it in 1963, roughly the setting of *Durango Street.* Coming into South Central was like entering another country, he writes. Every available flat surface was covered with graffiti—buildings, fences, concrete—a testament to the indisputable sovereignty of gangs in the area. Many shops had been boarded up. Many had been destroyed or marred by firebombs and bullets. The few stores that remained open kept steel security bars over the windows and doors, even during working hours. Bars and bullet holes marked the run-down houses. It was hard to find any building without at least one broken windowpane.

In the middle of the day, a tense, eerie quiet prevailed on the streets themselves with only the constant noise of freeway traffic surrounding the area. At night, when one might expect darkness and quiet to en-courage rest, there was the screech of cars, sirens, and human voices; the staccato of bullets; the deafening racket of low-flying helicopters; and the blinding white glare of searchlights.

ADULT MALES AND YOUTH GANGS

The main protagonist of *Durango Street* is a young African Ameri-can boy who, at the novel's opening, is serving time in a detention work camp for stealing a car. Rufus is prone to gang-related crimes and violence, especially fighting and shooting out store windows.

With extreme difficulty, his mother is rearing him, his younger brother, Curtis, and his sister, Janet, alone, her husband having left the family years before.

Despite the handicaps typical of a boy living in a poverty-stricken, gang-ridden neighborhood like the Coast City Flats, Rufus has positive forces in his life capable of lifting him above his environment. The camp counselors recognize Rufus as intelligent and capable of leadership. He loves to read and aspires to be a teacher because of his love of books and children. Moreover, although he has no father in his household, there is a constant theme in Rufus's existence that gives him hope: in the private recesses of his life is his hero worship of Ernie Brown, a famous football player. Ernie Brown is not just an athlete-hero for Rufus, however; he may actually be the real father he has never met. When Rufus was 12, his mother revealed that when she was only 16, she and Ernie were married briefly before their parents had had the union annulled, and that Rufus is the famous athlete's son, whom he supported until Rufus's mother remarried. Whether the story is true or something his mother makes up, hoping it will change his life, Rufus cannot determine. But it does give him a distant male role model whose qualities have the capacity of inspiring him to better things. Ernie inspires Rufus to think about finishing high school and working for a football scholarship to put himself through college because he realizes how crucial an education will be to his leaving the neighborhood. Rufus's most-cherished possession is the scrapbook on Ernie Brown that he has kept since he was about 12 when his mother first told him that Ernie was his father. Inside the front cover, he had written "My Big Ernie Book, Facks an' Pitchers collected by his son, Rufus H. Brown" (149). Most of the boys around him have no fathers, but Rufus keeps the connection with Ernie alive through the scrapbook. It becomes a magical holy scripture, representing the best part of his life. It is an emblem of identity and self-worth, a spiritual guide, a hope for something better.

At the same time, some thoughts of his presumed father are troubling to him. His mother told him that Ernie contributed to the support of his son only until she remarried, and Ernie, if he is Rufus's father, has made no attempt to find or know his son since then. Nor can Rufus escape the fact that while Ernie basks in the luxury and fame available to a highly paid professional football hero, his son Rufus and Rufus's family live in abject poverty and perpetual fear. Rufus thinks that if he can look Ernie in the eye he will know "whether to hate him for letting them live like this while he drove Cadillacs and owned a big house, or to be proud of being his son" (83).

In addition to his natural talents and the aspirations inspired by Ernie, Rufus has something else working in his favor: he meets Alex Robbins, a social worker, who refuses to give up on him and finally becomes a viable male role model who can lead Rufus out of gang violence.

Fear rises in Rufus as he is being released from detention camp and is told that his family has moved to Coast City, where notorious street gangs hold the neighborhood in perpetual terror. As he leaves camp for home, his counselor says to himself, *"Good luck, Rufus...You'll need it"* (14). At home, his mother is so afraid she keeps the blinds drawn at all times, never issues out of the house after she gets home from work, and doesn't want to be left alone at night. Nor does she want her children to go out of the house in the evening because she knows that some youngster is beaten up by gangs every night.

At home again, the issue of street gangs arises repeatedly as his overworked parole officer stresses that joining a gang will be a violation of his parole and as his little brother, Curtis, tells him that he plans to join a gang called the Little Warriors. His mother is ashamed of and depressed by Rufus's past gang activity, but sadly resigned to the inevitability that he will again join a gang in their new neighborhood.

On Rufus's first evening back home, he is forced into a confrontation with a gang when he goes to the store with his sister to buy his mother a bottle of milk. A carload of Gassers cruise through the shabby downtown area, intruding on territory actually belonging to the Moors. The Gassers, believing he has told the police they have thrown glass bottles onto the road, corner him in an alley, armed with cement chunks, planks, an iron pipe, and beer-can openers, the weapons of choice. But Rufus is already street smart. He has prepared himself with a weapon of his own—the broken milk bottle that he presses against the stomach of their leader, Simon Jones. With this, he holds the Gassers at bay, realizing at the same time that they will now be a real and present danger to him and his family.

After deliberately writing off the job his parole officer had lined up for him, when his boss continually calls him "boy" and "jailbird," Rufus seeks out the "fighting gang" called the Moors. He knows that his friend, a tough but kindly giant named Baby Gibson, belongs to the Moors. But Rufus and the Moors's leader, Bantu, form an immediate hatred of each other. Much to Rufus's surprise, Bantu orders the others to beat him up as a form of initiation and vows that he'll be beaten again if ever he decides to leave the gang. The police arrive to stop what they see as a disturbance, arrest the group, and call Rufus's parole officer. The parole officer, in turn, calls Alex Robbins, a social worker with the Group Service Council, whose job it is to break the cycle of violent gangs.

Robbins, with police cooperation, goes through the folders on the Moors, finding that each of these boys has been thrown out of schools, playgrounds, and clubs and that "not one in ten has a father" (75). Robbins surprises the Moors by appearing the following night at their gathering place on the housing-project roof. His approach to the gang is easier in that Bantu is still in jail. His leverage to get them to work with him initially is to promise he'll persuade the police to be more lenient with them. Rufus, who assumed leadership in Bantu's absence, decides that it will be to their advantage to agree to meetings with Robbins. At the first meeting, Robbins secures their cooperation by agreeing to take them to a professional football practice, a prospect that captures Rufus's attention because he's read that Ernie Brown has recently joined the team.

After Rufus pulverizes Bantu in an altercation, the gang members acknowledge him as their new leader, and meetings begin taking place in his house. Rufus proposes that the Moors seek an alliance with the Aztecs and the Bloods to provide the Moors with alibis if they decide to drive the Gassers from their territory. When Rufus returns home for meetings with the other gangs, he finds that the Gassers have attacked his little sister, Janet, and cut off one of her pigtails, which they are now flying from their car aerial. Rufus is so furious that he refuses to listen to Alex Robbins's wisdom about the need to report crimes and the need to break the endless cycle of revenge.

But he does think that the Moors need to use cunning rather than guns and knives to enact a revenge that won't result in the Moors going to prison. To this end, they carefully plot their strategy, familiarizing themselves with and preparing their battleground. They stretch wire across a field to trip up the Gassers who are provoked to chase them, and they bury small dynamite buttons to go off under them. Once they trap the Gassers, they beat them up, confiscate their fancy car, and push it over a concrete embankment. When the police arrest the Moors, the Bloods provide them with an alibi, as Rufus had hoped they would do.

Alex's plan to ease gang tensions is to invite the Gassers to go on the football-practice trip with the Moors. The gang members reveal themselves to be clumsy athletes, despite their street smarts. Only Rufus gets to show off for the hero he believes to be his father. At a follow-up practice that Ernie Brown and Alex put together for the gangs, Simon Jones, the leader of the Gassers, shows up with Rufus's precious scrapbook that he has stolen from his house, and he loudly reads the inscription in which Rufus claims to be Ernie's son. Ernie gently dismisses Rufus's claim, and he and Alex break up the fight that ensues and take Rufus home. Rufus, feeling destroyed and exposed, tells Ernie to keep the scrapbook. After what appeared to be some progress in "fixing" gang violence, the incident sparks renewed gang activity as the Moors get drunk on vodka, threaten to beat up one of their own gang members, order him to steal a gun, envision sniping and bombing the Gassers's cars and houses, and plan a dance for the express purpose of luring the Gassers into a trap to be beaten again.

As the Moors become involved in and excited about the dance, they forget about attacking the Gassers and try to think of ways of excluding them so that the rival gang doesn't ruin the party. Rufus realizes the change that has come about:

> What was wrong was that this dance, which was essentially a self-destroying weapon like a hand grenade, had mysteriously come to life for him. The thought of the Moors' big plans being wrecked made him sick. A tender, protective feeling, much like his affection toward Janet and Curtis, had developed in him where the dance was concerned. (177)

The dance became a turning point. The Gassers do crash the party, start a fire, and try to start fights, but they are checked by the police. Afterward, the party continues with great success as everyone begins to dance. Three days later Rufus, the Moors, and Alex are still basking in the success of the party. Other developments mark the possibility of a positive change in Rufus's life. His mother, who had given up on him after he returned from detention camp, has begun going to meetings with Alex and other parents to discuss what can be done to help their children. And there is a distinct prospect that Rufus will return to school.

PROTECTION FOR THE PRESENT; HOPE FOR THE FUTURE

In *Durango Street,* two ideas battle against each other with no easy resolution. On one hand is the grim unavoidable reality that no boy can survive in the Flats in Coast City without the protection of a gang. On the other hand, there is the hope that boys in these neighborhoods can abandon the gang life with the help of dedicated and wise guidance from people like Alex Robbins.

Rufus and the other young boys in the Flats, all living in one-parent households, have no fathers to protect them from the violence of street life. Tough and street smart as Rufus is, his feeling of vulnerability is revealed in his frequent fantasies that Ernie Brown rises up to protect him. Not long after his parole officer has dropped him off in the neighborhood (the very name of which caused his stomach to drop in terror), Rufus takes a nap and dreams of being surrounded by 12 boys. Rufus fights desperately but is no match for the boys, who are "swinging aerials, brandishing knives" (30). In his dream, Ernie Brown appears on the scene as his protector, his savior:

> Big Ernie Brown!
>   With a backhand blow, Ernie decked four of the boys, tire irons, knives, and all! (31)

Later that evening, when in reality the gang of Gassers has him trapped alone in an alley, Rufus again imagines Ernie Brown coming to his rescue:

> Against the bricks stood an enormous man, black from head to foot and at least seven feet tall! It was like a miracle. Big Ernie had come up through the pavement to save him. Standing there, he seemed to say:
>   Like the way you handle yourself in a scrap, Rufus. (46)

But all of Ernie's saving rescues dwell solely in the realm of dream and fantasy. In reality, Rufus is alone and exposed. There is no way for a boy in the Flats to avoid a hostile—perhaps deadly—encounter with a gang. On the Greyhound bus back home from detention camp, Rufus thought:

> Mr. Rubio could harp till he was blue in the face about staying out of gangs. But every boy at Pine Valley knew that the only way to stay alive in a big-city jungle was to join a fighting gang—before some other gang decided to use you for bayonet practice. (15)

Even his little brother's decision to join the Little Warriors is for protection from other gangs. Experience confirms Rufus's view about the need to join a gang for protection when the Gassers attack him on his first evening in the Flats. Social worker Alex Robbins acknowledges this at his first formal meeting with the Moors: "That's why you all swing together—cause you're afraid to go it alone" (88).

Counter to the fatalistic view that gang membership, even gang violence, is necessary for survival is the conviction of Alex and the Group Service Council that gangs should be redirected or even "busted." Alex uses several strategies to accomplish this. He forces them to meet with him to set up a formal structure where leaders are chosen by vote rather than determined by brute force. He introduces legitimate activities into their agendas, like football training, summer camp, and dances. These serve as alternatives to shooting out store windows and fighting from sheer boredom. Alex arranges meetings so that parents can talk to one another about ways to counter gang behavior. He studies the history and situation of each boy to help with practical problems. And he hammers them with the message that violence begets more violence endlessly. At one point the Moors are convinced that Alex, to avert violence, has stolen the gun they planned to use in an attack on the Gassers.

The final paragraph, despite Rufus's cynicism, suggests that Alex has had some success in "fixing" Rufus and the Moors. But the nagging reality persists: how will Rufus and the other Moors survive attacks from other violent gangs without using violence themselves?

BIBLIOGRAPHY

Baker, Donald. *Crips: The Story of the LA Street Gang from 1971–1985*. Los Angeles: Precocious Publisher, 1987.

Bing, Leon. *Do or Die*. New York: HarperCollins Publishers, 1991.

Bonham, Frank. *Durango Street*. 1965. New York: Penguin Putnam, 1999.

Curry, Clifton. *Juvenile Crime: Outlook for California*. Sacramento: Legislative Analyst's Office, 1995.

Klein, Malcolm W. *A Structural Approach to Gang Intervention: The Lincoln Heights Project*. Los Angeles: University of California, Los Angeles Youth Center, 1966.

Mowry, Jess. *Way Past Cool*. New York: Farrar, Straus and Giroux, 1992.

Phillips, Susan. *Wallbangin': Graffiti and Gangs in Los Angeles*. Chicago: University of Chicago Press, 1959.

Sanders, William B. *Gangbangs and Drive-bys: Grounded Culture and Juvenile Gang Violence.* New York: Aldine de Gruyter, 1994.

Skolnick, Jerome H. *Gang Organization and Migration: Drugs, Gangs, and Law Enforcement.* Sacramento: State of California Department of Justice, 1990.

16

South Central Los Angeles: Kody Scott's *Monster* (1993)

FROM "IN LOS ANGELES, IT'S SOUTH-CENTRAL NO MORE."

New York Times, *10 April 2003.*

South-Central Los Angeles, the neighborhood that became infamous in recent years for riots, gang violence and poverty, is no more—at least according to the Los Angeles City Council.

The council voted unanimously today to rename this 16-square-mile district South Los Angeles as part of an effort to erase the image of South-Central as the scene of race riots in 1965 and 1992 and the setting for films featuring gangs and drug dealers like *Training Day*, *Colors*, and *Boyz 'n the Hood*. (14)

Gang violence, the bitter fruit of poverty, racial discrimination, and family collapse, literally and psychologically demolished hundreds of thousands of African American young men, innocent bystanders, and communities in the last three decades of the twentieth century. The damage inflicted by the African American gang fell not on affluent and middle-class America, not on white America, but on poor blacks, the gang members' own people. In the 1970s, violence reached horrific proportions that neither Jamal nor Randy, in *Scorpions*, would ever have been able to imagine. The most gang-infested area in the United

States came to be not Harlem or Brooklyn, but South Central Los Angeles, home of two warring gangs called the Bloods and the Crips. The notoriety of South Central became so horrendous that on April 9, 2003, the city council of Los Angeles unanimously voted to change the name of the area from "South Central" to "South Los Angeles" on all city documents, plans, correspondence, and maps—a move designed specifically to change the area's image as a gang wasteland. A further indication of the extent of gang violence in the area is the decision of the army's medical corps to use South Central Los Angeles hospitals to train medics for battle conditions in Iraq (Reported on *CBS News with Dan Rather* 12 April 2003).

Monster: The Autobiography of a Gang Member is the memoir of a man who grew up in South Central. The author, whose given name was Kody Scott and gang-given nickname, Monster, took the new name of Sanyika Shakur after his reformation and religious conversion to Islam. In the preface, Shakur explains that at 29 years old, he is writing his autobiography from prison during one of numerous periods of incarceration. For more than 22 years, he writes, a war raged in South Central, culminating in the riots there in 1992 after policemen were exonerated in the beating of a black man, Rodney King. Shakur describes a 22-year war on a battlefield with helicopters hovering overhead; the sounds of automatic weapons, sirens, and explosions; the surge of troop movements, raids, and intense fighting. The battles have decimated the area. Few buildings, including houses, have escaped being burned by fires deliberately set or being torn by ammunition from automatic weapons. Every store and house left standing is like a fortress, with barred doors and boarded-up windows. No one is safe on any street at any time where most males over the age of 11 carry guns and anyone in or out of houses are liable to be shot when gang members exchange fire on a daily basis, over territory or for revenge.

The main activities of these gangs were, before 1979, primarily robbery and extortion, but, since then, have expanded to a vast cartel involving the selling and delivery of narcotics, a "business" that brings vast sums of money to the dedicated gang members who survive the violence and imprisonment. According to Shakur, who had been a gun-carrying gang member since he was 11 years old, the deaths in this war in South Central run into the thousands, and the injured and "missing" are thousands more than that. At 29, Shakur had been shot seven times and had murdered more people than he could count.

The gang war is nominally between the two major gangs, the Bloods and the Crips, but as Shakur points out, by the 1990s, wars between different "sets" within each gang increased dramatically. These intergang wars are the everyday reality, and by the 1990s, Shakur declares, more Crips are killed by Crips than by Bloods. Every time one of the Crips catches sight of a member of a rival Crips set, he tries to kill him—on the street, in a store, in a car, in a park, in a house. Shakur explains how gang activity skyrocketed between 1980 and 1990:

> The worst enemies were Crip and Blood sets. Today, of course, Crips are the number-one killer of Crips. In fact, Crips have killed more Crips in the last twelve years than the Bloods have killed in the entire twenty-two-year conflict. And, too, sets in the Crip and Blood communities have increased twenty-fold—so that there is literally a gang on every street. Also, there are the huge conglomerate sets spanning hundreds of city blocks at a time, extending themselves into other cities and counties. It's not at all unusual for one of these huge conglomerate sets to be policed by five separate divisions of both the LAPD and the sheriff's department. (20)

Most families of young men and women in South Central are without the steady presence of a father. Mothers rule the house and often accept and even encourage gang violence. When Monster's friend Twinkie is killed by a member of another Crips set, Twinkie's mother calls all his 14-year-old friends to her house, provides them with guns, and tells them it is incumbent upon them to get revenge for his death. Shakur, at 29, looks back with regret on "the type of father mine had been to me," and concludes that "absentee fatherhood was despicable" (372).

His story begins when, at the age of 11, he drops out of school and is initiated into the Crips. His initiation, which he compares to an African tribal rite into manhood, consists of his stealing a car, getting beaten up by his new "friends" and "family," and firing eight bullets, one of which kills someone, in response to a raid on their shack by the Bloods or Brims. The "set" that he joins in the 1970s had at that time 75 to 80 members. By 1992, gang sets in South Central had over 1,000 members each.

In 1977, at the age of 13, he is given the honorific nickname "Monster" after stomping a man into a coma. Craving a reputation that includes the designation "O.G.," for Original Gangster, he kills as often and brutally as possible. At 14, he had his own weapon instead of having to use a gang-owned gun.

Most of Shakur's life is a sorry, endless repetitious cycle of murder and imprisonment. He never finishes school, never has or advances in a trade or profession, never participates in a community larger than the small world of the gang neighborhood, and never has a stable home. In short, he goes nowhere but down and is nameless and invisible to everyone except the residents of South Central.

After years of multiple murders, wars, and arrests that sent him to Juvenile Hall, Juvenile Camp, and Youth Detention, he is sent to prison repeatedly—San Quentin, Chino State Prison, and Folsom Prison. In prison, he is introduced to the philosophy of Malcolm X and the Black Muslims. This philosophy discouraged gang violence against other African American gangs and the African American community. As a consequence, Shakur takes the very hard course of cutting himself off from the Crips on one of his times outside prison.

Before he encountered Malcolm X, Shakur had never been aware of the political implications of his gang-ridden life, never seen that gang violence had ultimately been the inevitable result of poverty and discrimination. Having realized this, however, he fails to assume personal responsibility for his own past actions and remains ambivalent about violence. Malcolm X, unlike Martin Luther King, seems to have taught him to choose war above peace, separation above brotherhood—not to relinquish violence, but merely to switch targets from rival gangs to the white establishment, especially the police.

Still, the 29-year-old Shakur ends by expressing an antiviolent philosophy counter to that of Malcolm X:

> How do we come to grips with the fact that this thing has gotten way too real, out of control like some huge snowball rolling down a hill, threatening to smash and kill all in its path, including those who originally fashioned it? Time is of the essence, and every thinking person with a stake in life— especially those involved in the fighting—should put forth an effort, something more concrete than a "media truce," to deal with this tragedy. The children deserve to have a decent childhood where they live. They shouldn't have to be uprooted to the suburbs to experience peace. We cannot contaminate them with our feuds of madness, which are predicated on factors over which we have no control. (383)

In a conversation with Cheo Hodari Coker in June of 1996, Shakur spoke of the changes in his own philosophy since the publication of

Monster, insisting that one's ideology has to evolve and change, as his had done. He laughed at the man he was when he emerged from prison in 1988, declaring that he was more a militant than a true revolutionary. Unity alone is not enough to save black people, he claims; one has to have unity around the right issues, and those issues seem to Shakur to be ridding the community of criminality, drug addiction, and gang violence.

BIBLIOGRAPHY

Baker, Donald. *Crips: The Story of the LA Street Gang from 1971–1985.* Los Angeles: Precocious Publisher, 1987.

CBS News with Dan Rather. CBS. 12 April 2003.

Klein, Malcolm W., and Lois Y. Crawford. *Groups, Gangs, and Cohesiveness.* Los Angeles: University of Southern California Youth Studies Center, 1967.

Scott, Kody. *Monster: The Autobiography of a Gang Member.* New York: Atlantic Monthly Press, 1993.

17

Barrio Gangs of the 1960s and 1970s: Luis Rodriguez's *Always Running, La Vida Loca: Gang Days in L.A.* (1993)

FROM "LOS ANGELES STREET WARS GROW DEADLIER."

New York Times, *11 April 2002.*

Truces between gangs, forged and maintained over the last decade, are unraveling. New gang members carry with them only dim memories of the devastating violence that prompted the creation of the pacts in the first place.

"Unfortunately, people my age and younger, they're not worried about people killing each other," said James Scott, 21, a member of the Bounty Hunters, one of the many subsets of the Bloods. "As long as it's not them dying, they're not losing any sleep over it."

Struck by the gangs themselves to quell a surge of killings in the early 1990s, the truces range from informal cease-fires to signed treaties, some of which have lasted as long as a decade. Communities have reinforced the peace, often using government money to hire former gang members as mediators who push for dialogue when tensions flare.

But even some longstanding truces have begun experiencing strain. With an air of celebration last April, gang leaders dragged a conference table into the middle of a street in the Watts neighborhood to expand a nine-year-old treaty between Crips and Bloods. The pledge they signed condemned the "barbarous acts that have outraged the conscience of mankind." Since then, however, gang-related crimes in the area have increased more than 43 percent, according to police statistics. (18)

Always Running, a biographical account of Luis J. Rodriguez's life in the gang world of East Los Angeles in the 1960s and 1970s, has as part of its subtitle *La Vida Loca,* Spanish for "the crazy life," in reference to gang life in the barrios, or neighborhoods populated largely by Mexican Americans. Four major themes emerge from the work: the social and economic conditions that foster gangs; the devastation that Mexican Americans inflict on each other through gang violence; the counterproductive responses to the problem on the part of mainstream society in general and schools and law enforcement in particular; and the social changes that might have a chance of diminishing street-gang activity.

Rodriguez was a gang member from the time he was 11 until he was 17. By the time he exited gang life, 25 of his friends had been killed. Rodriguez began his book as an argument for social change, a "reorganization of American society—not where a few benefit at the expense of the many, but where everyone has access to decent health care, clothing, food and housing, based on need, not whether they can afford them" (10).

SOCIAL CONDITIONS THAT BREED VIOLENT GANGS: THE MEXICAN AMERICAN IN EAST LOS ANGELES

It was the cheap housing that became available in the 1920s that first attracted a rainbow array of the working poor to East Los Angeles. Among those who had begun to inhabit the area were Mexicans who, rather than living in existing housing, built their own shacks in the ravines at the foot of the hills. In the 1930s, members of non-Hispanic cultures began moving out, and the number of Mexicans moving in accelerated. East Los Angeles came to be one of those places where new immigrants settled first.

What attracted immigrants from Mexico to the United States were jobs. Mexicans typically worked in the agricultural fields, but in World War II, they were also needed as workers in the defense industry. After the war was over, they worked chiefly in aircraft and auto-assembly plants, in garment and furniture plants, in food-processing plants, and for restaurants and railroads.

Although opportunities and living conditions in general were improvements over what was offered them in Mexico, housing and services in the area were substandard compared with the rest of the United States. Before World War II, most of the many neighborhoods of East Los Angeles had no running water, no sewage, no paved streets, and no gas lines. Even up until midcentury, some of the unincorporated barrios still did not have access to these services.

In the 1970s, at the same time that East Los Angeles experienced a tremendous increase in immigration from Mexico, employment for residents of its Los Angeles barrios took a turn for the worse. While high-tech industries were moving in, bringing many new jobs to Los Angeles, this was work requiring skills that Mexican laborers did not possess. At the same time that high-tech jobs were moving in, heavy-industry jobs, including those in steel and auto assembly were folding or moving to other areas, even other countries, and out of California. The jobs that were left, many of them in restaurants, offered starvation wages.

So while the rest of the area was experiencing a boom, most of East Los Angeles's residents lived below the poverty line, in the bottom 10 percent for income in the area, in the bottom 10 percent for quality of schools. Now overwhelmingly Mexican, East Los Angeles had one of the highest levels of welfare dependence and school dropouts and one of the lowest levels of home ownership.

The surge in immigrants to the area brought other problems. Chief among them was the need to educate children who spoke no English. At the height of immigration in the 1970s, 38–45 percent of the residents of East Los Angeles spoke no English, a ratio that increased throughout the 1980s.

By the mid-1990s, East Los Angeles had one of the highest dropout rates in the nation. Schools were so poor that even those who graduated from high school had an education too inadequate for the most basic clerical jobs. Not surprisingly, the youth unemployment in the area was 75 percent.

Under such conditions, street gangs flourish. Young men with no skills and no job prospects can pick up easy money working in businesses involving drugs and prostitution. As Luis Rodriguez observes, even a boy of 10 can pick up $100 a day as a lookout for drug dealers.

Among groups of other immigrants, conditions have improved; they have moved out of slums and out of poverty, and gangs among their youth are no longer a problem. But areas settled by Mexican American immigrants seem stuck in poverty. New immigrants continually arrive to East Los Angeles, so the cycle of adjustment and finding work in a foreign land is always beginning anew. But even those who immigrated decades ago experience continual difficulty in finding a livable wage and continual difficulty in being able to move into mainstream America. This also means that these neighborhoods continue to be plagued by gangs.

The forerunners of the present East Los Angeles Chicano gangs can be found among the Mexican settlers there in the 1920s. For two decades, these groups of young men were regarded by the community as just neighborhood, barrio boys, not as criminal gangs. They included the *pachucos*, or zoot-suiters, and groups that focused on athletics, usually arising out of the church. The activities of these barrio groups, while rarely criminal, were not exempt from violence, for their chief activity was fighting other barrio boys with their fists at parties and dances.

The 1940s brought a tragedy involving Chicano gangs in the Los Angeles area. This decade also brought profound changes in the character of East Los Angeles gangs and their relationships with law enforcement. After a single Chicano youth was killed in 1940, hysteria seemed to seize the police, the press, and the public with regard to gangs. Twenty-two barrio boys were arrested, each on the charge of conspiracy to commit murder. Seventeen were convicted—12 of murder and the rest on other charges. Panic reigned as police dragnets brought in over 600 Chicanos, and as groups of Anglo service men, new to the area, began a rampage attack on anyone they could find in the area wearing a zoot suit, gang member or not. As cooler heads examined the situation afterward, the public began to see the lack of wisdom and racial discrimination in the riots. In 1944, all the convictions of barrio boys were overturned.

Whether directly related to the Zoot Suit Riot or not, what had been groups of barrio boys, at the worst fighting with each other at parties, now became organized gangs. Heroin use was introduced to the young men of the East Los Angeles barrios in the late 1940s. Along with drugs, the use of guns and violence escalated throughout the 1950s and 1960s.

In the 1970s, violence took a horrific and impersonal turn as gangs introduced drive-by killings. In that decade, gang killings constituted 16 percent of all Hispanic homicides, as compared with 7 percent for other groups. In 1991, East Los Angeles was the home to 800 gangs and 100,000 gang members. In that year alone, 600 gang members had been killed.

By 1990, South Central and much of East Los Angeles looked like Middle Eastern battlefields: helicopters flew overhead, shining infrared lights, and armored vehicles crawled through the streets. These neighborhoods were under martial law.

While gangs certainly constituted a problem, police handling of gangs only worsened matters. In the 1980s, police turned to their own impersonal strategy after what was suspected to be a gang-related murder in an affluent white neighborhood. Their policy was to do a broad sweep through South Central Los Angeles and East Los Angeles, arresting every young male they found. By 1988, there had been 563 arrests. The *Los Angeles Daily News* reported that up to October of 1991, 57 people had been shot that year by police, all of them unarmed or shot in the back. Eighty percent of those were people of color.

THE DESCENT AND REBIRTH OF LUIS RODRIGUEZ

The preface to *Always Running* introduces the reader to the grim perpetuation of gang life. Luis Rodriguez begins to write the memoir of his own gang captivity in Los Angeles at a time when his 15-year-old son, Ramiro, continues his involvement in Chicago with gangs he had joined in East Los Angeles. As Rodriguez writes the book, his son is getting expelled from more than one school for being in the middle of gang fights between the Insanes and the Maniacs, two warring groups of the Folks. Father and son have fought over Ramiro's gang activities; Ramiro has lived in the streets for several weeks, ending up in a shack where his father finds him, and has spent two months in a psychiatric institution. Ramiro's tribulations are the more immediate reasons why Rodriguez takes up the project of writing the story of his own life in East Los Angeles.

His life in the United States begins when he is 2 years old, after his highly educated father's repeated failures in Mexico. After a brief residence in the Spanish section of Watts on the outskirts of Los Angeles, the family ends up in a section of East Los Angeles called South San Gabriel. It was an area made up of many rival neighborhoods or barrios located in the flatlands and hills. The most prominent barrios in Rodriguez's story include Las Lomas and Sangra. At 10 years old, he witnesses the first death of a friend when the two boys climb over a fence to play basketball in a school yard. Two sheriffs' deputies begin chasing them, and Tino, Luis's friend, falls through a skylight to his death.

Luis's gang activity begins innocently enough when he is 11 and forms a club with four other friends his age as a means of protection against other clubs. He is soon attracted to a gang of older boys called the Mystics, whose members ride up in low-slung cars one day to terrorize the school by brandishing chains, bats, and metal pipes, firing .22 rifles, throwing rocks through school windows, and beating up some kids who get caught in the middle. Garvey Junior High School, with a 50 percent dropout rate, is the turning point for Luis, whose gang activity, like that of most boys, increases significantly at this age. He joins other students in intimidating his teachers, making instruction impossible, and causing disharmony in his household. Part of gang life even at this young age is drinking and smoking dope.

By 13, he and his friends graduate to an older, more deadly gang called the Animal Tribe and are embroiled in a gang war between gangs in the Sangra and the Los Lomas barrios that will last for decades. Gang involvement turns risky when Luis and his friends become involved with an older gang member who has already spent considerable time in juvenile hall. Yuk Yuk, as he is called, introduces them to what Luis describes as "organized stealing" (73). Earlier, he and his friends had shoplifted or randomly stolen fast food. Under the tutelage of Zuk Zuk, they break into homes to steal anything that isn't nailed down and use guns to rob truckers and store owners.

Luis's gang activities, which now include taking pills and sniffing aerosol cans, cause his mother to exile him to the unheated garage without plumbing. He does little better at school, where his gang provokes an all-out war with the Anglos and Asians who are his schoolmates. He is pursued by a jeep of boys with bats outside school, and in-school fighting continues for several weeks, with police arriving in a futile attempt to keep order and ambulances pulling up to take away the wounded. Finally, to his great satisfaction, because he hates school and loves fighting, Luis is expelled.

Luis is initiated into the newly organized Lomas gang that had taken over from the Animal Tribe and is recruiting new members. At a party, he is "jumped in," beaten and kicked for several minutes. Later in the evening, as another part of his initiation, he must stab a man with a screwdriver. Not long after, at the age of 15, he is introduced to heroin.

Luis remains a staunch member of Las Lomas until he is 18 years old, but he felt, he writes, that "the violence was eating us alive" (113). He observes many things and participates in many things that frighten, disgust, and disillusion him: his gang's firebombing of a house, his sister's being targeted by rival gang girls, the high incidence of rapes of girls as young as 12, and the collapse of all codes, rules, and honor.

In 1970, when Luis is still in his midteens, several events and circumstances begin to introduce the seeds of change that will eventually undermine the power of gangs in Luis's violent, drugged-out life. His parents persuade him to return to high school for a brief time. It is far from being a satisfactory experience, and he drops out during a teachers' strike. During his time there, however, he discovers the library and literature written by and about people like himself—poetry by Amiri Baraka, Claude Brown's *Manchild in the Promised Land,* and, especially, Piri Thomas's book about Spanish Harlem, *Down These Mean Streets.* From this point on, he becomes a voracious reader of a wide range of literature.

At about 15, he is also introduced to community groups working to fight against gang violence, to stem the tide of deaths and terror. The community center also opens to him the world of politics and social action on behalf of the poor and gives him the incentive to recapture the Latin heritage of art and music. A young social worker named Chente, seeing promise in Luis, offers him a job working for the community center, on the condition that he return to school. From this point on, Luis becomes less involved in drugs and gang activities. He begins to train as a boxer. He attends a study group to discuss politics, philosophy, and economics.

The high school, with its new principal, also makes positive changes in Luis's life. The principal is determined to make improvements in the lives of the Chicano students, who make up 40 percent of the student body. These students are encouraged to form a club that meets once a week to address their particular problems. They have a Chicano Student Center and two sympathetic adult staff members, bringing Mexican students into the activities of the school. Not long before graduation, however, several matters set Luis against Mr. Madison, the principal: one of their sponsors, Mr. Perez, is fired, and an Anglo history teacher gets by with calling a Mexican student a whore in class. Only after intense student agitation, led by Luis, is Mr. Perez hired back and the history professor forced into early retirement. But by the time of Luis's graduation, the confrontations and shutdowns he has inspired have embittered the principal.

The third event in 1970 was the "largest anti-war rally ever held in a minority community" (Rodriguez 160)—a demonstration held in East Los Angeles against the Vietnam War. Luis sees it as more than an antiwar rally; it is a rally against violence—an expression of community outrage, an organized demonstration for social change. After the rally, gang violence abated.

With all the positive reinforcement, at 17 Luis is still deeply involved with gangs. In retaliation for an attack on a member of his gang, he joins others in hunting down a group of bikers and shooting one of them in the backside with a Ruger Long .22 semiautomatic rifle with a scope. He escapes an attempted murder charge after his friends at the community center get him out of jail because the bikers refuse to identify him. When he intervenes to stop a cop from beating a woman, he is arrested and has to serve a few months in the county jail.

When he gets out, it is as if he has made little progress in shaking the gang life, but his mentor Chente, urging him to leave East Los Angeles, tries to impress on Luis the smallness of the gang member's world. On the map of the world, he tells Luis, "Lomas is so tiny, nameless, it doesn't even warrant a dot" (236). And all the killing is for nothing. But Luis is convinced he can and should help his brothers, the homeboys, stop the cycle of violence. Just after he experiences some encouragement when some of the gang members follow him in refusing to inhale angel dust, a frightening experience devastates him: a car full of his gang brothers drives up to shoot at him.

> The homeboys tried to kill me, *vatos* whom I had known as brothers, with whom I scurried down muddy streets and slept next to in jail, with whom I partied and hung out in front of courthouses and the fields; they were dudes I fought for. (238)

The experience opens his eyes to the futility of trying to "save" his gang brothers. He speaks of it as a time of "conscious rebirth" (238).

He must immediately go underground to escape from the gang with his life. When he emerges, he lives in other, far-removed Los Angeles neighborhoods for a few years before moving to Chicago. Twenty years later, still actively working to reach street-gang members and help stop the cycle of violence, he nevertheless finds little hope in the barrios of urban America.

COMMUNITY BLINDNESS AND SELF-DESTRUCTION

From his own experiences as a gang member in the barrio, Rodriguez isolates several issues necessary to understand and combat violent gangs. First, in looking back on his own experiences, he emphasizes the self-destructiveness of the Mexican American community as members of rival Chicano gangs kill one another. Second, he stresses the failure of society in general and of schools and law enforcement in particular to respond wisely to the population out of which gangs arise. Finally, he discusses the social changes that he thinks might serve the Chicano community and diminish street-gang violence.

The tragedy of barrio gangs that unfolds in Rodriguez's story is that they are their own worst enemies. It is the gangs themselves that inflict the worst damage on the Chicano community, especially on its young people. An occurrence on the night that Luis is "jumped into" the Las Lomas gang is representative of the community's self-destruction. High on drugs, alcohol, and gang pride, the Las Lomas boys jump in a truck to drive into a rival gang neighborhood, where they surround a car of young strangers. Luis thinks they look like nice fellows, "like hard-working recreational lowriders out for a spin" (110). They respond to the Las Lomas gang members that they don't want any trouble. But Las Lomas attacks them, destroying the car, beating them with tire irons and two-by-fours, and stabbing the driver with a screw driver.

Another instance that unsettles Rodriguez is the firebombing of a house. In retaliation for an attack by Chava, a rival gang leader, a group of Las Lomas gang members throw firebombs into his mother's house, putting all his family members—parents and children—in jeopardy. They plan this attack, knowing full well that Chava probably will not be there. Chava is later ambushed and permanently maimed.

There is also gang destruction of the neighborhoods where they live—the trashing of community centers, schools, and streets.

Finally, Rodriguez shows his readers that gang members not only kill Mexican Americans in rival gangs, but they kill members of their own gangs, a truth that is brought home to Luis when he is shot at by his own friends.

Structures maintained by the dominant Anglo society worsen the lives of the Chicano poor and contribute to the rise of street violence. Schools are discriminatory and particularly unresponsive to the poor. Luis is frustrated by the schools' insistence on rigidly maintaining two academic tracks: one for upper- and middle-class Anglos and Asians, and one for the poor, including all Mexicans. In his junior-high years, he and other Mexicans are automatically restricted to vocational courses and barred from courses in history and literature, even when they plead to be allowed into academic courses.

Schools also make little effort to include Mexican Americans in the social and athletic life of their institutions, even when, as in some East Los Angeles neighborhoods, they make up half of the student body.

The schools' insensitivity exacerbates tension and misunderstanding between students of different cultures. These practices not only restrict Luis, they label him. In junior high school, he feels that he keeps trying to escape the label, but that the school keeps applying it.

Always Running is also an indictment of police brutality, especially within the Chicano neighborhoods of Los Angeles. The police, even Chicano police, are hostile toward all Mexican American boys. One tells Luis that their plan is to just bring in as many boys as they can, charging them with loitering, if nothing else. "In the barrio," he writes, "the police are just another gang" (72). One aim of the police is to keep Mexican Americans from intruding into Anglo territory. When a group of young teenagers dares to go on an outing at a public beach usually frequented only by Anglos, they are rounded up by beach police and taken to jail, where they must be retrieved by their parents. Another police tactic is to encourage ill feeling between rival gangs. In Chicago, police round up members of one gang and take them to the territory of a rival gang where they are made to paint over local graffiti. Then they are abandoned, being placed at the mercy of their rivals. In East Los Angeles, Luis is convinced that police stage an attack on two Las Lomas gang members, making it appear that the attack was by their rivals, the Sangras.

The brutality of law-enforcement officers is an everyday occurrence. A sheriff's deputy called Cowboy is typical. He is notorious for beating prisoners. Another law-enforcement officer, Fred Coates, guns down Luis's unarmed friend in his own house while hunting someone else. A jury finds Coates innocent.

Despite a brutal system of law enforcement, Rodriguez sees many people working for a variety of reforms designed to lessen self-destructive gang violence. Community centers were the best hope for East Los Angeles. The centers themselves provided places for teenagers to hang out and often gave them work for which they were paid and causes for which they could volunteer. They ran welfare and drop-out programs and food co-ops. They sponsored athletic activities for the neighborhood youth. The personnel of the centers involved themselves in barrio affairs, even going to houses to defuse domestic conflicts.

Community centers educated local people about the fundamental causes of their poverty and tried to engage young people in politics to empower the community. With the encouragement of these activists, Chicano student associations were formed that provided some young people with more-positive alternatives to street gangs.

Art centers, mural programs, Latin musical groups, and Chicano magazines served to rechannel energy into productive, creative endeavors, and to build confidence and cultural pride.

Luis is at the center of a movement to improve schools for Mexican American students in East Los Angeles. With the encouragement of a progressive principal, the students join forces to improve the physical condition of the school and to involve Chicano students in the extracurricular activities and governance of the school. They present a petition for a class in Chicano studies taught by a Chicano teacher. Most impressive of all, they meet with students at other schools to discuss ways of ending gang warfare in the barrios.

The discouragement is that most of these programs depend on local, state, and federal funding, which is rarely forthcoming. As a result, as Luis returns to East Los Angeles a few years later, he finds the community centers closed and taken over by street and prison gangs, some of them now hiding places for users of PCP or angel dust, which has become the scourge of the barrios. All but a few murals have been destroyed.

Rodriguez concludes in his epilogue that in his experience, gangs arise as alternatives to decent recreation, decent education, and jobs with living wages. He is confident that few young men would choose the way of death offered by gangs if they had better choices.

On the subject of family and gangs, an issue that has arisen so frequently in discussions of African American gangs, Rodriguez has this to say:

> But "family" is a farce among the property-less and disenfranchised. Too many families are wrenched apart, as even children are forced to supplement meager incomes. Family can only really exist among those who can afford one. In an increasing number of homeless, poor, and working poor families, the things that people must do to survive undermines most family structures. (250)

BIBLIOGRAPHY

Mazon, Mauricio. *The Zoot Suit Riots: The Psychology of Symbolic Annihilation*. Austin: University of Texas Press, 1965.

Moore, Joan W. *Going Down the Barrio*. Philadelphia: Temple University Press, 1991.

————. *Homeboys: Gangs, Drugs, and Prison in the Barrios of L.A.* Philadelphia: Temple University Press, 1978.

Rodriguez, Luis. *Always Running, La Vida Loca: Gang Days in L.A.* 1993. New York: Touchtone Press, 1994.

Romo, Ricardo. *East Los Angeles: History of a Barrio.* Austin: University of Texas Press, 1983.

Sweeney, Terrence. *Streets of Anger, Streets of Hope: Youth Gangs in East Los Angeles.* Glendale, CA: Great Western Publishing, 1980.

Virgil, Diego. *Barrio Gangs.* Austin: University of Texas Press, 1988.

18

Filipino Americans: Brian Ascalon Roley's *American Son* (2001)

FROM BOB HERBERT, "L.A.'S STREETS OF DEATH."

New York Times, *12 June 2003*.

I don't know which is more bizarre, the agonizing extremes of violence, much of it gang-related, in places like South and East L.A., or the passive acceptance of this enormous tragedy by so many people inside and outside the blood-drenched neighborhoods, who view it as simply "the way things are." Last year Los Angeles led the nation in homicides, and it is estimated that over the past 20 years some 10,000 young people have been killed. (33)

Brian Ascalon Roley's novel *American Son,* about a Filipino American family, is a study in the social and moral descent of two brothers, Tomas and Gabe, under the influence of gang values in Los Angeles in the 1990s. In this setting, the star-studded lives of those living in affluence stand in glaring contrast to the lives of those marginalized by poverty and discrimination. Ironically, it is a sense of responsibility and protectiveness toward his mother that has drawn the older brother, Tomas, into crime. The gangster life provides him with the money necessary for his mother's decent material existence. It also gives him a dubious kind of self-worth.

Tomas's 15-year-old brother Gabe, who tells the story, hates the violence and crime that are destroying his brother, and Gabe strenuously and futilely resists being pulled into the same life. Despite all Gabe's efforts, he cannot prevail against Tomas's determination to drag him into his own violent world.

THE FILIPINO DIASPORA

Tomas and Gabe's mother had left the Philippines with her American husband when her boys were barely school-age. Although she and the boys are thoroughly Americanized, her ties to the Philippines are strong and, throughout Gabe's story of his family in the summer and fall of 1993, the prospect of returning to the Philippines raises a constant threat. At the end of the story, their mother has finally agreed with her brother's demands that the boys return to the place of her birth, even though there is little prospect that she can actually force them to leave.

The economic problems and political chaos that continue even into the twenty-first century to plague the Philippines have contributed to the wholesale immigration of families to the United States. The real beginning of Filipino immigration came in 1898, after the Spanish American War, with United States annexation of the Philippines.

The first great surge of Filipino workers occurred between 1900 and 1935, when males without their families came to work in the agricultural fields. But anti-Asian sentiment and intense competition for low-wage jobs in the United States led to discriminatory practices. For example, Filipinos and Chinese were barred from union membership.

After World War II, the Philippines lay in literal and economic shambles. Added to this was the constant, violent internal conflict. Rebels challenged exclusive ownership of land by the privileged few in the Philippines, calling instead for collectivism and the end of tenant farming. Finally in 1955, land was more equitably redistributed to lessen the size of huge tracts of land and provide acreage to landless farmers. But economic hardship, rampant crime, absolute dictatorship, and widespread and violent rebellion continued, making life in the Philippines not only difficult, but dangerous. Adding to the problems of poverty and rebellion was corruption at the highest levels. Corruption was generated on one level by the smuggling, chiefly of cigarettes, from the Chinese underworld through the Philippines. Elpidio Quirino, who became president of the Philippines in 1948 had an alliance with Chinese triads involved in smuggling. And the dictator who followed him, Ferdinand Marcos, who was forced to flee after draining the country of billions of dollars, worked closely with the Chinese triads, who plied the smuggling trade from 1945 until the mid-1970s. Martin Booth, in *The Dragon Syndicates,* writes of his belief that even well into the twenty-first century, the Philippine government is buttressed by its Chinese population with links to criminal triads (253).

A new wave of Filipino immigration to the United States began in 1970 as conditions in the Philippines worsened and the U.S. economy required many more lower-level laborers. In the 1980s, Filipinos and South Koreans constituted the greatest numbers of Asian immigrants.

When Gabe's family goes back to the Philippines for a visit in the late 1980s, the poverty and filth they find there remind his mother of why she never wants to return to live there. Manila, she says, smells like cockroaches. And, though her brother in his letters continually boasts of his own privileged situation in the Philippines, he grudgingly admits that serious problems continue for most of the Philippine population. The country, he writes, is "overrun by communists, and San Pablo more crowded and dirty than we ever knew it to be" (134). His recommendation that she will find life improved contains an alarming suggestion: "And though Manila has more traffic and people than ever, armed guards keep the poor people and crime out" (134). His letters make reference to the reasons for the emigration of so many Filipinos—"austerity and dependency" and "unpleasant memories." "Indeed," he writes, "our country must have seemed a sad and unpromising place to raise children then, and for most Filipinos it is even worse now, but my circumstances have improved" (135). He admits further that "the problems of kidnapping are greatly exaggerated, mostly confined to Chinese Filipinos, and though the crime is great in Manila generally, here in Forbes Park we are very secluded" (58).

Typically, many Manila women work as maids in the United States. After the desertion by her husband, Tomas and Gabe's mother, even with the support of her wealthier relatives, works hard at two low-wage jobs to maintain a bleak existence on the outskirts of Los Angeles, where poverty and discrimination are breeding places for the most prolific and powerful gangs in the United States.

THE DEGENERATION OF TOMAS AND GABE

Fifteen-year-old Gabe's family consists of his 17-year-old brother, Tomas; his mother, who has been abandoned by her Caucasian husband; and his mother's well-to-do relatives—her brother, Betino, still living in the Philippines; her sister-in-law Jessica, who pays for Gabe's Catholic schooling; his mother's sister, Tita; Tita's daughter Dina; and her son Matt, Gabe's Harvard-educated cousin. Other significant characters in the novel include the celebrities to whom Tomas sells the attack dogs he trains; the people who take Gabe under wing when he runs away from home (especially Stone, the tow-truck operator); Father Ryan, who is principal of Gabe's school; the "yoga mom" who harasses their mother and her son Ben; and Eddy Ho, a man whose car the boys break into.

The story that Gabe tells about his family is introduced by and interspersed with four letters, written to his mother by her brother, Betino, from the Philippines. The consistent theme of each letter is Betino's concern for Tomas and Gabe, his two nephews, who, Betino is convinced from his sister's reports, are being corrupted in California and need the rigid discipline of a Catholic schooling in the Philippines: "I suggested to you then that he come to live in the Philippines with me where I could send him to a true Catholic school, one with discipline and supervision, not as those permissive ones which you will find in America" (57).

These letters reflect the downward spiral of Tomas and Gabe's lives as Uncle Betino at first urges his sister to return both boys to the Philippines and later decides that Tomas, and perhaps even Gabe, are beyond redemption.

The letters also keep in the forefront the family's connection to the Philippines, keeping alive the family's constant transitional state. Though the family has permanently left the Philippines when Gabe was a small boy, and visits back to the Philippines convince them that they don't want to return, Uncle Betino's letters continually hold out the threat of a forcible return. Moreover, their mother is Filipino by birth, upbringing, tradition, and appearance. While the family wants to be thoroughly Americanized, they know that whites like their father and the tow-truck operator do not regard them as Americans, but as foreign interlopers.

Just as the family is suspended between two countries, the family members shift uneasily between several ethnicities, not completely identifying with any single one, and somewhat uncomfortable, even antagonistic toward all. The boys are half white, but have no personal or cultural connection with their white father or his family and history. Gabe uneasily pretends to be white in the company of the tow-truck operator, and Tomas's Filipino relatives urge him to accentuate his whiteness, something he refuses to do. Even as Filipinos, they partake uneasily of several competing cultures—Spanish, Malay, Indian, and Asian. Yet Tomas and Gabe are not considered either Spanish or Asian. Tomas distances himself from Spanish people and has little understanding of Spanish language. He also fights with Asian boys his age.

> If anyone tried calling him an Asian he beat them up, and he started taunting these Korean kids who could barely speak English....Each time my brother taunted a Korean kid Father Ryan would call our mother in to pick Tomas up....Finally Tomas got kicked out of school for smashing a Japanese boy's car window with a tire iron. (30)

Much to his extended family's disgust, Tomas has constructed his own identity by embracing Mexican friends and Mexican ways, at the same time necessarily associating himself with a Mexican gang. His uncle, in the first letter in the novel, deplores the time Tomas is spending with Mexicans. Taking his personal style from his gangster buddies, he drives a "Mexican" car—"the type Mexican gangsters prefer" (30).

So the boys' identities are constantly being destabilized. This is shown not only by the ambiguities of ethnicity, but by the absence of their father, who makes one last abusive return home and is humiliated and booted out by Tomas. In this moment, Tomas becomes the undisputed male head of the family. He is the provider—but through thievery and deception. He is the family protector—but through violence and cruelty. And he is his younger brother's male guide—coercing him into crime.

Because the story is told by his younger brother, Gabe, who is not a gang member, Tomas's gang in *American Son* is not portrayed as having an immediate presence as gangs have in other gang novels. For example, Tomas's friends in the gang make few appearances, and organized gang activities remain in the remote background. Nevertheless, Tomas's gang involvement is richly implied. By his tattoos, he broadcasts that he is a member of the 18th Street gang. And Uncle Betino's coy reference to Tomas's association with "poor Mexican children" (12) overlooks the fact that they are members of barrio gangs in areas around Los Angeles. The family lives in Santa Monica, an area settled by Mexican workers for the streetcar lines, and while the main village of Santa Monica was transformed from fields to wealthy suburbs, South Santa Monica continued to be a barrio of poor Mexicans. Tomas has adopted the gang appearance, the badge of the Mexican gang. He keeps his head shaved and is extensively tattooed.

The tattoo on the back of my brother's neck—a black rose whose stem is wrapped by vinelike barbed wire—emerges from beneath his stretched T-shirt collar. . . . The tattoos are mostly gang, Spanish, and old-lady Catholic. As he leans forward, the thin fabric of his shirt moves over his Virgin of Guadeloupe tattoo that covers his back from his neck down to his pants. She wears a black robe and has deep, olive eyes. Crushed beneath her feet are the Devil's horns. (17)

The gang presence in Tomas's life is also suggested by his activities, chief among which is the training of attack dogs, a trade prominent among gangs who provide dogs for drug dealers and for the illegal blood sport of animal fighting. In 2000, for instance, a prison gang in California was found to be running a ring, in the business of training dogs to fight each other, from prison. Tomas runs what appears to be a legal business of training dogs to guard the homes of the rich and famous. He skirts the law only in passing off local Americanized dogs he buys from slum dwellers as expensive German breeds.

By the end of the novel, Tomas's criminal activity, involving stolen goods and break-ins, has expanded and intensified. The living room is piled high with stolen stereos he is fencing, and much of the house furniture, even the bathroom lavatory, has been stolen in break-ins.

The only glimpse the reader is afforded of Tomas's acquaintances comes when he takes Gabe to some gatherings enhanced by drug use. Here, Gabe hears stories of how his brother and his brother's friends took the opportunity of the Los Angeles riots to set a house on fire and engage in wholesale looting.

The story that Gabe tells begins in April of 1993 in South Santa Monica where the family lives. As Tomas teaches a client to handle an attack dog he has trained and later, after they deliver an attack dog to another client at his palatial mansion, Gabe reveals how cruel Tomas is to him and how terrified he is of the brother who was once his friend. Tomas is both psychologically and physically abusive. On leaving the mansion, Tomas knuckles Gabe in the mouth, hits him in the stomach with his fist, and grinds his shoe into Gabe's face after he has knocked him down.

The second part of Gabe's story occurs three months later when, in a desperate attempt to escape his brother and the home life his brother has created, Gabe steals Tomas's car and his favorite dog, Buster. He sells Buster for several thousand dollars cash and heads north toward Oregon. On the way, he encounters a more rural, homogenized world than he has known. Strangers are instinctively friendly to the small teenager. Stone, a tow-truck operator who takes him to Oregon, insists on taking him under wing, buying him lunch, and finding him a motel. During the ride, Stone obsessively talks to Gabe of his hatred of the Mexican and Asian immigrants who have settled southern California, making it unfit to live in. Gabe finds himself openly joining in the bashing of people very like himself. But Gabe's game will soon be up, for Stone has solicitously summoned Gabe's mother to come to get him. At first, Gabe whispers to Stone that this dark-skinned woman is his maid, but Stone learns the truth and tells Gabe's mother what Gabe has said about her. Relations between Gabe and his mother are never the same after that.

In part 3, entitled "A Dirty Penance," Tomas has forced Gabe to take part in his thefts and break-ins to make up for the theft of the dog. On one caper, Tomas makes Gabe break into a man's van to steal his drugs.

Their mother shoulders the heavy burden of Gabe's being ashamed of her and of Tomas's humiliating her at a family gathering with his rude, drugged-out behavior. She is also daily humiliated by the Caucasian population. A rich suburban mother chews her out in front of the school on two occasions for bumping her car and then repeatedly harasses her over the phone. At a shopping mall, a saleswoman chatters to a friend, ignoring Gabe's mother who is waiting to be served. Her desperation over the boys has led her finally to agree to send them to her brother in the Philippines.

Shortly after Gabe discovers this latest letter from his uncle in his mother's drawer, Tomas forces the protesting Gabe to come with him on another caper. This time, as it turns out, they go to the house of the woman who has been harassing their mother for an exorbitant amount of money to fix a tiny scratch on her bumper. They grab the woman's son Ben, a decent boy whom Gabe knows, and they beat him savagely, telling him that if he ever tells anyone, they will do the same thing and worse to his mother.

This last episode in the novel is a telling culmination, revealing the depths to which Tomas has sunk, and the depths to which Tomas has dragged Gabe. Gabe is horrified that "in a scary way I realize I like" attacking Ben (215).

IRONY

The issues in the novel are fraught with irony. At the forefront is the conundrum of race and ethnicity wherein the Filipinos, who meet with discrimination in a white society, despise the Asians and Mexicans because of their race and poverty. Tomas turns his back on his Filipino heritage and his white heritage by identifying with a gang of Mexican Americans, whom his own people despise. And Gabe tries to escape his life as a Filipino by running away in the car and agreeing with Stone's excoriation of immigrants of color in southern California, hoping that Stone can't detect his ethnicity in his dark skin and narrow eyes.

> Suddenly I notice my reflection in the mirrored glass and it appears so obviously Asian I almost stop in my tracks. My eyes look narrow, and my hair straight and coarse and black....I might even look Mexican, but not white. (90)

To make the picture more puzzling, Tomas, who has adopted a Mexican persona, is contemptuous of and rude to his client's Mexican wife, thinking she is his maid.

Behind Tomas's and Gabe's assumptions and pretenses are class and ethnic shame and the overwhelming longing for respect. Their mother, who is constantly demeaned, and regarded and treated as little more than an animal, still holds out some expectation of earning the respect of her relatives. Tomas's blatant gangster behavior—showing up at a family party stoned and pulling out his gun—destroys what little respect she can hope for from her own well-to-do family.

While Gabe seeks respect through deception about who he is, Tomas seeks respect through the physical intimidation of a gangster. Tomas has always declared he would attack anyone who was not respectful of his mother, and now, after the "yoga mom" mortifies and terrorizes her, he enlists Gabe's help in doing what he has always vowed he'd do. Tomas, ignoring his own part in humiliating his mother at the relative's party, takes Gabe to get gang-like revenge on the woman who has shown disrespect to her.

There is further irony in Tomas's youthful assumption of the role of family protector. His father is an abusive drunk who leaves the family to fend for itself. When, on his last return to the family, the father threatens to hit their mother, it is Tomas who protects her. And it is Tomas who takes on the responsibility of seeing that the family has enough money to augment his mother's meager salary. Yet he is irresponsible in his role as family head. He fulfills what he sees as his duty through criminal, gang behavior—pushing his little brother, against his will, toward gang involvement; putting his little brother in danger;

and setting up their house and Gabe for a drive-by attack from Ho and his friends.

There is also the typical ironic gang equation, in Tomas's mind, between manhood and gang violence. He taunts Gabe for his "womanly" cowardice when Gabe resists participating in the break-ins and thievery. Only after Gabe is forced to break the window of Ho's van, is almost knifed, and then crawls over Ho's mangled body to steal a stash of drugs does Tomas think he is man enough to no longer deserve taunts and man enough to meet Tomas's friends. And only when Gabe has joined him in bashing in Ben's head does Tomas give him a fatherly pat. In a twisted way, this brutality has finally appeased Tomas and brought the two brothers closer. Only by having his self-respect, his peace of mind, and his sense of decency taken away and replaced with emptiness and sorrow can Gabe make peace with his brother.

BIBLIOGRAPHY

Asis, Maruja Milagros B. *To the United States and into the Labor Force: Occupational Expectations of Filipino and Korean Immigrant Women*. Honolulu: East-West Center, 1991.

Battistella, Graziano, and Anthony Paganoni, eds. *Philippine Labor Migration: Impact and Policy*. Quezon City, Philippines: Scalabrini Migration Center, 1992.

Booth, Martin. *The Dragon Syndicates: The Global Phenomenon of the Triads*. New York: Carroll and Graf Publishers, 1999.

Moore, Joan W. *Homeboys: Gangs, Drugs, and Prison in the Barrios of Los Angeles*. Philadelphia: Temple University Press, 1978.

Roley, Brian Ascalon. *American Son*. New York: W.W. Norton, 2001.

San Juan, Epifanio. *From Exile to Diaspora: Versions of the Filipino Experience in the United States*. Boulder, CO: Westview Press, 1998.

Scharlin, Craig. *Philip Vera Cruz: A Personal History of Filipino Immigration and the Farmworkers Movement*. Los Angeles: UCLA Labor Center, 1992.

19

Vietnamese Gangs and Skinheads: Sherry Garland's *Shadow of the Dragon* (1993)

FROM KEVIN FAGAN, STEPHEN SCHWARTZ, AND J. L. PIMSLEUR, "SEVEN HURT IN CHINATOWN SHOOTING. POLICE BLAME GANG DISPUTE OVER FIREWORKS."

San Francisco Chronicle, *1 July 1995*.

Seven people were shot, including a pregnant woman and her mother, when gang rivalry over sales of illegal fireworks in San Francisco's Chinatown erupted in violence last night, police said.

The two women, whose wounds were not life-threatening, appear to have been innocent bystanders in the shooting that began when one group of gang members caught sight of another gang on opposite corners of Stockton and Clay streets shortly before 6 p.m. on the eve of the July Fourth holiday weekend, according to police.

Only one group appeared to have been armed and opened fire on the others as the second group tried to run away, said Commander Dennis Martel. When the shooting stopped at 5:52 p.m. seven wounded people lay on the sidewalk or street, drilled with bullets that appeared to be from 9mm. 45-caliber and 223-caliber weapons as well as a shotgun.

"There were gunshot wounds on virtually every part of their bodies," said Philip Harvey, a captain in the paramedic division of the San Francisco Department of Public Health. "We have no idea how many shots were fired. There were too many."

. . .

"When I got there... people were lying all over the street, groaning and crying for help," he said. "There was blood all over them and some people weren't moving. One woman lay there and screamed and screamed." The 32-year-old pregnant woman was shot in the back and left foot. She and her 51-year-old mother, who was shot in the left side and the right arm, were in stable condition at San Francisco General Hospital. (A1)

. . .

According to Deputy Chief Diarmuid Philpott and Central Station Commander John Willett, the shooting grew out of a battle between the Jackson Street Boys and a Tenderloin gang over lucrative sales of illegal fireworks in Chinatown.

Willett said the Jackson Street Boys is an ethnic Chinese group and the other group is made up of people of Chinese and Vietnamese descent. Neither Willett nor Philpott nor other investigators would say which gang is suspected of opening fire last night.

On Wednesday, there had been a shooting and knifing in the same area over the same problem, investigators said, adding that the shooting last night may have been revenge for the earlier incident. (A15)

As we have seen in African American communities, the nature of the family has a direct impact on the rise of violent street gangs and the ability of individual boys to renounce gangs. Such is also the case in the Vietnamese community portrayed in Sherry Garland's novel, *Shadow of the Dragon,* where tradition and a strong family buttress Danny Vo, the young hero of the story. Danny's family has to be strong to overcome a crippling national history and to survive attacks by a Vietnamese gang (to which Danny's newly arrived cousin, Sang Le, is attracted), as well as a gang of skinheads. The clear issues in the novel are: the impact of the Vietnam War and the hardships of immigrants on the rise of gangs; the damage that the Vietnamese gang inflicts on the Vietnamese community; and the gangs' need for revenge, which creates an endless cycle of violence.

A VIOLENT PAST IN VIETNAM

The Vietnam War is the formative event in the story of the immigrant family, the Vietnamese gangs, and the skinheads in the novel.

The war had erupted as a struggle between the Communist-held North Vietnam and an unpopular military dictatorship in the South. The direct American military involvement in what was, in essence, a civil war lasted a decade. The magnitude of the war can be suggested by numbers alone. Fifty-eight thousand Americans died in an unpopular war fought far from home. Three hundred thousand were injured. Hundreds of thousands of young Americans came home from the war psychologically damaged. Many returning soldiers and their families were embittered by the U.S. government that had involved them in Vietnam, embittered as well by their own fellow Americans who had not supported the war and did not seem to appreciate what soldiers had been forced to sacrifice. While they were in battle, many of their own countrymen were objecting to what the government was requiring soldiers to do, and, as returning veterans, they were not welcomed back and celebrated as were veterans from other wars.

The war had inflicted tremendous suffering on the Vietnamese as well. Over 350,000 South Vietnamese and from 500,000 to 1,000,000 North Vietnamese died in battle and millions of Vietnamese civilians also lost their lives during the war.

As the war wound down, there was every reason for citizens of South Vietnam to find a way out of the country. By March 1975, the government of South Vietnam was giving way before diminishing U.S. support and North Vietnamese incursions. In that year, the South Vietnamese army was decimated and hordes of civilians died as North Vietnamese invaded. In what was called the "convoy of tears," hundreds of thousands of South Vietnamese fled their homes to escape to other areas of Vietnam or to leave the country altogether. It was after this North Vietnamese assault that Hue, the home of Danny's grandmother, was destroyed, forcing the family to relocate to Da Nang. On May 1, 1975, U.S. helicopters airlifted out the remainder of U.S. personnel in Saigon and an estimated 150,000 South Vietnamese in Saigon who had worked against the North. These first refugees from Vietnam were professional people, well-to-do businessmen, and South Vietnamese army officers. Some of these refugees brought with them to the United States their experience as narcotics traffickers. The South Vietnamese who had no way to escape the country were in genuine peril. Chaos moved in when the American presence left. The looting, raping, and murdering during this period was replaced by the despotic oppression of the Communists. South Vietnamese who were even suspected of cooperating with the Americans were brutalized and killed by the Communists. Others, like Danny's cousin, Sang Le, were thrown into detention camps by the North Vietnamese.

Those who escaped death now faced a grim prospect. All the industries developed by Vietnam had been destroyed during the war, and the countryside of South Vietnam—millions and millions of acres—had been laid waste by napalm. And an estimated 21 million craters carved out by bombs scarred the landscape. The agricultural land of Vietnam was also poisoned by defoliants and herbicides.

The second wave of emigrants included the boat people like Danny's family. Thousands attempted to leave, crowded into tiny, leaky vessels, and many of them perished in the attempt. Among the boat people were many criminals escaping from the law.

Transition into American culture has been particularly difficult for Vietnamese immigrants, coupled with the difficulty they have in finding work. Only the most menial jobs are available to Vietnamese immigrants in the communities where they settle. They encounter some of the same problems that Chinese immigrants experienced in the nineteenth century. Their ability to eke out a living on very little money makes it possible for them to work for low wages, thus jeopardizing the workplace gains made by native laborers. Vietnamese workers, who presented serious competition for jobs, began to incur the displeasure of their working-class neighbors.

Except for the Vietnamese students who attend public school, recent immigrants have become isolated in Vietnamese communities and have had little contact with anyone other than Vietnamese because of their difficulties with the English language and other aspects of American culture. As the children of adult immigrants attend school in the United States, a generation gap occurs between grandparents, parents, and children.

Less that 3 percent of young people in Vietnamese communities belong to gangs. Still, Vietnamese and Chinese Vietnamese youth gangs plague many of these immigrant neighborhoods. A significant number of youths were members of gangs before they came to this country. Martin Booth describes these young people in *The Dragon Syndicates:*

> Housed in orphanages, fostered out or living alone in a strange land, alienated and lost, they formed burglary gangs, sometimes with friends they had made in Hong Kong's crowded and secure refugee camps, in order to survive and give themselves a sense of identity. Inured to violence by the Vietnam War, they were exceedingly ruthless

and, as the Chinese youth gangs had been before them, were utilized by Chinese criminals. (310)

Some Vietnamese gang members were the mixed-race offspring of American soldiers who fought in Vietnam. These unfortunate children were abandoned by their fathers and despised and ill-treated by the Vietnamese.

Many Vietnamese youths were already organized into gangs when they reached the United States, or they became organized shortly thereafter. They took western names like the Saigon Cowboys, the Thunder Tigers, the Pink Knights, the Vietnamese Youth, or the Born to Kill.

Frequently, gang members were runaways or school dropouts. Typical Asian gang members were also isolated in public housing or "Asia Towns" where gangs already existed. They were often those rejected by American natives, schools, and other Asians, and found it difficult to secure employment. When the youth in these gangs grew into manhood, they graduated from youth gangs into adult syndicates, at war with Chinese syndicates.

In many areas, Vietnamese immigrants are at the mercy of gangs called skinheads as well as Vietnamese gangs. Skinheads, who first emerged in England, reached the United States in the 1970s, springing up, often from the housing projects, in American midwestern, southern, and western cities. Most skinheads are teenagers who have not yet entered the work force. In Britain, skinhead groups sprang from the working class, but in the United States a large number of skinhead youth are middle-class suburbanites who still live with their parents and have not had to get jobs. They are known for their shaved heads, pro-Nazi tattoos, and work boots. Skinheads are self-proclaimed neo-Nazis, most of whom preach against all nonwhites and make them the target of their attacks. Calling themselves Aryans, they display swastikas and make a hero of Adolph Hitler. Jack B. Moore, in *Skinheads Shaved for Battle*, lays out the skinhead ideology:

> Skinheads should believe that ignorant, lazy, drug-ridden, sexually hyperactive blacks, linked with Jew or members of other "mud" races or with gays, are responsible for much of America's present sorry, decadent state, as though they are part of a pestilence visited on the land because of white passivity and failure to perceive the crisis in American life. (87)

Skinhead racism has especially targeted the Vietnamese. Their behavior is based on the erroneous conviction that all Vietnamese immigrants are Communists who are responsible for the deaths and crippling of American soldiers. They found friends and supporters among the American Nazi Party and the Ku Klux Klan. Danny's girlfriend, Tiffany, and her skinhead brother Frank have seen what the Vietnam War has done to their father. Typical of many Vietnam veterans, he gets into fights, has been hospitalized with mental illness in the Veterans' Administration facility, and abandons the family because he can no longer take responsibility for them. Frank, the skinheads, and his father hold all nonwhite people, especially the Vietnamese, responsible for their suffering.

There is another reason, supported by the novel, why skinheads resent all Asians: highly focused, disciplined, and ambitious Vietnamese students, like Danny Vo, with strong family support, pose serious scholastic competition for the native population. The skinheads' resentment of the ability of the Vietnamese students to win science and math prizes is typical of the response of some Caucasian students. In the novel, Calvin describes the reaction of a skinhead to the results of the science fair: "He entered the science fair two years ago. Man, he really got mad when he came in third place. That was the year Trung Tran won, and that big bag of blubber almost jumped down Trung's throat" (104). As the novel suggests, students such as Danny challenge the theories of Aryan superiority cherished by the skinheads.

Such attitudes are obvious in the many well-documented accounts of attacks on Asians by skinheads. In August 1992, for instance, a premed student in Coral Gables, Florida, was beaten to death by a group of skinheads who called him "Vietcong." And in Alpine Township, Michigan, on June 18, 1995, a Vietnamese student died after he was attacked by skinheads. In June 1990, in Houston, Texas, skinheads stomped a 15-year-old Vietnamese immigrant to death. And in Raleigh, North Carolina, in 1989, a Chinese American man, mistaken for a Vietnamese, was killed by skinheads.

THE TRIALS OF DANNY VO

The characters in *Shadow of the Dragon* include Danny Vo, the 16-year-old main character who came with his family to the United States when he was 6. Danny is the oldest boy in his family and has, thus, had to be strong and responsible. He is successful in living between two cultures. While he respects Vietnamese tradition, he has also become an American in his speech and dress. He is an excellent student and anticipates going to college on scholarship. His family consists of his hard-working mother and father; Kim, his defiant teenage sister; his younger brother and sister; Ba, his difficult grandmother; his uncle and aunt; and Sang Le, his cousin, who arrives in Houston from Vietnam shortly after the novel opens. The other main Vietnamese characters include members of the Cobra gang and Hong and Cuc, two teenage girls who have recently arrived in the community.

The non-Vietnamese in Danny's life are his best friend, Calvin; his girlfriend, Tiffany; Tiffany's brother Frank; and Frank's skinhead friends.

Life in Vietnam after the war and the cultural and religious traditions of Danny Vo's family are powerful forces that have shaped his life, setting him apart from most of his schoolmates. Although Danny is thoroughly Americanized, having been in the United States since he was 6 years old, his family's memories of a past in Vietnam constantly intrude on his life in Houston, Texas. Vietnamese tradition also impacts Danny during family celebrations—upon the arrival of a relative from Vietnam, the coming of the Vietnamese New Year, called Tet, or the birth of a baby—all take precedence over everything else, even in their new world. These rituals also bring meaning and order to their difficult, fragile lives, lived in transition.

At 10 years old, Danny learned that when he was an infant the family had fled the Vietnamese Communists in the dead of night in a fishing boat. The turbulence of the ocean, the unsettling darkness, and the group's terror at patrolling motorboats have become embedded in his psyche. After coming to the United States, the family—Danny's mother and father, and his uncle and aunt—struggle in menial jobs to get enough money to open businesses and are now dreaming of getting out of the projects and into a house. Life is a continual cycle of borrowing and lending money to help others get on their feet. As the story opens, the family has spent half their savings to get Danny's cousin, Sang Le, to the United States. As a consequence, their dream must be deferred again.

In contrast to family, tradition, discipline, and order are the violence and chaos of the Vietnamese gangs that lurk in their community like lords of misrule. The novel opens when 16-year-old Danny Vo encounters members of the Cobras near the Vietnamese market, where he and his mother have gone to shop. Danny spots four young men in their late teens threatening two terrified Vietnamese girls who have recently arrived in the United States. He suspects the men have just emerged from the pool hall, called *bida*. When he notices the emblem on their expensive silk jackets—"a golden cobra with blood-red eyes, its head raised off the ground, full-blown and poised to strike" (17)— he knows the men are members of a Vietnamese gang called the Cobras. Danny, who keeps himself in excellent physical shape, also keeps his head to avoid a serious confrontation and rescues the girls, pretending to be their brother and pushing them into his car to drive them to safety. His finesse in handling the situation prompts the Cobras to fold up their butterfly knives and let him go, but one boy assumes the stance of a cobra and hisses at Danny as a warning. Danny also notices their expensive gold jewelry and shudders to think how the boys have acquired it.

His mother recognizes the boys as dangerous and reminds Danny of what he already knows: "Those boys are very bad. Stay away from them. They're no good. They belong to a *toan du dang*. They're like pieces of trash in the gutter. We used to see them in Da Nang during the war" (20). Danny is puzzled when she trembles and continues to repeat the warning. He wonders what's wrong with her and becomes annoyed that she is making him upset. He thinks that she and his father have always trusted his choice of friends. Why, he thinks, is she becoming so nervous now? What Danny learns months later is that his mother and her sister have both been raped by members of a *toan du dang* in Da Nang, and that his aunt had committed suicide after the incident.

When Danny and his mother return home from their market excursion, they are confronted with two unsettling situations: Danny's teenage sister's fight with their grandmother over the clothes the girl is planning to wear out and the impending arrival of Danny's cousin from Vietnam. Both are examples of cultural collisions that propel young people, caught in the middle, toward gang association. Danny, as the oldest son, is called upon to send his rebellious sister to her room, a reprimand that causes her to refuse to go to the airport to greet their cousin.

Sang Le, the cousin, arrives at the airport thin and wasted, in ragged clothes, but sporting a generous and joyous spirit. But as Danny discerns Sang Le's gaunt face and haunted eyes, he has a foreboding that the arrival of his cousin is going to create havoc in his life.

The impending doom of the Vietnam gang in the Vos' lives is suggested on the night of Sang Le's arrival, when during the party for Sang Le, Danny discovers that his sister has slipped out of the house. Danny takes Sang Le with him in the car to look for her in Houston's

Chinatown, more appropriately described as Asia Town. In this area that becomes dangerous after dark, Danny spots his sister Kim and the four Cobra members at the same time. After he has dragged her to the car, he asks whether she associates with the Cobras and finds that she knows the brother of one of the gang members and refuses to take seriously the danger of involvement with the Cobras. Later, she runs away and lives with the brother of one of the Cobras, a boy, Danny learns, she had met on the night Sang Le arrived in the United States.

Gangs insinuate themselves into the Vo family in another way on this night. Danny had let Sang Le out of the car in Chinatown while he drove ahead to search for his sister. Not until some time later does Danny learn that, in the brief time Sang Le was by himself, he had made contact on the street with Tho, a Cobra member who had also been his friend in the same refugee camp in Hong Kong where Sang Le had lived for two years.

Several circumstances drive Sang Le into secret Cobra association. He arrives in the United States with great hope and enthusiasm, and with unmistakable artistic talent. But he quickly finds that learning English is becoming an overwhelming task. The school offers courses in English as a Second Language, but the difficulty of learning English is made more laborious and mystifying by the teachers' lack of knowledge of the Vietnamese language. Moreover, all except his art course depends on his mastery of English. On top of his academic difficulties, Sang Le faces financial problems. He has no money for clothes, no money for transportation, and no money to pay the family back for his passage from Vietnam. And his immigrant status and lack of ability to speak English stand in the way of his getting a job. Not surprisingly, Sang Le begins talking about quitting school, and on the first day of the Tet celebration, Danny finds Sang Le chatting with the members of the Cobra gang whom Danny had encountered earlier. They accuse Danny, who has come to America as a child, of not being a true Vietnamese.

Danny is unable to convince Sang Le to refuse the gang's invitation and come to the family celebration instead. He tells Sang Le that his friend Tho is "*du dang*—a gang leader. They call him Cobra. Man, he's just a punky hoodlum" (161). But Sang Le answers him that the boys in the gang need him more than the family does at this moment. After his cousin leaves with the gang members, Danny tells Calvin: "if Sang Le gets involved with Cobra, he would probably be a lot better off if he had stayed in Vietnam and slept with the rats" (162).

Sang Le meets a variety of discouragements by allowing his smoking, drinking, and gambling at the pool hall to get out of hand. At a *bida* that Sang Le has insisted on going into, Danny argues against the Cobras for his cousin's soul. One of the gang members in the pool hall pulls a gun on him. But Sang Le is convinced that accepting the gang's offer of a job will be best for him and for his family, who needs money.

Danny halfway convinces himself that he shouldn't worry about his cousin's choice of friends, but he soon encounters horrific evidence to the contrary. After he storms out of the pool hall, he goes to his uncle's video store. He is shocked to see that the store has been ransacked. Not only has the store been torn apart and the inventory destroyed, but his aunt's fingernails have been chopped off down to the quick and she is bleeding from a cut on her neck. All this has been the work of the Cobras.

Despite this, there is nothing Danny can do to stop the gang's involvement with his family. At the same time that his sister disappears with the brother of a gang member, Sang Le drops out of school and begins coming home with tremendous amounts of cash, which he puts into a bank for his grandmother. Proof of Sang Le's involvement with the Cobras comes when Danny spots him in a group of Cobra members on the television news reporting a murder in Chinatown. He has several talks with Sang Le, in which Danny promises not to tell their grandmother about Sang Le's gang membership if Sang Le will leave the gang. But, as Sang Le tells him later, extricating himself from the gang will not be easy because the leader finds him to be too valuable and realizes that Sang Le knows too much about their activities, some of them murderous. Instead, his engagement with the gang becomes even more intense. Their grandmother finds out about his gang membership and confronts him with it, telling him that his mother was raped by such gangs in Vietnam, and that she, his grandmother, will burn the money Sang Le has made. Only then does he agree to take the money back and extricate himself from the gang. Even though he is tempted to continue working with the gang, Sang Le does return the money, returns to school, and stays home with Danny at night. But, despite his having tried to turn his life around, he is, shortly after, found mortally wounded.

It is not his Vietnam gang that has killed Sang Le, however; it is a gang of skinheads that has done the deed. And the Cobras retaliate for the murder of Sang Le by killing Brian, the leader of the skinheads.

The skinheads become prominent in Danny's life shortly after Sang Le's arrival, when he learns that Frank, the brother of his girlfriend, Tiffany, is a skinhead. He noticed him and his buddies for the first time in the school cafeteria. All these boys have shaved their heads, sport many tattoos on their arms, and wear military boots. Calvin knows them to be part of a group that hates all nonwhites and call themselves Nazis. As Danny and Tiffany come home from their first date, she tells him that her brother is at home and that he now hangs out with really "creepy" friends and will be angry if he sees Danny. Still, Danny takes her to the front door and kisses her. In those few minutes, he sees into Frank's room, where posters of German soldiers and swastikas adorn the walls.

Tiffany is so afraid of what her brother and his friends will do that she avoids having another date with Danny. She explains Frank's particular hatred of Vietnamese people, saying that "Frank blames all Vietnamese for our dad leaving" (230). Predictably, when Danny manages to persuade her to go to a dance with him, he encounters trouble afterward. Her brother Frank and his gang of skinheads, shouting insults and threats, beat up Danny. Only when Frank's mother comes out to yell at him, comparing him to his father, does Frank stop the attack. After Danny returns home, he finally tells Sang Le who has attacked him and explains that the skinheads "hate anybody who isn't white" (270).

Tiffany is so terrified that the skinheads will kill Danny that she refuses to be seen with him, despite all his efforts to talk to her. Finally, on the night that Sang Le has told Danny he is going out for a pack of cigarettes and will return shortly, Danny tries to call Tiffany, knowing that Frank is never at home on the weekends. He learns that she is at a nearby house and that Frank, who was supposed to be taking care of their wheelchair-bound brother, has also left the house. On his way out to reach Tiffany at her friend's house, Danny finds his wounded cousin Sang Le.

Danny is able to survive the gangs. His family is able to move out of the Vietnamese projects into a nice house in a nice neighborhood, and his prospects for a scholarship to go to college remain strong. But the skinheads ruin his relationship with the love of his life, Tiffany, for she refuses to testify that she had seen her brother and his friends talking to Sang Le shortly before he is beaten to death with a baseball bat and kicked with military boots, weapons that were also used against Danny outside Tiffany's house. Danny has the choice of protecting Frank and keeping Tiffany or turning in Frank and losing Tiffany. He chooses to tell the truth.

GANG ISSUES IN *SHADOW OF THE DRAGON*

Shadow of the Dragon focuses on several issues, some of which are peculiar to Vietnamese gangs and some of which are characteristic of most ethnic gangs. Vietnamese gangs in the United States have a distinct history, shaped by conditions in Vietnam during and immediately after the war. During the war, boys who had lost homes and families found themselves living on the streets in cities where civil law had been displaced by a bloody civil war. They banded together for survival, roaming the streets, making money by theft and extortion, and committing rapes and murders with little fear of retribution. In the chaos and mayhem that reigned immediately after the war was over, these gangs controlled the streets. The desperation and hunger in Vietnam after the war made younger children easy recruits for gang membership. Tho, leader of the Cobras in Houston, taunts Danny bitterly with this information:

> Do you know what it is like to be the one left behind while the rest of your family lives in wealth in America? While you beg for food on the street and sleep with rats, your cousins and aunts and uncles wallow in American greed? (159)

In the early days after the war, when Vietnamese immigrants came to the United States, members of these street gangs and children who had been brutalized by misuse, hunger, and disease, were among them. Other gangs originated in the so-called reeducation camps set up by the Communists who came to power in South Vietnam shortly after the war and in the refugee camps, like the one in Hong Kong where Sang Le has lived for two years. The cruelty and subhuman living conditions in both places drew the young inmates together and made violent animals out of some of them. This shared experience of reeducation and refugee camps draws the Cobras together in Houston. Tho, the Cobra leader, speaks of his experience there shared by Sang Le, "He wears the scars of the re-education camp, if not on his back or the bottoms of his feet, then in his heart" (159). And Sang Le tells his cousin Danny, "Cobra was in re-education camp like me.... he was in a Hong Kong refugee camp, too. He understands me" (237).

The loneliness, humiliation, and desperation of the immigrant experience have also fostered gang membership. Although Danny speaks perfect English and is an excellent athlete and student, he himself has been ridiculed because he is Vietnamese. At one point in high school, a bigoted and ignorant classmate taunts Danny by asking if, when he was a kid in Vietnam, Danny had ever shot an American in exchange for a candy bar, never mind that Danny had not been born until after the war, that his family had despised the Vietcong and Communists, and that he had left Vietnam when he was an infant. The humiliations experienced by recent immigrants are more intense. Rumors circulate that Sang Le had been in prison in Vietnam for murdering someone. And the two young girls who have recently arrived from Vietnam, wearing their old-fashioned clothes and struggling with English, are the frequent targets of ridicule. That this humiliation drives some young immigrants to gangs is seen in the situation of Sang Le, who says that the leader of the Cobras "doesn't laugh at me because I don't speak English or because I flunked American school" (237).

Sang Le's fundamental reason for coming to America is to find work. He discovers that he will never find a job because he is defeated in school, especially in his attempts to learn English, and refused even the most menial jobs because of his status and inability to understand English. The store owner within walking distance of the Vos' apartment would rather hire lazy and dishonest boys who speak English than a hard worker, willing to work for half the pay, who doesn't speak English. So Sang Le, like many other young immigrants, turns to a gang, the Cobras, who *are* able to give him lucrative work.

Like many gangs with different histories, however, the Cobras seek their cruel pleasures and blood money by targeting their own people in their own neighborhoods. In the novel, this practice is traced to gangs during the war who rape Danny's and Sang Le's mothers. The opening chapter provides one example, when Danny sees several members of the Cobras menacing two young Vietnamese immigrants.

Even at this point, Danny knows something about gangs. Everyone in the neighborhood knows that members of the Cobras harass shop owners and fight over territory. He tells Sang Le, only half facetiously, that the job the Cobras have for him is likely "stealing social security checks from old women" (183). Shortly afterward, he witnesses what the Cobras have done to his uncle and aunt, who resisted paying protection money to them. Not only have they destroyed the store, they have physically attacked his aunt and threatened the little children. Soon Danny comes to believe that the Cobras are not only bullies and thieves, but murderers, involved in killings at Vietnam Plaza. As Danny's family observes, the Cobras not only kill innocent Vietnamese, but each other—"Those bad *toan du dang* are killing each other off" (236). Once Danny is convinced that Sang Le is involved with the Cobras and that the Cobras are killers, he tells Sang Le what he thinks his friend Tho has perpetrated on the Vietnamese community: "He steals and extorts and who knows what else. All the time in the news I hear about somebody getting hurt or killed in Chinatown. You know Cobra thugs are behind some of it. What are you going to do when Cobra tells you to smash up Uncle Dao's store downtown? Will you destroy your own family?" (237–38). Danny has seen so much evidence of the Cobras victimizing their own people that he believes at first that they have murdered Sang Le just because he was trying to extricate himself from the gang.

Like other gangs, the Cobras and skinheads are constantly propelled by the need for revenge. The suffering of both groups has been so great that they are compelled to place blame on and seek vengeance against those they regard as their tormentors. In attacking the Vietnamese, the skinheads believe they are getting revenge for what the Vietcong did to American soldiers during the war:

> Why don't you go back to your rice paddies and jungles where you belong? If it wasn't for you, Americans wouldn't have died. (264)

Danny, fearing the cycle of revenge will start again, refuses at first to tell Sang Le that the skinheads have beat him up. As Danny feared, when Sang Le learns the truth, he goes to the Cobras to get revenge. "My friend Cobra can take care of them like that.... They are mere children compared to Cobra. Don't worry, we will take care of them" (270). But Danny knows that revenge is the stuff of gang warfare and refuses to let Sang Le initiate this line of action.

It is their lust for revenge against all Vietnamese that has led the skinheads to beat Sang Le to death. Seeing the hatred in the eyes of the Cobra members at Sang Le's funeral, Danny pleads with them not to perpetuate the cycle of revenge. But soon the skinhead leader, Brian, who had killed Sang Le, is dead at the hands of the Cobras, and the cycle of violence and revenge goes on.

BIBLIOGRAPHY

Bass, Thomas A. *Vietamerica: The War Comes Home.* New York: Soho Press, 1996.

Booth, Martin. *The Dragon Syndicates: The Global Phenomenon of the Triads.* New York: Carroll and Graf, 2000.

Do, Hien Duc. *The Vietnamese Americans.* Westport, CT: Greenwood Press, 1999.

Du, Phuoc Long. *The Dream Shattered: Vietnamese Gangs in America.* Boston: Northeastern University Press, 1996.

Freeman, James W. *Hearts of Sorrow.* Stanford: Stanford University Press, 1989.

Garland, Sherry. *Shadow of the Dragon.* New York: Harcourt, Brace, 1993.

Lacey, Marilyn. *In Our Fathers' Land.* Washington, DC: Migration and Refugee Services, 1985.

McKelvey, Robert. *The Dust of Life: America's Children Abandoned in Vietnam.* Seattle: University of Washington Press, 1999.

Moore, Jack B. *Skinheads Shaved for Battle: A Cultural History of American Skinheads.* Bowling Green, OH: Bowling Green State University Popular Press, 1993.

Rutledge, Paul. *The Vietnamese Experience in America.* Bloomington: Indiana University Press, 1992.

Tran, De, Andrew Lam, and Hai Dai Nguyen, eds. *Once Upon a Dream: The Vietnamese-American Experience.* Kansas City, MO: Andrews and McNeel, 1995.

20

Chinese Gangs: Dan Mahoney's
The Two Chinatowns (2001)

FROM JIM DOYLE, "CREW SAYS SMUGGLING FORCED BY CHINESE."
San Francisco Chronicle, *29 March 2001.*

The smuggling ship that made a daring run into San Francisco Bay last month had been commandeered by a group of armed Chinese men in Hong Kong and forced to carry hundreds of Chinese passengers across the Pacific, crew members have told investigators. (29)

. . .

Kyaw Swa Oo Sai, the Burmese second engineer, told an INS investigator that on the evening of March 26, while the ship was in Hong Kong, he awakened to find a group of Chinese climbing aboard the Pai Sheng armed with knives.

According to Tse-Hsiung Hsieh, the Taiwanese chief engineer, the men "threatened the crew with knives." From that point on, crew members said, two men were always on the bridge with knives. (A14)

FROM PAMELA BURDMAN, "HUGE BOOM IN HUMAN SMUGGLING—INSIDE STORY OF FLIGHT FROM CHINA."
San Francisco Chronicle, *27 April 1993.*

Early in February 1992, the Coast Guard received a perplexing tip:

Three men had come to the Marina Village Yacht Harbor in Alameda to buy a 57-foot yacht called the *Liberated Lady*.

. . .

The Coast Guard put the *Liberated Lady* under surveillance, and three weeks later investigators were watching as the yacht made a midday rendezvous with a Taiwanese fishing trawler off Long Beach. When they raided the yacht that night, they were stunned by what they found.

In a cabin designed for 12 people, 85 Chinese citizens were crammed into cupboards, stuffed under the sink and doubled over on top of each other in the bathroom. The *Liberated Lady* was a smuggling ship, and the cargo was human.

. . .

Some estimate that more than 100,000 Chinese are being smuggled into the country every year.

. . .

The repercussions are startling:

The traffic in Chinese immigrants has become a $3 billion-a-year business, with tentacles reaching from Hong Kong to San Francisco, New York, and Paris.

. . .

Some immigrants prosper in America, but usually they must first toil for years in restaurants and garment-industry sweatshops to pay off smuggling fees of $30,000 or more. Those unable to pay on time have been kidnapped and beaten by gang members working for the smugglers. (A1)

Dan Mahoney, an author and 25-year veteran of the New York City Police Department, describes the workings of Asian gangs, not from the viewpoint of the gang member, but from the perspective of the policeman in his novel *The Two Chinatowns*. The two Chinatowns in question are in Toronto, where the novel opens, and New York City, where its main character, Cisco Sanchez, works as a detective. Mahoney's novel is a police procedural that provides an overview of the character of Asian gangs—from youthful street gangs to powerful international criminal syndicates. The novel stresses several aspects of Asian youth gangs that are true of all gangs: they serve the needs of older mobsters, and the people they harm most profoundly are those in their own culture.

TRIADS, TONGS, AND GANGS

Despite some of the similarities among gangs of any ethnic makeup, Asian gangs, like those in Mahoney's novel, differ markedly from other immigrant gangs in their composition, their relationship to the community in which they operate, and their international character. Triads and tongs are fundamental to Asian cultures. Some of them are not involved in criminal activities, but many of them are. The most powerful, organized criminal gangs are called triads, which operate internationally and usually have Hong Kong as their headquarters. Triads began hundreds of years ago in China as secret societies. One of the most prominent groups arose at the turn of the twentieth century, with the purpose of overthrowing the Chinese government. Numerous triads developed over the next decades, most of them international criminal syndicates involved in the heroin trade, extortion, counterfeiting, prostitution, and smuggling. An especially prominent triad business is smuggling illegal aliens into Canada and the United States. Though concentrated in Hong Kong, triads operate, often hand in glove with Asian businesses and government officials throughout Southeast Asia. Some 50 triads with approximately 80,000 members are believed to still be operating in Hong Kong. Some of the most notorious triads in Hong Kong include Sun Yee On, the largest, with the strongest ties to mainland China; Wo Group, the oldest in Hong Kong; 14K, one of the most powerful and prominent triads in Mahoney's novel; and Big Circle Gang, made up of former members of the Red Guard who specialize in robbery.

Each triad has its identifying concentration in some criminal activity: loan-sharking, protection rackets, jewelry and gold robberies, or bank robberies. The head of the triad is called the Dragon Head, or sometimes Mountain Lord. Once "elected" to his post, he is in absolute power, like the captain of a ship, administering the multiple branches of the organization, each of which is led by sublords. Others close to the Dragon Head (sometimes called the Vanguard or the Incense Master) administer finances or oversee rituals for him. More often than not, youth gangs are hired to do much of the dirty work involving kidnapping, maiming, torture, and murder.

One of the most insidiously harmful of the triads' activities is the heroin trade. In the 1960s, 1970s, and 1980s, triad operatives oversaw the manufacture of drugs and, in cargo ships, smuggled opium from Burma, Thailand, Laos, Vietnam, and various provinces in China (embracing opium's Golden Triangle), to markets the world over. Triads also sold opium to Hong Kong's population, almost 40,000 of which are addicted to heroin.

Protection rackets and extortion are also important sources of triad revenue. In large cities in Asia and in urban areas with large Asian populations in the Western world, triads prey on restaurant owners and other businessmen in various Chinatowns, extorting hundreds of thousands of dollars a week.

The extent of their criminal empires and the violence of their activities led Hong Kong in 1994 to pass the Organized and Serious Crimes Ordinance, which outlawed triads. Events leading to that law are the subject of Mahoney's *The Two Chinatowns.*

Working in close proximity with the triads are tongs, which literally means "meeting places." The rationale for the creation of tongs is thoroughly situated in American history. In the mid-nineteenth century, the Chinese tradition of international trade, on top of the appalling political and economic conditions in China and the hope for better lives in the United States, drew 100,000 Chinese workers to America. Many were attracted to California, where they found work in the newly discovered gold mines and, later, on the transcontinental railroad, completed in 1869 to connect the western United States with the eastern United States. The great wave of nineteenth-century Chinese immigration was between 1850 and 1882. As more settlers came from the East to California, owners of huge agricultural spreads also hired Asian Americans for field work. For the most part, Chinese Americans found themselves at the bottom of the socioeconomic ladder. Jobs in the mines and on the railroad were plentiful for them because they would work for starvation wages, far lower than those accepted by white workers. Thus, they faced not only racial discrimination and mistreatment by owners and managers but resentment from white workers because they drove down wages. Asian Americans, in general, were ridiculed as "chinks" and demonized as part of "the yellow peril." Their culture, so radically different from that of the Western world, made assimilation difficult and subjected them to stereotyping and ridicule. In the 1870s and 1890s, Asian Americans were targets of nativist violence. Official discrimination continued when, in 1882, the United States Congress placed a ban on Chinese immigration, which remained in place until 1943. As a result, Chinese tended to withdraw from the general population and ban together in isolated neighborhoods—Chinatowns. In the early twentieth century, Chinese Americans were prohibited from owning property in San Francisco, even in Chinatown, and laws were passed for a brief period segregating Chinese American children in the public schools. As labor unions grew in influence to improve the position of workers, Chinese Americans were excluded from them.

It was in the setting of nineteenth-century hardship and discrimination that tongs developed in San Francisco, adopting the facades of other secret or social organizations in the United States like the Masons or civic fraternities. The legitimate purpose of many tongs set up by respectable Chinese businessmen was to protect the interests of new Chinese residents. But other tongs in these early years exploited opportunities to make money by criminal means in a society made up overwhelmingly of young, single males. The infamous opium dens of San Francisco and, later, New York City, were run by tongs. They also generated revenue with prostitution rings and gambling dens.

Tongs spread to other large U.S. and Canadian cities with substantial Asian populations. With the waves of Chinese immigration following World War II and the lifting of the ban on immigration in 1943, tongs grew more numerous. Even into the twenty-first century, rival tongs often go to war over territory, killing and injuring each other and innocent Chinatown residents who get in their way. Some criminal tongs work hand in hand with Hong Kong triads, sharing in the violent work and in the ill-gotten profits. The most prominent Asia criminal tongs are the Hip Sings and On Leongs, who are bitter enemies.

Youth gangs, a third level of organized Asian crime, did not appear in large numbers until the 1960s. Frequently, criminal tongs control youth gangs, but a few gangs operate independently of the tongs and triads. As Asian populations swelled in the United States and Canada in the 1970s and 1980s, so did Asian youth gangs. There is a hierarchy within those gangs that work directly for the triads. In larger gangs (usually with more than 50 members), a "Red Pole" leads the gang. The "White Paper Fan" is the gang member who keeps the books. The "Straw Sandal" is the messenger and sometimes organizer. Those at the bottom of the hierarchy, hoping to become initiated into the gang, are called "49s." In *Chinatown Gangs,* Ko-lin Chin details the relationship between the powerful adult triads and the Chinatown youth gangs:

> There also appear to be functional economic relationships between youth gangs and adult organizations. Chinese youth gangs often are hired by adult organizations for lucrative work, such as protecting gambling and prostitution houses, collecting debts, and working as "street soldiers" in economic and territorial affairs. Their involvement in these enterprises, under the influence of adult crime groups, provides them with income and access to a career ladder within the illegal organizations, which decreases their dependence on extortion and other forms of business exploitations. The adult groups also exert considerable control over the gangs and discourage their involvement in nonsanctioned extortion and violent activities that might jeopardize the adult organization's enterprises. Social control is maintained by the implicit threat of exclusion of gang members from the more lucrative work. (viii)

Usually as part of their work for a particular triad, youth gangs are also involved in gambling, prostitution, armed robbery, trafficking in heroin, loan-sharking, and kidnapping for ransom. In New York City in 1995 there were, for example, 34 *reported* kidnappings in the Asian community. And those who have made a study of the Asian community claim that only about 10 percent of the kidnappings are ever reported. The extent of the crime of Chinese youth gangs can be seen in another set of figures. Police estimate that over 90 percent of Asian businesses in the United States and Canada are subject to extortion, most of which goes unreported and is just accepted as part of the reality of life in Chinatowns.

The Chinese are not the only Asians who make up youth gangs. Tens of thousands of Vietnamese, Cambodians, and Laotians immigrated to the United States after the Vietnam War and, as Mahoney portrays in the novel, formed youth gangs before and after they arrived in the United States and Canada. The situation of Vietnamese immigrants was especially hard as they met with discrimination, not only from American whites but from the now-better-established Chinese Americans as well.

CISCO VERSUS THE ASIAN GANGS

Mahoney's story opens in Toronto, where we find hundreds of Chinese men and women working for starvation wages in sweatshops in the factories and warehouses in the industrial area of the city. To collect past-due money from aliens they have transported to America, the triad called 14K depends on street gangs based in New York City, in this case a group called Born to Kill, whose members are of Chinese descent but Vietnamese upbringing. Three members of Born to Kill—the leader, Johnny Chow; Nicky Chu; and David Phouc—show up near one of the Toronto sweatshops, looking for one of the illegals working there. Their usual strategy is to kidnap the debtor and torture him to force him or his family in China to come through with the money. In most cases, he is eventually killed. David Phouc eagerly anticipates this caper because killing the worker they have come for will be his initiation rite into Born to Kill. Previously, he had merely hung out with the gang leaders and helped them in their kidnappings.

Coincidentally, a New York City detective named Cisco Sanchez is also in Toronto at the same time as are these Born to Kill gang members. Cisco already has connections to Asia. In New York, he has worked on cases involving Asian gangs and knows something about them. More important, he has fallen deeply in love with a Chinese woman named Sue, and to win her affections, he has steeped himself in Chinese culture and learned to speak both Mandarin and Cantonese. The two of them have become engaged and visit a Chinese restaurant in Toronto owned by Sue's Uncle Benny. Here, the paths of the Born to Kill trio and Cisco cross, for while Sue and Cisco are in the restaurant, Nicky Chu and Johnny Chow force their way into the kitchen, where they torture the dishwasher who is behind on his payments and then proceed to kidnap him. In the struggle that follows, Sue is brutally murdered, and Cisco kills Chu and Chow and has a shootout with David Phouc before Phouc drives away. The fatal incident plunges Cisco into the complex world of Asian gangs. From Sammy Ong, a businessman who was also having dinner in the restaurant, and from Harry, an illegal working in the kitchen, he learns that his fiancée's death can ultimately be attributed to the Hong Kong–based 14K triad and its Dragon Head, or leader, Johnny Eng. He learns that 14K charges each illegal alien $35,000 for his transport, which he or his family pays off at the rate of $300 a week. He also learns of the conditions aboard ship where they are hidden, crowded in huge containers. A number of them die along the way and are dumped overboard. It is to be expected that any illegal who objects to conditions aboard ship will mysteriously disappear. Once in an American city like Toronto, he learns, they are placed in filthy rooming houses where two men must share one bed, and one toilet serves an entire hall of residents. Tongs find them hard work at rock-bottom wages in restaurants or factories. Any alien who complains or falls behind in his payments stands the risk of being killed or having one of his family members in China killed. Harry, the illegal alien working in the restaurant, tells Cisco that gang members in China have probably already killed the wife of the dishwasher targeted by Born to Kill members. Harry also tells him the story of another ship, the *Golden Venture*, hired by 14K in 1993. When this ship went aground off the coast of New York, many illegal Chinese trapped in the containers were drowned.

From Sammy Ong and Connie Li, a New York detective on the Asian Gang Task Force, Cisco and Robert E. Lee, a Chinese detective in the Toronto Police Department, learn that 14K uses members of New York City's Vietnamese gangs as hired killers, and the specialties of the Born to Kill are kidnapping and torture. Sammy Ong also tells him of the connection with a tong called Hip Sing in the lives of the illegal aliens. Sammy himself belongs to Hip Sing, a civic organization made up of highly respectable, influential Asians who, nevertheless, skirt the law by their involvement in illegal gambling. Sammy also has to confess that Hip Sing and other tongs are fully aware of the arrival of illegals in containers, that they provide transport for them to the substandard rooming houses, and that they hire them in their factories and restaurants, working 12 hours a day, 6 days a week, for $400, $300 of which goes to the triad.

The killings in the restaurant have upset this complex arrangement: the illegals have decided that they will no longer cooperate with the Born to Kill collectors, and the Hip Sing object to the involvement with the Born to Kill members. Partially as a result of this and the bungled Toronto restaurant job, the triad targets Born to Kill members. The young driver, who had just been initiated into Born to Kill, is found dismembered, and two others are beaten and forced to return to New York. Cisco and Lee close in on the New York street gang, arresting all the Born to Kill members and releasing the victims they've kidnapped.

Police also take into custody four 14K operatives, two of whom are high-ranking members who agree to help the police destroy the 14K in exchange for reduced jail sentences. The highest-ranking member of the four is Boris, second in command in 14K. From these informants, police learn that their job will be much harder because of internal corruption in the Chinese government, which is reluctant to move on triads in Hong Kong. Many high-ranking government officials in

Hong Kong and China are deeply involved with triads and benefit from their activities. From these informants, police learn that at that very moment the crew of a transport ship will begin killing hundreds of illegal aliens on 14K orders, for fear the ship will be intercepted and searched upon arrival in an American port. The FBI immediately intercedes with helicopters that hover over the ship, forcing the crew to surrender and land at the U.S. Guantanamo Base in Cuba. From the ship's crew, the police discover that 14K is also running heroin.

To unsettle Johnny Eng, the Hong Kong leader of 14K, Cisco circulates a rumor that the police have an informant. Eng, believing that the informant is a man named Bing Ho, has Ho's entire family slaughtered, including his two tiny children and his servants.

Cisco and Lee get a break in the case when they learn from Murray, Boris's lawyer, that Johnny Eng's name in Mandarin is Jonathan Ng. Under that name, he had been arrested in New York City, so the police and FBI have a complete file on him that enables them to bone up on the triad boss's entire life. They learn that Ng, aka Eng, was reared in Taiwan, where his well-to-do family had supported Chang Kai-shek. Later, Boris enlarges on this chapter in Eng's life. Eng's father had been head of a triad called the Green Gang and later became head of Chang's secret police. Eng had been educated at the University of California, Berkeley, after which he immigrated to Toronto, Canada, where he was able to open a garment factory. Soon, he moved as a legal alien to New York City, where he assumed an important position in the tong called Hip Sing and secured contracts with three casinos to transport Chinese gamblers from Manhattan to Atlantic City in the buses he had purchased. Eng's fortunes improved when he was named vice president of an Asian-run international banking cartel with headquarters in New York. His luck took a turn for the worse when, to expand his bus business to other casinos, he tried to get rid of his competition by hiring the most important street gang in Chinatown, the Ghost Shadows, to intimidate his rival. They stole and set fire to his competitor's property. It was not until the other businessman's daughter was kidnapped that Eng got his way. Only after extensive worldwide investigations did the New York police learn that the girl had been kidnapped by thugs connected to Hong Kong triads, and only then did they realize how deeply Eng was involved in Asia's organized-crime scene. The police and FBI got their information about Eng, the kidnapping, and the triads after they arrested Tommy Gan, a member of the Ghost Shadows, for shooting a member of another youth gang—the White Dragons—in the leg. An attempt to force the casinos to nullify their contracts with Eng failed when Eng's lawyer, Murray, responded by suing the casinos.

Only through the dedicated work of one officer had the government been able to build a case against Eng for using his bank to launder money from the Asian triads. But Eng was able to post the million-dollar bail and, in a year, quietly disappeared from New York.

With this file, put together almost a decade earlier, Cisco in New York and Lee in Toronto set out to question Boris and bring down Eng and 14K. Boris begins his confession by claiming to be a double agent, working for both the Chinese Communists and 14K, which China has paid him to infiltrate. Boris provides them with further details about the general workings of the triad, including the practice of using Chinese and Vietnamese street gangs to do their collections, kidnappings, tortures, and killings. Such gang members are called "snakeheads." The triad's hirelings who work the emigrant trade inside China are called "snaketails." Even as they question Boris, members of a street gang called United Bamboo tail the law-enforcement officers and are arrested. Inspector Kwan, the Shanghai policeman on the team, nails down important evidence by obtaining a tape of Eng's phone conversations, in which he orders various murders.

From Boris, they learn that 14K is planning to drop billions of counterfeit U.S. dollars into western markets, a criminal action that would devastate the economies of several countries. Boris gives them the location of the current counterfeiting plant and the warehouses where the bills are stored, enabling Cisco and the other police in the international community to avert this disaster. In the process, they find that the head of China's Public Security Bureau is in on the scheme.

Eng, who has ordered the murder of Bing Ho and his family, now orders the death of the leader of Born to Kill and slips away from his Hong Kong mansion, leaving a look-alike in his place. From his research, Kwan is convinced that Eng will flee to Guam. There, the team meets the boat on which Eng has hidden in a container. When cornered, he shoots himself. The government of Hong Kong seizes all the assets of 14K. And Cisco is satisfied that he has his revenge for the death of Sue.

THE DISTINCTIVE CHARACTER OF THE ASIAN GANG

As Mahoney's novel illustrates, though Asian gangs have many things in common with other ethnic gangs, the character of the Asian gang is fundamentally different. Most apparent is the international dimension of Asian gangs, which view the countries of the entire world as their places of operation. The world of a gang on the streets of Chicago and New York was often restricted to the block they defended as their territory. Even a Los Angeles gang in the twenty-first century may typically be restricted to the gang members' South Central neighborhood. But members of 14K and Asian youth gangs move with regularity from Far Eastern countries—Hong Kong, China, Vietnam, Thailand, and the Philippines—to major cities throughout the West. The businesses and the terror of a single triad reach into many countries. Even the New York–based Asian street gangs in the novel move across national borders, from Toronto to New York City, and have personal histories that include connections to China, Vietnam, Hong Kong, and Taiwan. This means that the markets for their illegal goods and services are much more extensive. It also means that their ability to move across borders makes them much more elusive.

Both Asian and non-Asian mobsters typically assign untried youths to lower-risk jobs like courier until they prove themselves with a murder. But the dynamics between adult and youthful gangsters is somewhat different in Asian gangs. Adult gangsters in other cultures did and do sometimes court and promote promising young men in street gangs, openly expressing their desire to recruit them into adult mobs. In the Asian structure, it is the members of the youth gangs who court their elders in the hope of rising through the ranks of gang membership to a tong or to the inner sanctum of a triad. But the triads have little concern for the youth gangs other than to employ them for their dirtiest work. In *The Two Chinatowns,* when police and Asian businessmen in Toronto become angered at the behavior of the Born to Kill gang, the triad thinks nothing of having the young driver, who aspired to official gang membership, killed and dismembered, and having his two companions so severely beaten that they are admitted to a hospital.

The Two Chinatowns also makes clear a tragic irony of Asian gangs: the extent to which these gangs exploit and target members of their own culture and community. All the murder victims in the novel are Chinese. The primary victims of Asian gangs in the novel are the destitute Chinese who believe they will have a better life in the United States and Canada, and who are mercilessly killed when it is to the triad's advantage. On a typical voyage, 300 Chinese, crammed into containers, are taken on a four-month voyage. They have only rice and water to consume and are routinely beaten and raped. Once in the

United States, the immigrants are exploited by the tong-controlled restaurants and sweatshops, and are threatened and murdered by Chinese and Vietnamese gangs, on orders from the triad, when they can't pay. Moreover, members of the immigrants' families in China are held hostage. Chinese immigrants aren't the only victims of the gangs. In their protection rackets, the tongs make their living by selling protection—extorting money from Chinese businesses.

The invasion of the Chinese restaurant near the beginning of the novel represents this exploitation in a single incident. Benny and his daughter, who run a restaurant in Toronto's Chinatown, know full well the violence brought to the neighborhood by the gangs working under 14K orders. So terrorized are they that neither owners nor workers lift a finger to call the police when known murderers move into the restaurant, burn the head of a dishwasher, and try to kidnap him. The gang members attempt to leave, having killed Sue, an innocent Chinese bystander.

In the police pursuit of Johnny Eng, the grisly murders of Asians by Asians pile up, ending with Johnny Eng's decision to murder all of Bing Ho's family and the discovery of the dismembered bodies of gang leader Louie Sen and his family, including his 3-year-old son and 10-month-old daughter.

Well-organized Chinese youth gangs in the United States specialize in break-ins and burglaries of Chinese residences. There are several reasons why Asian gangs target the Asian American population. One is the well-known Chinese tradition of investing heavily in jewelry and gold. A visit to any shopping area attracting Chinese customers will reveal extensive offerings of jewelry. New arrivals, unfamiliar with a foreign banking system, especially tend to keep money, gold, or jewelry in their homes, making them ideal targets for thieves.

Chinese gangs also target their own people because, of course, illegal immigrants don't want to draw attention to themselves by reporting crimes against them to the police. But even legal immigrants are reluctant to report a crime to the police. In the minds of those who have lived in China and other areas of the Far East, the police are connected to the political oppression they have tried to escape. Furthermore, even Chinese Americans of long-standing residence in the United States are hesitant to report a crime and admit to non-Asian authorities that their own young people are criminals. In their minds, their community loses face when it is known that a Chinese person has been robbed by an Asian gang.

An even more powerful reason why residents of a Chinese community are reluctant to report crimes by gangs is fear of violent retaliation in the form of brutal attacks on the victims themselves or on their families in the United States or in China.

The novel is especially skillful at showing the particular difficulties in controlling Asian gang activity and the measures that police departments have taken to deal with gangs. For instance, Chinese officers serve on the police force in both Toronto and New York City, and both police departments have created a task force to deal with gangs. Several Caucasian police officers, including Cisco, the main character, have learned to speak Chinese. The police are able to zero in on the Born to Kill gang by planting a Caucasian who understands Mandarin in the hospital room of two gang members. Many officers make a point of learning about Asian culture and the workings of Asian gangs by keeping up contacts with officers in Singapore and Hong Kong, as Cisco does. By learning from Kwan and Collins, he is able to succeed at the difficult task of earning the cooperation of Ruth Fong, the attorney general in Hong Kong. And Cisco gains valuable information by earning the trust and honoring the confidences of both important and humble members of the community—Sammy Ong, the businessman, and Harry, the dishwasher.

BIBLIOGRAPHY

Alexander, Claire. *The Asian Gang*. Oxford, UK: Clarendon Press, 1996.

Black, David. *Triad Takeover*. London: Sedgwick and Jackson, 1991.

Booth, Martin. *The Dragon Syndicates: The Global Phenomenon of the Triads*. New York: Carroll and Graf, 2000.

———. *The Triads*. New York: St. Martin's, 1991.

Chin, Ko-lin. *Chinatown Gangs: Extortion, Enterprise, and Ethnicity*. New York: Oxford University Press, 1999.

Mahoney, Dan. *The Two Chinatowns*. 2001. New York: St. Martin's Press, 2002.

Seagrave, Sterling. *Lords of the Rim*. New York: G. P. Putnam's Sons, 1995.

Index

About the Author

CLAUDIA DURST JOHNSON, now an independent scholar, was a Professor Emeritus at University of Alabama, where she served as Chair of the English Department for over ten years. She is the series editor for this series as well as Greenwood's *Literature in Context* series for which she wrote more than 12 casebooks. She is also the co-author of *The Social Impact of the Novel* (Greenwood, 2002).